MW00653826

"Malcolm Yarnell is someone whose scholarship I hold in high regard. He is careful, judicious, and thorough. He is also biblical and orthodox. In *God the Trinity: Biblical Portraits*, the full array of his scholarly skills is on display. This is a welcome addition to the field of Trinitarian studies and one I am glad to commend without hesitation."

Daniel Akin, president, Southeastern Baptist Theological Seminary

"Malcolm Yarnell has provided us with a masterful introduction to Trinitarian theology. Historically informed, carefully crafted, and well researched, Yarnell's work not only provides a faithful hermeneutical model to help us move from Bible to theology, but it brilliantly affirms why the renewal of Trinitarian theology is exegetically and existentially essential for the people of God. Pastors, teachers, and students alike will find insightful guidance from this constructive presentation. It is a joy to recommend this fine book."

David S. Dockery, president, Trinity International University/Trinity Evangelical Divinity School

"This book is a gallery of eight masterpiece biblical texts on the Triune God interpreted by a scholar steeped in theology and art. He writes with confidence but never arrogance, blending heart and head, aesthetics and systematics. Do not miss the epilogue—it proclaims the necessity of the Triune doctrine with a ring of worship and awe."

Rodrick Durst, professor of historical theology, Golden Gate Baptist Theological Seminary

"Unlike most of his predecessor Baptist theologians, Malcolm Yarnell decided to write a monograph on the Trinity. He could have merely reviewed the course of Trinitarian theology up through Augustine or could have opted for interreligious dialogue with Jewish and Muslim scholars on the Trinity. Instead he has chosen, in authentically Baptist fashion, to address the biblical dimensions of the Trinity with a focus on eight particular texts, the post-Enlightenment exegesis of which takes the discussion beyond Arthur W. Wainwright's conclusion (i.e., the Trinity is a 'problem' in the New Testament) to the conclusion that the doctrine of the Trinity is both biblical and necessary."

James Leo Garrett Jr., distinguished professor emeritus of theology, Southwestern Baptist Theological Seminary

"True followers of Jesus Christ worship the one eternal God who has forever known himself and who, in biblical revelation, has revealed himself to us as the Father, the Son, and the Holy Spirit. This fresh study of God the Holy Trinity is a welcome addition to the renaissance in Trinitarian theology among Baptists and evangelicals today. I commend it to all the Lord's people everywhere."

Timothy George, founding dean and professor of divinity, history, and doctrine, Beeson Divinity School

"In *God the Trinity*, a skilled theologian traces the patterns of Scripture that undergird post-canonical formulations of the Trinity. Malcolm Yarnell carefully exegetes key biblical texts and interacts with a wide range of interpreters throughout the Christian tradition. I am pleased to recommend this important contribution to the field of Trinitarian theology."

Adam Harwood, associate professor of theology and McFarland Chair of Theology, New Orleans Baptist Theological Seminary

"In *God the Trinity: Biblical Portraits*, Malcolm Yarnell not only shows that the Trinity is a biblical doctrine but he displays how the Trinity serves as the very idiom of Scripture. Yarnell advances the dual truth that there is equality and order within the Trinity. Written to persuade evangelicals that the Trinity is indeed an indispensable biblical truth, this winsomely written work is a treasure for Christians of all stripes."

Daniel Keating, associate professor of theology, Sacred Heart Major Seminary

"Is the doctrine of the Trinity biblical? Malcolm Yarnell sets out to explore this important question in this immensely learned yet eminently accessible volume. His study is a model of scholarship: deeply grounded in biblical teaching and expertly synthesizing the scriptural data into a coherent whole. Highly recommended!"

Andreas J. Köstenberger, senior research professor of New Testament and biblical theology, Southeastern Baptist Theological Seminary

"All true Christian theology, worship, and discipleship is Trinitarian in shape and substance. Regrettably, many evangelicals often fail to reflect on the importance of the Trinity in defining the contours of Christian theology and the Gospel. In this book, Malcolm Yarnell has given the church a lucid and compelling defense of the doctrine of the Trinity, while also giving evangelicals a sense of why the church must continually and unashamedly confess its faith in the one God who is Father, Son, and Spirit."

R. Albert Mohler Jr., president, The Southern Baptist Theological Seminary

"Having been assured that Trinitarian theology is the warp and woof of the Christian faith, the vast majority of people in evangelical churches accept it as true; but when they read books on the subject, they mostly scratch their heads wondering what all of these philosophical discussions about intellectual minutiae have to do with the Bible and with faith. Malcolm Yarnell has done the unthinkable. He simply explicates the Scriptures in a most enlightening way. Clearly an accomplished theologian has done his work, but there is something new here. The theologian is also a preacher and a pastor, and he appropriately believes that in God's Word, we can find clarity on most issues. This book becomes mandatory for every pastor and every theologian to have and to read."

Paige Patterson, president, Southwestern Baptist Theological Seminary

"There is no task more important in contemporary Trinitarian theology than that of clarifying its biblical character. Count Malcolm Yarnell among the theologians who have rightly identified this, and watch how he throws everything he's got into the task. This book engages the Bible's Trinitarian idiom creatively, and summons evangelical theologians and Bible scholars to join in the joyful work of learning to discern just how deeply and directly *God the Trinity* has spoken in Scripture."

Fred Sanders, professor of theology, Torrey Honors Institute, Biola University

"Biblical exegesis is the native soil in which the Christian doctrine of the Trinity flourishes. In this learned and beautifully written book, Malcolm Yarnell plays the role of skillful gardener, tending the Holy Scripture and cultivating the fruits of knowledge and love of the Triune God. I found the last chapter on the book of Revelation especially instructive, but am confident that the entire book will be a blessing to readers."

Scott R. Swain, professor of systematic theology and academic dean, Reformed Theological Seminary

"Instead of heading directly to Nicaea, Yarnell takes us on a canonical tour of the Bible's artistic depictions of God the Trinity. His close theological reading of eight biblical portraits of God leads him to suggest that God the Trinity is not the explicit propositional teaching of the Bible but the Bible's implicit idiom, an insight that leads him to rethink the way many evangelicals read the Bible. *God the Trinity* combines a Baptist commitment to biblical authority with literary sensitivity, imagination, an openness to premodern patterns of interpretation, and a little art history to boot. What's not to like?"

Kevin J. Vanhoozer, research professor of systematic theology, Trinity Evangelical Divinity School

MALCOLM B. YARNELL III

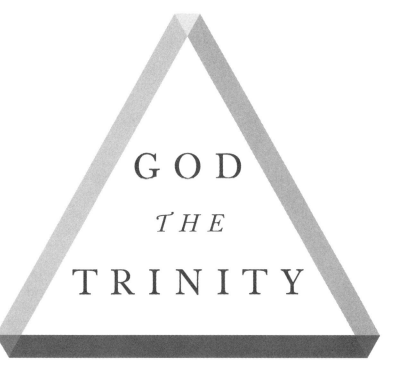

GOD *THE* TRINITY

BIBLICAL
PORTRAITS

ACADEMIC
NASHVILLE, TENNESSEE

CONTENTS

PROLOGUE

E vangelicalism in America has amalgamated for scholars in the
organization known as the Evangelical Theological Society. The
two parts of its "doctrinal basis" concern the Bible's truthfulness and
God the Trinity.[1] While some evangelicals have addressed the Trinity
in terms of systematic theology and others have employed the Trinity
in debates over gender relations, few monographs are dedicated to
evaluating the biblical source material for the Trinity. This is an odd
oversight for a people whose confession centers on only the Bible
and the Trinity. Anecdotal evidence, moreover, suggests such work
should begin in earnest, for if a recent survey is correct, most evangelical Christians in the United States are not necessarily Trinitarian.
One-fifth of American evangelicals claimed Jesus is the first creature
created by God, and more than half claimed the Holy Spirit is a force
and not a personal being.[2] That survey gives some credence to Curtis
Freeman's controversial claim that "most Baptists are Unitarians that

---

[1] "The Bible alone, and the Bible in its entirety, is the Word of God written and
is therefore inerrant in the autographs. God is a Trinity, Father, Son, and Holy Spirit,
each an uncreated person, one in essence, equal in power and glory."

[2] "Americans Believe in Heaven, Hell, and a Little Bit of Heresy" (LifeWay
Research, October 28, 2014, accessed 12 February 2015, http://www.lifewayre-
search.com/2014/10/28/americans-believe-in-heaven-hell-and-a-little-bit-of-her-
esy). Ligonier Ministries and LifeWay Research, *The State of Theology: Theological
Awareness Benchmark Study* (TheStateOfTheology.com, 2014), 11–12.

simply have not yet gotten around to denying the Trinity."[3] If evangelical scholars are Trinitarian, the people in the churches may not be.

In addition, there is some diversity among Christian scholars regarding whether the Trinity is a necessary doctrine. One well-known evangelical theologian, Roger E. Olson of Baylor University, says the doctrine of the Trinity is a true conclusion, but belief in the Trinity is neither necessary nor part of gospel proclamation.[4] Another, R. Albert Mohler Jr. of The Southern Baptist Theological Seminary in Louisville, Kentucky, to the contrary classifies the doctrine of the Trinity as "fundamental and essential to the Christian faith."[5] Leaving to the side the issue of "theological triage," which both theologians affirm, an evangelical equivocation regarding the Trinity remains. In writing this book, we set out to answer these two questions: Is the doctrine that God is Trinity a biblical doctrine? Is it, moreover, a doctrine that is necessary to believe? The following eight chapters contribute toward the answers.

In the midst of engaging in the close theological exegesis of eight important biblical texts, it became evident that a Trinitarian reading of Scripture also required an evaluation of Protestant hermeneutics. The method of Bible study many evangelicals are taught to use must be substantially revised if the Trinity and the Bible are to coalesce. As a result, there arose the need to wrestle with interpretive method as much as Trinitarian exegesis. Indeed, we almost adopted the subtitle, "The Trinitarian Revision of Biblical Hermeneutics." Karl Barth observed this difficulty and opted to diminish hermeneutics out of

---

[3] Curtis W. Freeman, "God in Three Persons: Baptist Unitarianism and the Trinity," *Perspectives in Religious Studies 33* (2006), 324. James Leo Garrett, however, refers to Unitarianism as an "incursion" into Baptist theology. James Leo Garrett Jr., *Baptist Theology: A Four-Century Study* (Macon, GA: Mercer University Press, 2009), 44–46, 549.

[4] Olson's position is indirect. On the one hand, "I think belief in the Trinity, that God is Father, Son and Holy Spirit and yet one God, is essential to authentic Christianity." On the other hand, "The doctrine of the Trinity, although extremely important as a landmark, if not a pillar, of Christian doctrine, is not essential to being Christian" (accessed February 12, 2015, http://www.patheos.com/blogs/roger eolson/2015/02/must-you-believe-in-the-doctrine-of-the-trinity-to-be-a-christian).

[5] R. Albert Mohler Jr., "The Pastor as Theologian," in *A Theology for the Church*, rev. ed., ed. Daniel L. Akin (Nashville, TN: B&H, 2014), 725.

concern that any interpretive criterion beyond the text necessarily distorts exegesis.[6] While there is much to learn from Barth, and his call to enter "the strange new world of the Bible" warms the heart of this free churchman in his own friendly remonstration toward Protestant evangelicalism, we have opted to revise rather than repress evangelical hermeneutical method.[7]

In the following study, comparison is made with the art of painting as a helping metaphor. This was deemed helpful on several accounts. First, it allows for a focused consideration of the various texts, treating each according to its own authorship, genre, and context. From a modern critical perspective, this properly takes the history and grammar of any text as a distinct phenomenon with utmost solemnity. Second, the appeal to art helps construct a bridge from the rationalism endemic among the practitioners of my own discipline in theology to the more holistic approach of the biblical writers. The critique of any work of literature requires both reason and imagination, but the theological interpretation of Scripture especially requires the graces of both *logos* and *pneuma*.[8] Third, the art metaphor allows this author to function as an appreciative if critical commentator upon each text as a great work of theological literature. Avoiding the extremes of the Enlightenment and Romanticism, we sought to weave a middle way through the judicious employment of both modern and premodern methods. Finally, the meticulous treatment of each text on its own later permits the epilogue to pursue a distinct canonical approach, as when art is gathered thematically for review in contemporary art

---

[6] Alan Torrance, "The Trinity," in *The Cambridge Companion to Karl Barth*, ed. John Webster (New York: Cambridge University Press, 2000), 75–78. Donald Wood reasons that although Barth minimized hermeneutics, he nevertheless engaged the discipline. "It was exegesis and not hermeneutics to which Barth called his students. But a recognition of the 'logical and material priority of biblical exegesis over hermeneutics' in Barth should not prevent us from recognizing that Barth did have a good deal to say about what scripture is and how it ought to be read, and from reading this material with care." Donald Wood, *Barth's Theology of Interpretation*, Barth Studies (Burlington, VT: Ashgate, 2007), x.

[7] Karl Barth, *The Word of God and the Word of Man*, trans. Douglas Horton (Gloucester, MA: Peter Smith, 1978), 28–50.

[8] For an in-depth treatment of the burgeoning discipline of theological interpretation, please see *Dictionary for Theological Interpretation of the Bible*, ed. Kevin J. Vanhoozer (Grand Rapids, MI: Baker Academic, 2005).

galleries.[9] On a technical note, all translations are my own, unless indicated otherwise at the beginning of a chapter.

Many wonderful people have enabled the completion of this study. Among professional theologians, there have been enlightening Trinitarian conversations through the years in biblical theology, historical theology, systematic theology, and practical theology with Gerardo Alfaro, David Allen, Craig Blaising, Robert Caldwell, Dongsun Cho, the late Ralph Del Colle, Rodrick Durst, Paul Fiddes, Madison Grace, Michael Haykin, Paul Hoskins, Marvin Jones, Dennis Jowers, Friedhelm Jung, Daniel Keating, Keith Loftin, Fred Sanders, Matthew Sanders, Jason Sexton, Scott Swain, John Webster, and Donald Wood. These scholars have inspired me to take up the biblical doctrine of the Trinity from a systematic perspective, but any errors are purely my own. Paige Patterson kindly asked me to share earlier versions of several of these studies in the impressive Southwestern Seminary MacGorman Chapel, and the trustees of Southwestern Baptist Theological Seminary granted a teaching sabbatical for the 2015 academic year—this book is the result of such generosity. Jim Baird, Andreas Köstenberger, Chris Thompson, and Chris Cowan at B&H Publishing have been helpful in bringing this book to the public.

Several PhD students deserve commendation: John Mann, my graduate research assistant, an established pastoral theologian and rising systematic theologian, has been instrumental in managing residual teaching responsibilities. David Norman, my assistant with the Center for Theological Research and the Oxford Studies Program, has helped juggle my continuing administrative responsibilities and kindly procured the odd book or article. Several graduate research students encouraged me to supervise their theses on the Trinity, including Heinrich Kehler on Stanley Grenz's development, Kent Warner on John Zizioulas's origination of the divine persons, and Hongyi Yang on evangelical lacunae in the Trinitarian gender debate.

---

[9] Others have also found the artistic analogy accommodating. Cf. Robert Alter, *The Art of Biblical Narrative*, rev. ed. (New York: Basic Books, 2011); Alter, *The Art of Biblical Poetry*, rev. ed. (New York: Basic, 2011); V. Philips Long, *The Art of Biblical History*, Foundations of Contemporary Interpretation (Grand Rapids, MI: Zondervan, 1994).

Thanks are also extended to the scores of theology graduate students who enthusiastically enrolled in three elective courses on God as three and one, as well as the hundreds who have listened to regular ruminations in the required systematic theology courses. Most of my students have been required to write expository sermons dealing with a Trinitarian text, in part out of the deep conviction that the Trinity must reclaim the pulpit and the lectern.

It has been a privilege to preach diverse series on the Trinity among large Texas churches—at Birchman Baptist Church in Fort Worth where Bob Pearle is pastor, Prestonwood Baptist Church in Plano where Jack Graham is pastor, and Lakeview Baptist Church in Granbury where Mark Forrest is pastor, as well as countless sermons in venues scattered too broadly to rehearse. The Men at Birchman, led by Monty Briley and Russ Deason, have allowed me to lead them through intensive weekly Bible studies in Genesis, Proverbs, Isaiah, Mark, Romans, Philippians, Hebrews, and Revelation. Without their attentive ear to hear biblical proclamation, I might have left the seminary for a pulpit years ago. They have also consistently offered prayers and personal encouragement regarding this book.

Most important, however, has been the personal involvement of my lifelong partner in Trinitarian imagery, my bride Karen Annette Searcy Yarnell. Even while you have been working on a graduate thesis on the Trinity in Dietrich Bonhoeffer, you have selflessly given of your time and effort to nurture our children and make our home a most wonderful retreat. This book is dedicated to you with the prayer that God will continue to grace you and our five children in Christ with glimpses of his glory through his Spirit.

Malcolm B. Yarnell III
Fort Worth, Texas

THE IDENTITY OF GOD: ΌΝΟΜΑ

> Going, therefore make disciples of all the peoples, baptizing them in the name [ὄνομα] of the Father and the Son and the Holy Spirit.
>
> Matthew 28:19

Truth through Idiom

Le plus savant physician ne pourrait rien reprocher à leurs analyses de la lumière.[1] "The most learned physicist could never find a difficulty with their analyses of light." In a moving essay written to celebrate the rise of the Impressionist movement in painting, Edmond Duranty made this startling assertion. The claim would not have been problematic to Duranty, an artist himself, but it would be and is somewhat shocking to those moderns whose primary idiom for speaking truth is found in scientific discourse rather than in art or in the more realist forms of art.[2] Duranty's challenge, written

---

[1] Louis-Edmond Duranty, *La Nouvelle Peinture* (1876; repr., Paris: Boucher, 2002), 17.

[2] The Greek adjective ἴδιος was used to indicate that which belongs to an individual. An "idiom" is now used to indicate a language or style that belongs to a small group.

1

to foster appreciation for the contributions of "The New Painting" among the academic painters who elevated detail, seems intentionally blunt. The difficulty in finding the proper medium for expressing truth—on display in the modern clashes between the various arts, between the various sciences, and between science and art—is as deep as the difficulty in discerning truth.[3] And the difficulty is compounded by the diverse ways human beings express the truth they perceive. Some believe truth is expressed through definitive, verifiable, and concrete propositions, as expressed in the language of fact, formula, and creed, while others express truth more readily through narrative, poetry, and hymn, or even painting, sculpture, and tapestry.

Capacities for Truth

John Ruskin, the famous proponent of natural history, political economy, and critical art, understood well the problems in bringing the arts and the sciences to a mutual understanding. From an early age Ruskin was fascinated with geometry and botany on the one hand but increasingly with engraving and poetry on the other hand. He went up from a middle-class family to read for a degree in classical greats at Oxford. Ruskin had a capaciousness of mind and spirit that is rare in any age, and from his struggles perhaps we can learn to see beyond the confines of our own limited idiom.

In lectures delivered in 1872, three years after being appointed the first Slade Professor of Art at the University of Oxford, Ruskin chided the physicist who told him that sight was "altogether mechanical." He lamented that that particular scientist's "physiology had never taught him the difference between eyes and telescopes." Ruskin believed human science was a wonderful and necessary human effort because it helped humanity discern order in nature. However, one must not limit human understanding to that which is merely physical. "You do not see with the lens of the eye. You see through that, and

---

[3] Perhaps this was the point being made cynically by Pontius Pilate, with his retort to Jesus, "What is truth?" (John 18:38).

by means of that, but you see with the soul of the eye."[4] Ruskin then appealed to Matthew 6:22–23 as a biblical basis for bringing together physical and spiritual perception: "The light of the body is the eye. If therefore, thine eye be evil . . ."[5]

Ruskin, who was reputed to have "the most analytic mind in Europe,"[6] recognized that "analytic power" was an intellectual faculty available to people who exercised "patience in looking," "precision in feeling," and "due industry," with only an average "memory" required.[7] His social politics were geared toward educating the common man to develop this faculty beyond the constrictive conventions of the modern age's dominant commercialism and industrialism, even as he recognized that some human beings were more gifted in some ways than in others. Earlier in his life, like his scientific interlocutor, he was able to see only the "hideous rocks" and a "small aspen" during his sojourn through a forest at Fontainebleau, France. However, as he began drawing the lines of a tree, he was privileged to see, if just for a moment, beyond the natural world into the beautiful, and through the beautiful into the eternal. Ecclesiastes 3:11 echoed around his mind during this epiphany.

> The woods, which I had only looked on as wilderness, fulfilled I then saw, in their beauty, the same laws which guided the clouds, divided the light, and balanced the wave. "He hath made everything beautiful, in his time, [he has also set eternity in the human heart,]" became for me thenceforward the interpretation of the bond between the human mind and all visible things; and I returned along the wood-road feeling that it had led me far;—Farther than ever fancy had reached, or theodolite had measured.[8]

---

[4] John Ruskin, "Lecture VI: The Relation of Art to the Science of Light," *The Eagle's Nest* (London: George Allen, 1900), 97–98. William Blake said similarly, "We ever must believe a lie / When we see with, not through, the eye." Malcolm Muggeridge, *The Third Testament* (New York: Ballantine, 1983), 68.

[5] Ruskin, *The Eagle's Nest*, 106.

[6] John Ruskin, *Praeterita*, ed. Tim Hilton (New York: Everyman's Library, 2005), 1:49.

[7] Ibid., 1:60.

[8] Ibid., 2:77.

Neither Romanticism with its idiom of "fancy" nor the Enlightenment with its "theodolite" (a precision surveying tool) could ultimately obtain for Ruskin his fleeting but evocative insight into the eternal. He came to see that the laws of both art and science point toward a deeper reality, but they cannot attain it except in shadow. His was an experience in natural theology that depended on the knowledge of special revelation for its proper interpretation.

For Ruskin, who was no mere evangelical and spoke freely of his "un-conversion" from Scottish Puritanism,[9] the copious reading and wholesale memorization of Scripture nevertheless provided the intellectual basis for discerning eternal verities through both art and science. Humanity may express the realities of this world through various idioms because God intends human discernment to testify to him. God provides humanity with the gift of perceiving him in sundry ways. The artist who received this grace could not conclude with mere aesthetics but must end in something more profound, which Ruskin called θεωρία, literally seeing God. The scientist could similarly receive the grace from God that would help him move beyond mere mechanics and glimpse the sublime.[10] In response we are to relay what we have seen, for the "use and function" of all our analytic efforts "is to be witness to the glory of God."[11] This also means that Scripture itself is to be read ultimately not simply in a scientific manner, though that is not inappropriate, but in a more holistic way, in a typological manner.[12]

---

[9] Ruskin was raised by a strictly evangelical mother, experienced his "un-conversion" after hearing a retrograde Waldensian sermon, but later experienced a "re-conversion." Robert Hewison, "Ruskin, John (1819–1900)," in *Oxford Dictionary of National Biography* (New York: Oxford University Press, 2014).

[10] John Ruskin, *Modern Painters*, vol. 2 (1846), in *The Works of John Ruskin*, ed. E. T. Cook and Alexander Wedderburn, 39 vols. (London: George Allen, 1903–12), 2:2.6.

[11] Ibid., 2:1.4.

[12] Ruskin appears to have learned typological reading through his mother's devotional guidance and the popular evangelical sermons they heard. These have been described as "treating objects as both real and symbolic at the same time, a key critical practice." In other words, through the simultaneously literal yet figurative language of Scripture, final truth is discerned. Hewison, "Ruskin, John."

The Bible's Own Idiom

In this book we hope to demonstrate that the Bible reveals the doctrine of the Trinity through its own idiom, an idiom that is conducive to typological hermeneutics responsibly deployed. Where Ruskin was fascinated to discover "patterns" as well as color and background in the world around him at an early age,[13] a way of perception that made him one of the sharpest critics of both art and science in the late nineteenth century, I hope the reader will come to see the pattern of the Trinity is woven into the biblical revelation in both micro and macro forms. Indeed, the Trinity ultimately appears to be the idiom of Scripture in both Testaments. This book does not assume to speak in an artistic manner, for I am not an artist but a scientist engaged in a lifelong analysis of theological discourse. However, we do employ the idiom of art at points as a way to demonstrate that the biblical text does not restrict the theologian to a mere Aristotelian perception of the mundane. On the other hand, through regularly (and primarily) employing Aristotelian-inspired methodologies, especially evident in evangelicalism's exegetical practices, we also demonstrate a necessary limitation to the flights of fantasy to which earlier Platonic-inspired methodologies may tend.

After reading the last paragraph, my family reminds me that my literary ventures become opaque through the use of demanding allusions and compressed vocabulary. For this I ask your patience and beg you to stick with my book as eventually I typically get around to speaking in an idiom that may suit the reader. So perhaps I must state what I mean more clearly at certain points, and this is a good point to do so with the general project. Let me use the analogy of a three-way conversation between scientists, artists, and theologians: The idiom of art may seem pointless to the scientist because the scientist speaks through a more propositional manner. Likewise, the idiom of science may seem difficult to the artist because the artist speaks through a more affective manner. This writer, an academic scientist through both training and temperament, has through time

---

[13] Ruskin, *Praeterita*, 1:14–15.

and exposure learned to see that the artistic idioms of poetry, painting, and plays are also valuable for conveying truth. If the scientist and the artist momentarily grant each other the benefit of the doubt regarding the truth that both are seeking to perceive and proclaim in their own ways, then they may perhaps realize that the theologian seeks the same. Moreover, in the midst of this three-way dialogue, perhaps even the theologians, who tend usually either toward the scientific or the artistic idiom, may see that the Bible has its own idiom. The Bible's own idiom, its own way of speaking, transcends art and science and the theological discourses that incline toward either. The biblical idiom, of which a few scientifically based yet artistically inspired portraits are considered in this book, is God the Trinity.

Discerning the Trinitarian Idiom

The purpose of this study is to examine some of the apparent Trinitarian patterns in Scripture. Trinitarian motifs are there to be seen, though perhaps not so clearly from a modernist propositional perspective. Different ages, cultures, and subcultures speak in different ways, viewing certain ways of speaking as proper or idiomatic, as we have seen for instance in the discussion regarding art and science. It is unfair to demand that each treatise of truth speak according to one's own learned or preferred idiom. The elevation of the rational proposition is an European and an American Enlightenment peculiarity, though the hubris in the elevation of one idiom above and even to the exclusion of others is not necessarily peculiar to modern Western scientific thinkers. In my own sojourns through many cultures, and into yet others through the miracle of the written word, it appears that the limitation of truth to a preferred form of thought and speech is a human problem that inflicts many cultures. However, I must speak critically to the community I know best, the Western Enlightenment culture, a culture that elevates the rationalist idiom. This vernacular becomes embarrassed when it begins to exegete the Christian doctrine of the Trinity, but the embarrassment may be the fault of the method more than of the doctrine.

Problems with Propositionalism

Elevating propositional claims to the exclusion of other ways of claiming the Trinity has three major problems. The first problem with elevating the propositional idiom above all others is that it does not correlate with the way Scripture itself speaks. Yes, there are propositions in Scripture, and they are important, even fundamental to Christian dogma. "God created" (Gen 1:1) and "Jesus is Lord" (1 Cor 12:3) are two such essential theological propositions. However, Scripture also places these propositions in a narrative, such that these two propositions receive their correlation and fullness of meaning within the narrative that orients them. The propositional claims that "God created" and "Jesus is Lord" make sense only if this particular human being is also the only God, who created human beings. The narrative of creation, fall, Israel, Jesus, Spirit, church, and judgment must be stated so that the propositions function together in a coherent manner. Moreover, besides narrative, there are other genres—proverbs, poetry, genealogy, apocalyptic, etc. We suggest, therefore, that theological propositions are not to be privileged, especially in an exclusive fashion, but to be correlated with other literary forms of truth telling.

The second problem with elevating the propositional idiom is that philosophical presuppositions alien to the biblical text may be and often are thereby introduced into Christian interpretation. If propositions are privileged as the only legitimate form of doctrinal revelation, oddly without a biblical proposition expressly promoting privilege, it must be queried as to why the interpreter believes that propositions should be privileged. Is it because the modernist paradigm demands the elevation of this one idiom? This raises yet other questions. What else within the modernist paradigm is being imported into the reading of Scripture?[14] For instance, is the modernist presumption that "monotheism" definitively excludes all complexity and movement

---

[14] The problem of philosophical invasions of theological formation is dealt with summarily elsewhere. Malcolm B. Yarnell III, *The Formation of Christian Doctrine* (Nashville, TN: B&H Academic, 2007), chap. 2.

within God naively taken to be true? Chapter 3 addresses the definition of monotheism more fully.

The third problem with elevating propositions unduly is that it
encourages a form of Bible study that can become self-defeating,
especially with regard to the Trinity. For example, the old method of
proof-texting the Trinity suffered when text critical studies addressed
the Johannine Comma. First John 5:7–8 states, "For there are three
that bear record in heaven, the Father, the Word, and the Holy
Spirit, and these three are one. And there are three that bear witness
in earth, the spirit, and the water, and the blood, and these three
agree in one." If there was a propositional claim for the Trinity in
the Bible, then the statement, "the Father, the Word, and the Holy
Spirit, and these three are one," would appear to be what was needed!
Alas, however, while the words were brought into Erasmus's *Novum
Testamentum* and incorporated into the Textus Receptus, it is nearly
universally accepted today, except among rigid fundamentalists, that
they were not in the earliest manuscript tradition.[15]

Another example concerns the rigid application of the modernist
method of demonstrating truth by earnest Christians. Samuel Clarke
famously and exhaustively, with the same method as used in the natural sciences, addressed every biblical text that seemed to teach the
doctrine of the Trinity. Clarke found more than 1,250 texts worthy
of consideration.[16] Alas, in spite of his efforts to the contrary, Clarke's
inelastic imposition of the scientific method on the Bible also brought
widespread and sustainable accusations of heresy.[17] Taken side by side,
the continuing fundamentalist advocacy of the Johannine Comma

---

[15] "That these words are spurious and have no right to stand in the New
Testament is certain." Bruce M. Metzger, *A Textual Commentary on the Greek New
Testament*, 2nd ed. (New York: United Bible Societies, 1998), 647–49.

[16] Samuel Clarke, *The Scripture-Doctrine of the Trinity, in Three Parts* (London:
1712). Clarke surveyed 1,251 texts, operating with the following principles: "No
Article of the Christian Faith delivered in the Holy Scripture, is disagreeable to Right
Reason," and "Without the Liberty of Humane Actions there can be no Religion."
John Gascoigne, "Clarke, Samuel (1675–1729)," *Oxford Dictionary of National
Biography* (New York: Oxford University Press, 2014).

[17] Maurice Wiles concluded Clarke was a "Moderate Arian." Maurice Wiles,
Archetypal Heresy: Arianism Through the Centuries (New York: Oxford University
Press, 1996), 110–34.

and the heretical work of Clarke oddly correlate in the unnecessary elevation of the propositional idiom to the detriment of textual integrity and/or theological orthodoxy. That these otherwise trenchantly opposed cultural war parties agree with one another in their method may rather poignantly be more a function of the age in which they reside than of the truth they examine.

Even among orthodox Christians who affirm the doctrine of the Trinity, there is a tendency to deny that the Trinity is revealed verbally in the Bible. Typically, what that writer really means is that there is no propositional claim in Scripture regarding the Trinity. Three examples will suffice to demonstrate that this is not an issue confined to the most acidic of the historical critics. First, Benjamin Breckenridge Warfield argued that the revelation of the Trinity "was made not in word but in deed." For Warfield, the double event of the sending of the Son and the Holy Spirit is the revelation, and this occurred after the Old Testament was written and before the New. "We cannot speak of the doctrine of the Trinity as revealed in the New Testament, any more than we can speak of it as revealed in the Old Testament."[18]

Second, in one of the few recent book-length attempts to examine the biblical basis of the Trinity, Arthur W. Wainwright similarly preferred to speak of the New Testament authors as responding to a "problem" rather than stating a "doctrine." We agree with Wainwright that there is "no formal statement of trinitarian doctrine in the New Testament as there is in the Athanasian Creed or in Augustine's *De Trinitate*."[19] But I would argue that there are more ways to reveal a doctrine than through formal proposition, even if formal propositions are our preferred doctrinal idiom.

Third, among contemporary American evangelicals, a renaissance of Trinitarian theology has been advocated most eloquently by Fred Sanders of Biola University. His efforts to further evangelical exploration of the Trinity in the fields of systematic theology, biblical

---

[18] Benjamin Breckenridge Warfield, *Biblical and Theological Studies* (Philadelphia, PA: P&R, 1952), 32–33.

[19] Arthur W. Wainwright, *The Trinity in the New Testament* (London: SPCK, 1962), 4.

theology, and historical theology are very helpful.[20] However, even the erudite Sanders can write, "We should not seek to construct the doctrine of the Trinity from the words of the New Testament alone, where it is not properly revealed so much as presupposed."[21] Fisher Humphreys of Beeson Divinity School would agree with the evangelical consensus that no doctrine of the Trinity is to be found in

---

[20] E.g., Fred Sanders, "Entangled in the Trinity: Economic and Immanent Trinity in Recent Theology," *Dialog: A Journal of Theology* 40, no. 3 (2001): 175–82; "The State of the Doctrine of the Trinity in Evangelical Theology," *Southwestern Journal of Theology* 47, no. 2 (2005): 153–75; *The Image of the Immanent Trinity: Rahner's Rule and the Theological Interpretation of Scripture* (New York: Peter Lang, 2005); "The Trinity," in *The Oxford Handbook of Systematic Theology*, ed. John Webster, Kathryn Tanner, and Iain Torrance (New York: Oxford University Press, 2007), 35–53; "Chalcedonian Categories for the Gospel Narrative," in *Jesus in Trinitarian Perspective: An Introductory Christology*, ed. Fred Sanders and Klaus Issler (Nashville, TN: B&H Academic, 2007), 1–41; "Trinitarian Theology's Exegetical Basis: A Dogmatic Survey," *Midwestern Journal of Theology* 8, no. 2/9, no. 1 (2010): 78–90; *The Deep Things of God: How the Trinity Changes Everything* (Wheaton, IL: Crossway, 2010); and "The Trinity" in *Mapping Modern Theology: A Thematic History of Recent Theological Reflection*, ed. Kelly M. Kapic and Bruce L. McCormack (Grand Rapids, MI: Baker Academic, 2012), 21–45. Dennis Jowers and Scott Harrower, whose works are considered elsewhere herein, have also been helpful in the recovery of classical Trinitarian doctrine.

From a general evangelical perspective, one should consult the slightly earlier works of Millard Erickson, such as *God in Three Persons: A Contemporary Interpretation of the Trinity* (Grand Rapids, MI: Baker, 1998); and *Making Sense of the Trinity: Three Crucial Questions* (Grand Rapids, MI: Baker, 2000). The most comprehensive contributions from a more Reformed evangelical perspective are Robert Letham, *The Holy Trinity: In Scripture, History, Theology, and Worship* (Philipsburg, NJ: P&R, 2004); and Bruce Ware, *Father, Son, and Holy Spirit: Relationships, Roles, and Relevance* (Wheaton, IL: Crossway, 2005). Erickson and his primarily Reformed interlocutors have become largely embroiled in American evangelicalism's complementarian versus egalitarian gender debates over the Trinity. We discuss these focused contributions in chapters 6 and 7.

One must also consult the legacy of the late left-wing evangelical, Stanley Grenz, whose contributions to the Trinitarian renaissance among evangelicals was cut short by his early death. Jason Sexton of Fullerton, California, recently completed a PhD dissertation for the University of Saint Andrews on Grenz's Trinitarianism, while one of my PhD students, Heinrich Kehler of Porta Westfalica, Germany, is currently writing another. The most sustained Trinitarian monographs by Grenz are *The Social God and the Relational Self: A Trinitarian Theology of the Imago Dei* (Louisville, KY: Westminster John Knox, 2001) and *The Named God and the Question of Being: A Trinitarian Theo-Ontology* (Louisville, KY: Westminster John Knox, 2006).

[21] Fred Sanders, "Trinitarian Theology's Exegetical Basis," 83.

the Bible. Humphreys, however, uses the historical critical method to argue that the Trinity is behind the biblical text.[22] A recent book-length contribution to the field of biblical Trinitarianism is more restrained in its evaluation of whether the doctrine of the Trinity is contained in the Bible. There is "no developed doctrine," but "the raw data to construct such a doctrine" is there.[23]

Against the academic presuppositions displayed in Warfield, Wainwright, and many American evangelicals, I hope to show through the texts analyzed in this book that the Trinitarian pattern is found across the various literary genres in the Bible. The Trinity is defini-tively revealed in the New Testament and, for those with sensitive enough ears, across both testaments. This book is intended to show the pattern at a few points and argue for a hermeneutical idiom more appropriate to the biblical text than appears in the dominant evangeli-cal critical method. Chapter 4 addresses the historical progress and regress of precritical and postcritical Christian exegesis of the Bible in more detail. While the arguments raised there are intended to chasten and limit the claims of the historical critical method that has found its home in evangelicalism, broadly understood, a critique of evangeli-cal exegesis is not a rejection of it. Indeed, this book employs that method, retaining its practice of making detailed grammatical and historical queries, even as it issues a call to hear other methods, meth-ods that are open to perceiving an idiom that is pervasive in Scripture, the Trinitarian idiom.

Along with Fred Sanders, we encourage modern exegetes "to reinstate large, comprehensive structures of meaning" in order to restore Trinitarian hermeneutics. A philosophical way of describ-ing what Sanders is advocating, an advocacy with which this author agrees, is that the close inspections demanded in the Aristotelian method of analysis should be balanced with the comprehensive

---

[22] Fisher Humphreys, "The Revelation of the Trinity," *Perspectives in Religious Studies: Journal of the National Association of Baptist Professors of Religion* 33, no. 3 (2006): 287.

[23] Ben Witherington III and Laura M. Ice, *The Shadow of the Almighty: Father, Son, and Spirit in Biblical Perspective* (Grand Rapids, MI: Eerdmans, 2002), xi. Witherington and Ice trace the revelation of the three persons within the biblical text, though they spend more time on the Father and the Spirit than the Son.

metaphysic favored in the Platonic method of analysis. This does not mean abandoning the historical critical method entirely, but it should reorient itself through canonical conviction toward an exposition of the God who transcends both testaments and by his Spirit inspires all the biblical writers. This will not be easy, for it demands certain faith presuppositions; but if we are true to both classical and evangelical Christianity, we must do the hard work. "Emphasizing one subtopic at a time, [the historical critical method] can only with difficulty climb back up to the level of the comprehensive judgment necessary to affirm the doctrine of the Trinity."[24] This book may help others see their way toward aiding in this venture, toward reconnecting the biblical theology of the church with the historical and systematic theologies of the church.

Strategies for Reading

Systematic, historical, and biblical theologians offer at least three strategies for reading the Bible in a way that helps one retain simultaneously classical orthodox Christianity and the evangelical historical-critical method. These include, first, recognizing and exploring the development of the Old Testament message about God and the Messiah into the New Testament. Sanders referred to this as recognizing the "trinitarian hinge" between the Old and New Testaments and the "hyperfulfillment" of Old Testament messianic prophecies in the Lord Jesus Christ. Richard Hays refers to this strategy as hearing the "echoes" of the Old within the writings of Paul and the Evangelists.[25] We have followed this strategy in nearly every chapter to some extent, but especially in chapter 3, regarding the primary Hebrew confession about the nature of God, the Deuteronomist's Shema. The Shema

---

[24] Sanders, "Trinitarian Theology's Exegetical Basis," 89.
[25] Ibid., 82–85, 87–88; Richard B. Hays, *Echoes of Scripture in the Letters of Paul* (New Haven, CT: Yale University Press, 1993); idem, *Reading Backwards: Figural Christology and the Fourfold Gospel Witness* (Waco, TX: Baylor University Press, 2014). Cf. G. K. Beale, *A New Testament Biblical Theology: The Unfolding of the Old Testament in the New* (Grand Rapids, MI: Baker, 2011); *Commentary on the New Testament Use of the Old Testament*, ed. G. K. Beale and D. A. Carson (Grand Rapids, MI: Baker, 2007).

speaks of God in a particular manner but not in the way often assumed in modernity, and the Hebraic way of recognizing God was taken into the identity of Jesus with God in the New Testament.

A second strategy that bridges precritical with postcritical exegesis was referred to by Carl Andreson as "prosopographic exegesis" and modified by Marie-Josèphe Rondeau as "prosopological exegesis."[26] It means asking such basic and relevant grammatical questions of personal identification as: Who is the person (πρόσω-πον) that is speaking? Or to what persons (πρόσωπα) is that person referring? The early church fathers were adept at asking these questions, and their results were transformative.[27] Among evangelicals, the previously cited work of Witherington and Ice, as well as a systematic monograph by a Southern Baptist colleague, Bruce Ware,[28] has followed this strategy. In my systematic theology lectures, I likewise provide a broad survey of how Scripture presents the Father, the Son, and the Holy Spirit as distinct yet divine. In chapters 5, 6, and 8 below, I follow a more focused literary version of this strategy in identifying from the Johannine corpus the divine persons who are speaking and the divine persons about whom they speak and their mutual relations with one another.

A third strategy for reading the Bible, in a way that is faithful to both the patristic (and medieval) and the evangelical methods of exegesis, is through discerning the nature of God through his activity. This method was highlighted by the early church fathers and was instrumental in the reclamation of Trinitarian theology in the twentieth century. Karl Rahner and Karl Barth, the twentieth century's exemplary theologians for respectively Roman Catholicism and evangelicalism, both employed this economic method. Responses to the economic perception of God in the Bible have yielded a spectrum of answers. On one end of the spectrum, Rahner verbalized an axiom that entirely equated God's acts with God's being. On the other end

---

[26] Michael Slusser, "The Exegetical Roots of Trinitarian Theology," *Theological Studies* 49, no. 3 (1988): 462–63.

[27] Ibid., 463–68, 470–75. Cf. Matthew W. Bates, *The Birth of the Trinity: Jesus, God, and Spirit in New Testament and Early Christian Interpretation of the Old Testament* (New York: Oxford University Press, 2015).

[28] Ware, *Father, Son, and Holy Spirit*, chaps. 3–5.

of the spectrum, within the twentieth century's biblical theology movement, evangelical theologian Oscar Cullmann promoted that discipline's prevailing presupposition that there is a stark difference between ontology and function. Jesus fulfilled a divine vocation in our salvation, says Cullmann, but we cannot speak of his being.[29] We consider the methodological issue of θεολογία and οἰκονομία at several points in this book, placing ourselves toward Rahner's end of the spectrum but without collapsing the distinction between God's being and God's act. We also follow the means of exploring divine being through divine act particularly in chapters 2 and 7. Chapter 2 provides a preliminary portrait of the Trinity through the works performed by the Trinity, while chapters 7 and 8 offer a sweeping cosmological panorama of the divine movement.[30]

Before moving into the various portraits of the Trinitarian God, portraits so pervasive in the biblical text as to be found in both testaments and through the various biblical genres with multiple authors spanning centuries of theological discourse, we consider perhaps the most explicit Trinitarian text in the Bible. Known as the Great Commission, Matthew 28:16–20 contains the command to baptize new disciples "in the name of the Father and of the Son and of the Holy Spirit." As the reader may have noticed with the customary perusal of the table of contents and perhaps a perusal of the first pages of the chapters, we have chosen to headline each chapter with a theological claim, a biblical text from which the claim arises, and an important biblical term from that text. The term we chose for this

---

[29] Oscar Cullmann, *Christology of the New Testament*, rev. ed., trans. Shirlie C. Guthrie and Charles A. M. Hall (Philadelphia, PA: Westminster, 1963), 3.

[30] We should mention here a similar strategy followed by Leonard Hodgson in the twentieth century and recently repeated by Fisher Humphreys. Hodgson, Regius Professor of Divinity at Oxford University, argued that the revelation of the Trinity is to be found in the events behind the biblical text. Humphreys summarizes Hodgson's project as a progressive revelation toward the Trinity, exemplified in the seriatim conversion of Peter. The revelation of the persons of the Trinity occurred in three historical events: the Shema, the incarnation of Jesus, and the revelation of the Spirit at Pentecost. It seems somewhat counterintuitive that Humphreys classifies the Shema, a confession, as an "event" in contradistinction to a propositional doctrine. It strikes this reviewer that the Shema participates in both event and proposition. Humphreys, "The Revelation of the Trinity," 290–91, 295–96.

chapter concerns the identification of God provided by Jesus Christ in the Gospel of Matthew. The Greek ὄνομα is best translated in English as "name," and Jesus's name for God tells us much about him/them.

Naming God the Trinity

"What's in a Name?"

In perhaps the most recited lines of any play in history, Shakespeare's Juliet pled for Romeo to forsake his name.[31] Alas, no matter how they tried to escape their appellations, which identified and divided their warring families, the lives of this Montague and that Capulet were determined to a great extent by the social relations they had received with their names. At one point Romeo averred that he would change his name through baptism if he could. "Call me but love, and I'll be new baptiz'd; henceforth I never will be Romeo."[32] Shakespeare was referring to the medieval practice of receiving a "Christian name" during baptism, which in turn likely mimicked the reception of a name during Hebrew circumcision (Luke 1:59).

The Christian ceremony of baptism and the Christian's personal identity became historically intertwined due to the biblical practice of baptizing "in the name of" the Lord Jesus (Acts 8:16; 19:5) and, more expansively, the Trinity (Matt 28:19). However, baptism in the biblical frame concerns not primarily the identity of the one who is baptized (though it does indicate a transformation in human character), but the identity of the God in whose name the human person is baptized. The historical practice of Christian baptism appears to mark personal identity in two directions. First, it identifies God as one who is both with Jesus and named in a threefold manner. Second, it identifies the one being baptized with the God in whose name baptism is received. We are primarily concerned with the first mark, the identity of the God who is named in Christian baptism.

---

[31] William Shakespeare, *Romeo and Juliet*, Act 2, Scene 2, lines 37–67.
[32] Ibid., lines 55–56.

Hans Bietenhard of Bern University said it is a universal cultural belief that a name describes the "indispensable part of the personality."[33] Gerhard Von Rad of Heidelberg University agreed.

> According to ancient ideas, a name was not just "noise and smoke": instead, there was a close and essential relationship between it and its subject. The subject is in the name, and on that account the name carries with it a statement about the nature of its subject or at least the power appertaining to it.[34]

In addition to granting or conveying an identity or authority, a name could take upon itself hypostatic qualities, standing in place of the subject to whom the name pertains. This hypostatization, or personalization, is also true for the covenantal name of Israel's God, Yahweh (יהוה, transliterated as *yhwh*, also known as the Tetragrammaton).[35] In other words, through knowing the name of God, Israel received knowledge about his nature and personhood.

According to modern exegetes, the proper use of the name of God made God present to his people. Suggestions for the meaning of Yahweh include "being present" and "being there." In Old Testament theology, rather than suggesting an absolute attribute of Yahweh, such as "self-existent," the name probably indicates God's relational nature.[36] God's gift of his name to people through revelation was no small thing. As a result of the divine presence and the relationship established through his name, it was understood that the name was "the very heart of the cult of ancient Israel."[37] Spanning both the Old and New Testaments, worship was understood as the context for remembering the name, and the name itself must be

---

[33] Hans Bietenhard, "Ὄνομα, [etc.]" in *Theological Dictionary of the New Testament*, vol. 5, ed. Gerhard Friedrich, ed. and trans. Geoffrey W. Bromiley (Grand Rapids, MI: Eerdmans, 1967), 243.

[34] Gerhard Von Rad, *Old Testament Theology*, vol. 1, *The Theology of Israel's Historical Traditions*, trans. D. M. G. Stalker (New York: Harper & Row, 1962), 181–82.

[35] Cf. Pss 54:1; 89:24; 118:12–12. "Ὄνομα," in *New International Dictionary of New Testament Theology and Exegesis*, 2nd ed., vol. 3, ed. Moisés Silva (Grand Rapids, MI: Zondervan, 2014), 517.

[36] Von Rad, *Old Testament Theology*, 1:180.

[37] Ibid., 183.

hallowed, or kept holy, through service and obedience in worship and action.[38]

Israel's zeal to hallow the name of God eventually brought them to cease using the covenantal name altogether, so that they lost its proper pronunciation. Instead, whenever יהוה was encountered in the text, they uttered the rarer Hebrew אדני (*adonai*), "Lord." The Hebrews drew upon the fact that when used of God in the Old Testament, the singular אדון (*adon*), which may be used of men, is rendered in the plural אדני (*adonai*).[39] In the Septuagint, the Greek translation of the Hebrew Bible, both Yahweh and Adonai were rendered as κύριος.[40] In a significant move, portending the coalescence of his identity with God, κύριος was later regularly applied to the human Jesus.

"The Name" in the Great Commission

According to Matthew, after his resurrection from the dead and prior to his ascension, the Lord Jesus commissioned his disciples to go to the nations, make disciples, baptize them in "the name," and teach them all of his commands. The third part of that fourfold command requires further portrayal here.[41] By most accounts Matthew 28:19 contains the clearest reference to what became known as the Trinity in the Christian Bible. As is widely recognized, the term "Trinity" (Latin *trinitas*; Greek τρίας) along with the related orthodox vocabulary of "one substance" (Latin *consubstantia*; Greek ὁμοούσιος) and "three

---

[38] Bietenhard summarizes his lengthy treatment of the divine name's cultic and ethical implications. "As the position of believers is declared in a specific attitude to the name of God and of Jesus Christ (in prayer, healing, proclamation, admonition, confession, suffering, reverence and praise), so unbelief is manifested in *blasphemein*." Bietenhard, "Ὄνομα," 279–80. Silva would add "holy war" to the means of hallowing the divine name (*New International Dictionary of New Testament Theology and Exegesis*, 3:517).

[39] Ken Hemphill, *The Names of God* (Nashville, TN: B&H, 2001), 22.

[40] Ibid., 31–34; Von Rad, *Old Testament Theology*, 1:187.

[41] I have treated the Great Commission from the exegetical, historical, and theological perspectives elsewhere. This chapter extends those earlier studies. Yarnell, *The Formation of Christian Doctrine*, 186–92; idem, *The Heart of a Baptist* (Fort Worth, TX: Center for Theological Research, 2005).

persons" (Latin *tres personae*; Greek τρία ὑπόστασεις) do not occur in Scripture. There is no propositional claim, or near claim, stating anything closely akin to "God is a Trinity of three persons sharing one substance." However, and this is the argument of this book, God the Trinity is revealed through word and deed in the Bible, even though not in our propositional form. In this important text God is clearly named, singularly but completely, "the Father and the Son and the Holy Spirit."

Kendall Soulen argues that there is a difference between proper names and other names. "A personal proper name is a very humble form of speech. Unlike other kinds of names (common nouns, titles, epithets, and so forth), the ordinary grammatical role of a proper name is not to describe but simply to point: this one and not another."[42] Furthermore, "a personal proper name acquires its sense from the person and history of the one who bears it, from his character, actions, and fate."[43] According to Soulen, the personal proper name for God in the Old Testament is Yahweh, and the meaning of his name came through his character and activity. In the New Testament, the proper name of Yahweh was now replaced with "the Father, and the Son, and the Holy Spirit," each of which was treated as the Lord. This threefold Lord is the one who later Christians called "God the Trinity."

Soulen and others agree that, in the Matthean perspective, this threefold name indicates the same God as Yahweh.[44] Jane Schaberg and Benedict Viviano have argued that Matthew 28 seems to be a midrash, or Rabbinic interpretation, of how God is presented in Daniel 7:13–14. "The Ancient of Days," who sits upon the divine throne, is approached by "One like a Son of Man." This "Son of Man," a popular self-designation of Jesus later in the Synoptic Gospels, is given universal and eternal authority to rule. It is promised that "every people, nation, and language" will serve him. The eternal authority that must

---

[42] R. Kendall Soulen, *The Divine Name(s) and the Holy Trinity*, vol. 1, *Distinguishing the Voices* (Louisville, KY: Westminster John Knox, 2011), loc. 194.

[43] Ibid., loc. 197.

[44] Using Philippians 2:5–11 as an example of how the New Testament alludes to Yahweh, Soulen found well over 2,000 references to the Tetragrammaton in the New Testament. Ibid., loc. 379. Cf. R. Kendall Soulen, "Yhwh the Triune God," *Modern Theology* 15, no. 1 (1999): 26–54.

be proclaimed to every people in Daniel 7 parallels the claims of Jesus to eternal authority and universal proclamation in Matthew 28. For Schaberg and Viviano, reaching similar conclusions in their several studies, the Ancient of Days becomes identified with the Father; the Son of Man becomes personified in Jesus; and the heavenly host, the Holy Spirit. Schaberg notes there are alternative interpretations of Daniel 7 in Jewish midrash, but the early Christians adopted this form due to their conviction that Jesus had transcended death into eternity.[45] (Our own understanding of the relationship between the Old Testament's Yahweh and the New Testament's Trinity, especially the Son, will be brushed out in chapter 3 below.)[46]

"The Name" and the Names

Throughout Christian history, both orthodox and heretical theologians have focused on the meaning of the threefold baptismal formula. The Council of Antioch in AD 341 argued that because three different names were given, each indicates a separate ὑπόστασις (person), and, significantly, to each is thereby assigned a particular "order and glory." The Arian theologians, Aetius and Eunomius, would go further and conclude, "Difference in names indicates difference in substance."[47] The orthodox theologian Athanasius disagreed and considered baptism as an act involving a single divine agency, not three separate agencies. Against the idea that there are three agents, he appealed to Ephesians 3:5, where Paul said there is "one Lord, one

---

[45] Jane Schaberg, "The Father, the Son, and the Holy Spirit: An Investigation of the Origin and Meaning of the Triadic Phrase in Matthew 28:19b" (PhD Dissertation, Union Theological Seminary, 1980). Benedict T. Viviano, "The Trinity in the Old Testament, from Daniel 7:13–14 to Matthew 28:19," in *Trinity—Kingdom—Church: Essays in Biblical Theology* (Germany: Universitat-Verlag, 2000); cited in Sanders, "Trinitarian Theology's Exegetical Basis," 84.

[46] Soulen organizes his book around three different "patterns" of Trinitarian naming, each of which he finds legitimate, but the first of which is primary: the theological (the Tetragrammaton), the christological (the Trinity), and the pneumatological (open-ended). Soulen, *The Divine Name(s) and the Holy Trinity*, 1:610–17, 638.

[47] Khaled Anatolios, *Retrieving Nicaea: The Development and Meaning of Trinitarian Doctrine* (Grand Rapids, MI: Baker, 2011), 145–46.

faith, one baptism."[48] When Basil of Caesarea addressed the Great Commission's use in worship, as we shall see in chapter 5, he viewed the three as placed by the text in a connumerative relation rather than a subnumerative relation.

Drawing on modern linguistic studies of the biblical Greek, there appear to be two significant hurdles against the heretical interpretation. First, the use of ὄνομα in the singular indicates primarily a unified identity. There are three different names provided—Father, Son, Holy Spirit—but "name" is either mistakenly or intentionally used in the singular. If intentional, it appears to indicate a singular identity for the three. That the use of the singular was a mistake by the Gospel writer runs against the modern understanding that the communal practice being reflected was widely accepted by the time of the Gospel's composition. If this was a mistake, there should either be early textual variances, or Matthew displayed an uncharacteristically haphazard concern with numbers. Yet there are no significant textual variances of which to report. And because of its placement at the conclusion of the Gospel, it is highly unlikely that the commission was treated carelessly.[49] Any discussion of ὄνομα should therefore begin with divine unity and only then proceed to considerations of diversity.

The second hurdle for the heretical interpretation is that it emphasizes differences between the three subjects being named. However, the common connective conjunction, καί, "and," must not be bypassed. According to Johannes P. Louw and Eugene A. Nida, καί most often indicates "a marker of coordinate relations."[50] A tertiary use of καί focuses on an "additive relation which is not coordinate," but even here the meaning lacks any hint of contrast.[51] If the Gospel

---

[48] Ibid., 146–47.

[49] The majority view of the Gospel's date is that it was written in the last quarter of the first century, while a well-argued minority view holds that it was written prior to the fall of Jerusalem in AD 70. R. T. France, *The Gospel of Matthew, New International Commentary on the New Testament* (Grand Rapids, MI: Eerdmans, 2007), 18–19, 1116–18.

[50] Johannes P. Louw and Eugene A. Nida, *Greek-English Lexicon of the New Testament Based on Semantic Domains*, 2nd ed., ed. Randal B. Smith and Karen A. Munson (New York: United Bible Societies, 1988–89), 89.92.

[51] Ibid., 89.93.

of Matthew had wished to place the possibility of contrast in the commission, the conjunction δέ would have been necessary,[52] rather than καί, which typically indicates a coordinate relation. However, Matthew seems to have chosen καί for a reason, and his use of a series of persons elsewhere may be instructive. For instance, in Matthew 13:55, four brothers are placed beside one another with the connective conjunction καί, the emphasis being on their common relation to another person. Due to these grammatical and historical factors, it appears that the proper understanding of the baptismal commission must place the three—Father, Son, and Holy Spirit—in a unity, first. Out of that basic unity, three coordinate relations then unfold. The identity of the God of the Great Commission is one in name, a name that encompasses three real relations.

A New Name

The transformation of humanity through the threefold baptism must now receive consideration. What exactly does it mean to be baptized "into the name," εἰς τὸ ὄνομα? Modern linguists do not discern a profound difference in the use of the preposition εἰς rather than the more typical ἐν, or the other possibilities of ἐπί, ἕνεκεν, or διά. Εἰς, however, is often coupled with πιστεύειν; salvation is through faith in the name of Jesus (John 1:12; 2:23; 3:18; 1 John 5:13). Because of the coordination of the ceremony of baptism with salvation in the New Testament, Matthew 28:19 likely indicates salvation is in the name of this God. An Old Testament background may lie in the use of the Hebrew preposition ב (be) with שם (shem), which may be roughly translated as "according to the name." In the Old Testament, to do something בשם (beshem) specified that the person being referenced granted the authority to conduct this activity. For instance, the Lord told Moses that prophets, some true and some false, would speak words "in my name" (Deut 18:18–20). To call בשם יהוה (beshem

---

[52] Ibid., 89.94.

Yahweh), "on the name of the Lord," was also often used in the context of worship (Gen 4:26; 12:8).[53]

The appeal to authority fits the context of the Great Commission,
but due to the nature of Christian salvation and its initial closeness
with baptism, εἰς τὸ ὄνομα probably indicates something more than
mere approval. First, note that calling on the name of Yahweh in
Old Testament cultic worship was now replaced with a calling on the
triune name in the cultic context of baptism. Baptism in the name
of the three is an act of worshipping the one in three. Second, other
apostles equally place the three (God the Father, his Son Jesus Christ,
and the Holy Spirit), the name of God, and Christian salvation in
relation to one another. Christians are "washed," "sanctified," and
"justified in (ἐν) the name of the Lord Jesus Christ and in (ἐν) the
Holy Spirit of God" (1 Cor 6:11). "But the Father will send him, the
Paraclete, the Holy Spirit, in (ἐν) my name," the Son said, to guide
the apostles and the church into all truth (John 14:26). It is likely
that baptism "into the name of the Father, and the Son, and the Holy
Spirit" indicated that the newborn Christian's entire life was now
brought into the context of this divine life. As one is born again by
the Holy Spirit through faith in Jesus Christ, one is able to enter eternal life with God. This God has been named "Father" by the "Son,"
and the "Holy Spirit" reveals the truthfulness of this divine reality to
the human heart.

The importance of names may be found from the beginning of the
Gospel according to Matthew. In Matthew 1:21, the Father grants to
his Son the name of *Iesus*, "Yahweh is salvation." In Matthew 1:23, it
is prophesied that his name will be Ἐμμανουήλ, "God is with us" (cf.
Isa 7:14). Intimations of the Trinity can also be found near the beginning of the Gospel of Matthew, for instance in the baptism of Jesus,
which was attended by the personal revelation of the Father and the
visible granting of the Holy Spirit (Matt 3:16–17).

---

[53] The Rabbinic לשם (*leshem*) may be properly translated as "into the name" or
"according to the name." לשם (*leshem*) was used with washing to declare the freedom
of a slave. Bietenhard, "Ὄνομα," 258–61, 267; *New International Dictionary of New
Testament Theology and Exegesis*, 3:517–19.

Locating the Great Commission's Trinity in the overall movement of Matthew and adopting evocative language from the realm of
the artistic senses, Soulen concludes,

> Like the sun finally rising above the horizon at dawn, the
> verse makes explicit the trinitarian nature of the passage
> that has been subtly signaled from the beginning; indeed,
> it makes explicit the trinitarian nature of the whole Gospel,
> which has also been prefigured since the opening chapters.[54]

With this portrait of God from the Gospel of Matthew, a portrait that may be justifiably described as Trinitarian, we now turn to
a metaphorical summary of the gallery that will be surveyed in the
remainder of this book.

Biblical Portraiture

We have chosen the concept of portraiture because Scripture itself
often speaks in visual, chromatic, and patterned terms. The late W. A.
Criswell made much of "the scarlet thread through the Bible" in his
preaching ministry.[55] The appeal to color and contrast is evident in
many places. Early in the book of Isaiah, it is prophesied, "Though
your sins are as scarlet, they shall be as white as snow" (Isa 1:18). The
Synoptic Gospels picture the Mount of Transfiguration as being cov-
ered with shimmering light (Mark 9:2–3 and parallels). The Gospel
and Epistles of John make much of the contrast between dark and
light, as we shall see. Vibrant colors are on display in Moses's instruc-
tions for the construction of the tabernacle and in the description of
the end in the Apocalypse of John. Scripture also provides patterns
that run through both Testaments, including the unity of God, God
as Creator, man as creature, man as sinner, the Messiah as Redeemer,
and the Spirit as Perfector. This book employs the idea of a portrait or
visible pattern to argue that God as Trinity is the transcendent pattern

---

[54] Soulen, *The Divine Name(s) and the Holy Trinity*, loc. 4399.
[55] W. A. Criswell, *The Scarlet Thread Through the Bible: God's Promise and Man's Deepest Hope* (Nashville, TN: Broadman, 1973).

in the entire Bible, mysteriously revealed in the Old Testament, and more fully revealed in the New Testament.

Framing

Professional artists and scientists understand that they must place their respective analyses within a context or a "frame" if they are to be properly conducted. Some artists expend a great deal of energy constructing the frame for their art. Before proceeding further, we need to determine the frame of the biblical portraiture offered in this book. First, a cursory glance at the book's subtitle, the opening section of this chapter, or this section's title may give the impression that this is a book intended to evaluate Trinitarian icons or other art featuring the Trinity. While I have an appreciation for Trinitarian art in its sometimes enlightening, sometimes stupefying manifestations, the reader will have to look elsewhere for analyses of such art.[56] We are using "portraiture" in a metaphorical sense to indicate the symbolic representation of the Trinity in the Bible through literary rather than visual means. This metaphor correlates with our contention in part that Scripture's literary revelation arouses an ability in human creatures to receive knowledge of the reality of God akin to the faculty of sight.

A second limitation regards the breadth of the subject matter. By no means does this book intend to discuss every Trinitarian text within the Bible. While a thorough review of all the biblical texts that allude to the Trinity may be (and would be!) beneficial, that task would require as many if not more volumes than what Samuel Clarke offered. Downsizing from Clarke's 1,251 texts, Fisher Humphreys restricts the field of Trinitarian references to 120 texts through excluding

---

[56] You may wish to begin with David Brown, "The Trinity in Art," in *The Trinity: An Interdisciplinary Symposium on the Trinity*, ed. Stephen T. Davis, Daniel Kendall, and Gerald O'Collins (New York: Oxford University Press, 1999), 329–56; Gesa Thiessen, "Images of the Trinity in Visual Art," in *Trinity and Salvation: Theological, Spiritual and Aesthetic Perspectives*, ed. Declan Marmion and Gesa Thiessen (New York: Peter Lang, 2009), 119–39; François Bœspflug, "The Trinity in Christian Visual Arts," in *The Oxford Handbook of the Trinity*, ed. Gilles Emery and Matthew Levering (New York: Oxford University Press, 2011), 472–86.

the Old Testament and bypassing some of the major texts, including some of those focused upon herein.[57] If one of the readers of this text sets out to accomplish such a gargantuan task, I would recommend a self-critical evaluation of hermeneutical method be conducted first. This particular book will hopefully add to the field of biblical studies of the Trinity, a field that needs to expand exponentially, but it does not deign to encompass or cap that field. I would also recommend interested readers consult *inter alia* Arthur W. Wainwright's *The Trinity in the New Testament*, Ben Witherington III and Laura M. Ice's *The Shadow of the Almighty*, Peter Toon's *Our Triune God*, and important articles by Robert W. Jenson on the Trinity in the Old Testament.[58] These scholars take more varying though complementary approaches to the "problem" or "doctrine" of the Trinity in the Bible than will be found herein. Other, narrower treatments of the biblical Trinity are yet available, and many of those will contribute to the portraits that follow.

A third limit regards the Augustinian advocacy, and subsequent Barthian declamation, of the *vestigia trinitatis*. Augustine famously used a psychological analogy to construct his highly influential doctrine

---

[57] Matt 1:18–23; 3:16–17; 4:1–3; 10:20; 12:18; 12:28, 31–32; 22:43; 28:19; Mark 1:10–11; 3:29; 12:36; 13:11; Luke 1:35; 1:15, 41, 67; 2:25–32; 3:22; 4:1–3, 14–19; 10:21; 11:13; 12:10, 12; John 1:32–34; 3:5, 34; 6:63–65; 14:15–17, 26; 15:26; 16:5–11, 12–15; 20:21–22; Acts 1:1–3, 7–8; 2:4, 11, 22, 33, 38–39; 4:30–31; 5:29–32; 7:55–56; 8:14–19, 29–39; 9:17–20; 10:38, 39–48; 11:15–17; 15:1–11; 16:6–10; 19:1–8; 20:21–23, 28; 28:23–25; Rom 1:1–4; 5:1–8; 8:1–2, 3–4, 9, 11, 15–17; 14:17–18; 15:12–13, 16, 18–19, 30; 1 Cor 2:6–16; 3:16–23; 6:11, 19–20; 12:1–3, 4–6, 12–13; 28; 2 Cor 1:21–22; 3:3, 4–6; 3:17–4:1; 5:5–7; 13:14; Gal 3:1–5, 6, 10–14; 4:4–6; 5:1–6, 21–25; Eph 1:13–14, 17; 2:18, 22; 3:5, 16; 4:4–6; 5:18; 6:10, 11, 17; Phil 1:19; 3:3; Col 1:7–9; 1 Thess 1:4–6; 2 Thess 2:13; 1 Tim 3:15–16; 2 Tim 1:3, 13–14; Titus 3:4–6; Heb 2:3–5; 6:4–6; 9:14; 10:29; 1 Pet 1:2, 3–12, 3.18, 4.14, 1 John 3:23–24; 4:2, 13–14; 5:5–9; Jude 20–21; Rev 1:4–6, 9–10; 2:1, 7; 3:21–22; 14:12–13; 22:16–18. Humphreys, "The Revelation of the Trinity," 292n. A quick survey shows that Humphreys' self-imposed limits exclude *inter alia* Genesis 1–2, Deuteronomy 6, and Revelation 4–5, and several texts identified herein in Ephesians.

[58] Robert W. Jenson, "The Bible and the Trinity," *Pro Ecclesia* 11, no. 3 (2002): 329–39; idem, "The Trinity in the Bible," *Concordia Theological Quarterly* 68 (2004): 195–206. Jenson concludes the latter article with the question, "Is the doctrine of the Trinity in the Bible?" "Yes indeed, and there is more of the Trinity in the Bible than has yet been recognized in the formulated doctrine."

of the Trinity.[59] Others have drawn on various other physical, psycho-logical, and/or social aspects of creation and humanity to construct a portrait of the Trinity. Karl Barth roundly criticized the project of discerning and discussing the "vestiges" or "marks" of the Trinity in creation. According to Barth, this method misuses general revelation by constructing an anthropological model for God, supplanting the only *vestigium trinitatis*, who is the Word of God.[60] While we would not be as trenchant in our critique of the use of Trinitarian marks in creation as Barth was, we would agree with his preference for putting our efforts primarily into biblical exegesis.[61] Barth spoke compellingly that there is a "strange new world within the Bible" waiting to be discovered by those who will hear.[62] This book paints a few represen-tations of the Trinity who has encountered the author in his readings of the Bible. We hope others may be encouraged to look and see for themselves if the God of the Bible graces them with a similar vision of himself.

Canvasing

Another responsibility in properly portraying a subject requires the treatment of that subject on the proper canvas. Biblical interpreters emphasize that a text must be understood within its particular con-text. In the portraits we consider, it will be understood, along with the historical critical method, that a text's interpretation requires knowl-edge and appreciation for its particular book, genre, and author, as well as date, audience, and other relevant historical factors. It will also be understood, along with the precritical method of the early church, that a text's interpretation requires appreciation for the canon, which

---

[59] Augustine, *The Trinity*, trans. Edmund Hill, ed. John E. Rotelle (Brooklyn, NY: New City Press, 1991), book 15.

[60] Karl Barth, *Church Dogmatics*, vol. 1, book 1, 2nd ed., trans. G. W. Bromiley, ed. G. W. Bromiley and T. F. Torrance (Edinburgh: T&T Clark, 1975), 347. Cf. David S. Cunningham, *These Three Are One: The Practice of Trinitarian Theology* (Malden, MA: Blackwell, 1998), 90–107.

[61] Barth, *Church Dogmatics*, vol. 1, book 1:333.

[62] Karl Barth, *The Word of God and the Word of Man*, trans. Douglas Horton (Gloucester, MA: Peter Smith, 1978), 28–50.

implies the work of the Holy Spirit in the reception of the church. A single painting is often perceived best in a gallery of similar works. We, therefore, intend to take what is best in both the evangelical and the early church exegetical models and apply them to the interpretation of these selected texts.

We have chosen texts from both testaments and several genres to evaluate, and they typically reflect on yet other texts throughout the Bible. This intratextual approach is necessary if one is to remain true to where the writers themselves located their own work. Among biblical scholars, it is becoming increasingly evident that the biblical authors drew heavily from one another in their various writings. Intratextuality becomes acutely important when Christians consider their Lord's own hermeneutical method. As the Gospel of Luke relates, Jesus portrayed the Old Testament writings, with respect to their generic division and across the entire textual apparatus, as being fulfilled in his own incarnation, ministry, life, death, resurrection, and final reign (Luke 24:13–48).

The Lord's need to open his disciples' dull minds is an indication that proper hermeneutics is ultimately a work he must perform in his followers' hearts. Thus a combination of both human intellectual effort and divine illumination appears necessary for the interpretation of the ultimate meaning of the biblical revelation. To speak in more human terms, the proper interpretation of Scripture involves both scientific measurement and artistic inspiration. Close attention must be paid to the details within the text, and the dynamic action within the text must drive any representation of the subject.

Authors and Artists

Turning to the individual portraits, we have chosen eight biblical texts to review. Comparing the biblical authors and their literary genres with some great artists and their styles may be instructive.[63]

---

[63] For an extensive and informative if dated interaction between artistic and biblical exposition, see P. T. Forsyth, *Religion in Recent Art: Being Expository Lectures on Rossetti, Burne Jones, Watts, Holman Hunt, and Wagner* (London: Simpkin, Marshall, 1889).

The first text, which we have considered in this chapter, is the premier Trinitarian baptismal text in the Great Commission of Matthew 28. Among the Gospels, Matthew is a favorite for teachers due to its structural detail. If the apostle Matthew, a tax collector, was the author of the Gospel, then his financial expertise certainly fits with the study discovered there. Similarly, among the great artists Michelangelo Merisi da Caravaggio has long been recognized as leading the Baroque movement. His eye for the gritty facts of human nature was especially favorable for scenes from the Synoptic Gospels and the book of Acts, for which he used the disreputable denizens of Rome as models. Like Matthew, whose life he portrayed in a famous cycle, Caravaggio achieved clarity in the presentation of that which humans could see with their eyes. Those granted eyes of faith may also see with Caravaggio and the Synoptic writers beyond nature into eternity. Caravaggio's *Supper at Emmaus*, now at the National Gallery in London, presents Jesus in the climactic moment that the disciples recognize him as the risen Lord, yet all the worldly tavern owner sees is a man.[64] Likewise, perhaps the only way for a human being to discern the orthodox Trinity in Matthew 28 is through eyes that are suddenly opened.

A suggestive relation might also be established between the writings of Paul and the Expressionism immortalized in the paintings of Edvard Munch. The apostle Paul presented God as Trinity in his movement of grace, love, and fellowship toward humanity, among other places in the benediction of Second Corinthians. A contextual exegesis of this text is the portrait drawn in chapter 2 of this book. Munch similarly focused on the internal processes set loose through the intimate encounters between persons. *The Scream*, which Munch painted after feeling "as if a scream was going through nature," is an iconic work valued in contemporary cultures throughout the world.[65] It is well known that Munch's art intends to express the

---

[64] A tragic figure in his own age, Caravaggio was a careful reader of the Synoptic Gospels, incorporating a detail from Mark 16 into his painting of the Emmaus scene from Luke 24. Andrew Graham-Dixon, *Caravaggio: A Life Sacred and Profane* (New York: Norton, 2010), 221–25.

[65] Edvard Munch, *The Frieze of Life* (1918), in *Edvard Munch: The Frieze of Life*, ed. Mara-Helen Wood (London: National Gallery, 1992), 13.

human soul, although his Expressionism was not understood in his beloved Norway for a long while. It is less known that he was raised in a Norwegian evangelical minister's home.[66] While relinquishing much of this heritage, he retained the desire to express the progress of the person within a comprehensive metaphysic. Munch's *Frieze of Life* displays a post-Christian οἰκονομία that moves from the beginning of life through love and anxiety to suffering and death.[67] That Munch could combine an intense personalism with a comprehensive metaphysic has similarities with the writings of the apostle Paul. Paul presents personal salvation within the dynamic working of God from creation through redemption to final consummation. Paul's metaphysical soteriology will be treated contextually in chapter 2, then more comprehensively and canonically in chapter 7.

Modern critics have expended a great deal of effort in peering behind the text of the Bible to get at historical details. In spite of some of the acidic and contradictory results the historical critical method has rendered, it is telling that the critics generally believe there actually is a recoverable history in the Bible. The authors of the Old and New Testaments relayed historical truth through their theological narrative. An analogous commitment to historical realism, along with narrative symbolism, is found in the paintings of William Holman Hunt.[68] Hunt embodied the goals of the Pre-Raphaelite Brotherhood, whose commitment to authentic detail he helped conceive in 1848.[69] Hunt's

---

[66] Sue Prideaux, *Edvard Munch: Behind the Scream* (New Haven, CT: Yale University Press, 2007).

[67] *The Scream* immediately follows *Golgotha* in the final Berlin exhibition of the frieze. Reinhold Heller, "Form and Formation of Edvard Munch's Frieze of Life," in *Edvard Munch: The Frieze of Life*, 34. Munch may have identified himself with the crucified Christ. Ibid., 104.

[68] His most famous work, *The Light of the World*, has been called a "protestant icon" due to its wide reception in the late nineteenth century. Judith Bronkhurst, "Hunt, William Holman (1827–1910)," in *Oxford Dictionary of National Biography* (New York: Oxford University Press, 2014).

[69] The four principles are, in short, "to have genuine ideas to express," "to study Nature attentively," "to sympathize with what is direct" in previous art but forsake the merely conventional, and "to produce thoroughly good pictures and statues." W. M. Rosetti, *Family Letters*, 1:135, cited in Bronkhurst, "Hunt, William Holman." Hunt saw himself as a priest whose duty was to present apostolic truth through meticulous paintings for the common man. Ibid.

paintings adhere closely to nature and history, and his representa-
tions of Jerusalem were some of the first to make the visual details of
that historic city accessible in the modern West. John Ruskin publicly
defended the Pre-Raphaelite Brotherhood's naturalist method in a
famous series of letters to *The Times* of London. Ruskin also lauded
Hunt for his rare simultaneous possession of intellectual capacity and
Christian commitment.[70] Hunt's continuing popularity is due to his
ability to combine stunning historical detail with rich theological
symbolism. Chapter 3 considers how the foundational theological
claim of the Shema was historically understood in ancient Israel and
subsequently received in the New Testament.

Modern academics tend to treat the Gospel of John skeptically
regarding its faithfulness to history, especially in comparison with
the Synoptic Gospels.[71] Like their scientific brethren, the European
art academies in the early nineteenth century were committed to
the realist representation of history and nature. When the French
Impressionists came on the scene, they were greeted with an incredu-
lity that paralleled that which modern scientific critics have displayed
toward John. The appearance of William Turner's paintings, whose
airy light inspired the leading Impressionist, Claude Monet, caused
similar outrage in England. A pseudonymous critic from America,
Petronius Arbiter, disparaged a piece from Monet's *Rouen Cathedral*
series as a "color stunt" and "deformation of a form," saying no
museum should buy Impressionist art, for it is "repellant," "absurd,"
and possesses "absolutely nothing of importance or of endurance."[72]
What that critic failed to understand was that Monet was not seeking
to copy a stone facade or express an emotion. He was apprehending
revolutions in light on the stone face of the cathedral. The academic
realists before him could relay only the "*relative*" contrasts between

---

[70] Ruskin was responding to Hunt's *The Shadow of Death* in a letter to the histo-
rian J. A. Froude. Ruskin to Froude, 1874; Ruskin, *Works*, 37:83.

[71] Following the work of C. H. Dodd, Leon Morris argues that while John is a
theological interpreter, he adheres closely to historical facts that can be verified. Leon
Morris, *The Gospel According to John*, rev. ed., New International Commentary on
the New Testament (Grand Rapids, MI: Eerdmans, 1995), 35–42.

[72] Petronius Arbiter, "A Trivial Work of Art: 'Rouen Cathedral' by Monet," *The
Art World* 2, no. 1 (1917): 66–67.

dark and light, and they did that well. However, Monet was painting "*absolute* values in a very wide range, plus sunlight, as nearly as he can get it," and that required a different style with bright colors.[73] Both the realists and the impressionists of light sought to impart the unity and diversity of visual truth but in radically different ways![74] Similarly, the apostle John, who identifies God with light, retains earthly reality even as he stretches human language beyond that of the Synoptic Gospels to speak of divine being. William Temple said the Synoptics "may give us something more like the perfect photograph; St John gives us the more perfect portrait."[75] Three chapters, 4–6, focus on the Trinity as portrayed in the Gospel of John, simply because it contains the plushest Trinitarian ontology in Scripture.

The biographers of Caravaggio, Munch, Hunt, and Monet relay the many difficulties each of those now widely revered artists had in being received by their contemporaries. Art connoisseurs today will have their preferences. (Caravaggio is my favorite due to his nearly propositional realism.) But none of these artists were esteemed as little as William Blake, whose chosen visual form, engraving, was considered pedestrian, whose poetry was confusing if compelling, and whose theology can be justly described as bizarre.[76] Blake is buried among honored dissenters at Bunhill Field, Finsbury, London, yet

---

[73] Henry G. Stephens, "Impressionism: The Nineteenth Century's Distinctive Contribution to Art," *Brush and Pencil* 11, no. 4 (1903): 282. His italics.

[74] The massive, rigid, impermeable structure of Rouen Cathedral serves as the principle of unification in Monet's famous "suite" of paintings. Monet's more appreciative critics have noted a "systematic impulse" in Monet to bring together "elementary diversity into a harmonious whole." His first biographer wrote, "All these shapes, all these shimmers order each other, saturate each other, influence each other with their mutual colours and reflections. . . . Hence the unity of his paintings." Gustave Geffroy, cited in Joachim Pissarro, *Monet's Cathedral: Rouen 1892–1894* (New York: Alfred A. Knopf, 1990), 6–8.

[75] William Temple, *Readings in St John's Gospel* (London: Macmillan, 1947), xvi; cited in Morris, *The Gospel According to John*, 42n.

[76] Blake wrote a faithful patron and friend, Thomas Butts, that on his good days he looked to Christ. At his death he is reported to have joyfully embraced "salvation through Jesus Christ." George Richmond to Samuel Palmer, August 15, 1827; cited in Robert N. Essick, "Blake, William (1757–1827)," in *Oxford Dictionary of National Biography* (New York: Oxford University Press, 2004).

fresh flowers are often found only on his relatively small gravestone.[77] As an artist Blake loved the Bible because it can be understood by everyone and is "addressed to the Imagination."[78] He is helpful in that he appreciated the visionary aspects of Scripture, though his own visions puzzled contemporaries. Some of his scriptural renderings, especially in the apocalyptic genre, show a respect for how "multiples and unities meld into one another."[79] Blake's penchant for colorful apparitions is conducive to the powerful vision of the enthroned Trinity in the fourth and fifth chapters of the Apocalypse, which as an eschatological text appropriately ends this book.

All the authors and the painters reviewed in summary here had to deal with interpreters who responded negatively to their various styles. Yet they were all committed to conveying truth as they saw it or heard it. While we may not grant the painters inspiration in the sense of authoritative revelation, we suggest parallel lessons are to be gained from their lives and work. Most of these are obvious and need not be labored. What I would like to stress is that each of our biblical texts conveys to the reader the doctrine of the Trinity but according to its genre. Moreover, as each chapter is read and remembered, it will be seen that they wrote with a common Trinitarian idiom. As we pause to listen carefully to the biblical text, putting aside our own stylistic preferences, perhaps we may hear each witness more clearly and through each become grasped by the triune God they heard and saw.

---

[77] As I write, there is a major exhibition, "William Blake: Apprentice and Master," at the Ashmolean Museum in Oxford, England.

[78] Paul Miner, "William Blake's Creative Scripture," *Literature and Theology* 27, no. 1 (2013): 42.

[79] See his graphite and watercolor, *The Four and Twenty Elders Casting Their Crowns Before the Divine Throne* (1803–1805), now at the Tate Modern, London. Martin Myrone, *The Blake Book* (London: Tate, 2007), 109. A biblical scholar, Christopher Rowland, argues that Blake perceived the complexity of Old Testament monotheism long before its rediscovery in modern scholarship. Christopher Rowland, "Exploring the Contraries in Divinity," in *Blake and the Bible* (New Haven, CT: Yale University Press, 2010), 73–85.

2

THE GOD WE WORSHIP: META

The grace of the Lord Jesus Christ, and the love of God,
and the fellowship of the Holy Spirit, be with [μετά] you all.
2 Corinthians 13:14 (NASB)

The second biblical portrait to be considered in this monograph is a miniature painted by Paul to conclude one of his largest epistles. In this chapter we shall focus less on methodological concerns and more on demonstrating a basic economic Trinitarianism in the New Testament with the apostle who wrote half of the newer part of the canon. In subsequent chapters we shall return to the methodological and hermeneutical questions that must be addressed alongside the theological exegesis of the various Trinitarian portraits. It may be helpful for the reader to have this miniature of the Trinity in mind before proceeding through the remainder of the gallery.

How and Whom?

Among contemporary Christians many arguments have resulted from and much thought and attention have been given to the question of *how to worship*. The so-called worship wars between traditional music (which is, in a twist of irony, historically quite innovative) and

contemporary music (which is frequently superseded in the next
generation) have created much anxiety. However, what often fails to
receive attention is the more fundamental issue of *whom to worship*.
This confusion of priorities is a detriment. Certainly, idolatry may
occur through worship inappropriately offered to the true God, so
human beings must be careful about how they worship. But idolatry
is absolutely bound to occur if we worship the wrong God! Moreover,
if Christians are careful to perceive *whom* to worship, then they will be
better able to perceive *how* they ought to worship.

So, who is this God that Scripture reveals to human beings and
commands them to worship? The "benediction"[1] at the end of Paul's
second letter to the church at Corinth, 2 Corinthians 13:14 (enumer-
ated as verse 13 in some versions) is a beautiful text for answering this
weighty question. Gordon Fee referred to this verse as "the most profound theological moment in the Pauline corpus."[2] That may be true.
Recognizably, this is not the only Trinitarian text in 2 Corinthians (cf.
1:21–22; 3:3, etc.), but it is the most profoundly doxological one.

The threefold movement of the benediction finds its unity in its
direction toward humanity, specified in the concluding preposition,
μετά. Μετά relates the three divine subjects with one another and
with their object, humanity. This text introduces the knowledge of
who God is through relaying how God relates to his creatures. How
God relates to humanity is, moreover, not confined to the mundane
trivialities that so often consume our attention. Rather, how God
relates to us is realized in how God originally created men and, after
the great human rebellion against God, how he saves them. The questions of "Whom?" and "How?" prompt the contemplation of two
critical truths theologians have long found beneficial to consider.

The first critical truth is that God is the one who reaches out to
humanity to enable our worship. Human salvation is from beginning
to end purely a work of divine grace. Scripture teaches us that God is
love, and when God acts in love, this we call "grace." Grace is God

---

[1] A benediction is a blessing that is often used in corporate worship. A non-
exhaustive list of other examples from Scripture includes Num 6:24–26; Rom 15:5–
6, 13; 1 Pet 5:10–11; Jude 1:24–25; Rev 22:21.

[2] Gordon D. Fee, *God's Empowering Presence: The Holy Spirit in the Letters of
Paul* (Peabody, MA: Hendrickson, 1994), 363.

moving toward humanity with blessing. He demonstrates grace by reason of his nature of love. Grace is seen in the Father's election of us, in the Son's sacrificial death for us, and in the Holy Spirit's application of personal salvation to us. Human beings respond in worship to him only because he has related to us in gracious ways, and his grace in turn enables the human response of worship.[3]

The second critical truth is that the knowledge of *who* God is, the so-called immanent Trinity, comes to us through the experience of *how* God relates to us, the so-called economic Trinity. Now, mind you, we are not speaking here of two different trinities; rather, in using this language we are distinguishing between *who* God is within Godself and *how* God relates to us. The "immanent Trinity" is also referred to as the "essential Trinity" or the "ontological Trinity"—these roughly synonymous terms refer to God's Trinitarian relations *ad intra*, or the internal relations within Godself.[4] To speak of the "economic Trinity" is a manner of describing how God relates to all that is not God—in this way systematic and philosophical theologians refer to God's Trinitarian relations *ad extra*, or the external relations of God to his creatures.

The proper way to formulate the immanent Trinity's relation to the economic Trinity has prompted a great deal of conversation, which we shall enter fully in subsequent chapters. For now, we note that Karl Rahner's famous "axiom" is a beginning point for many contemporaries within this discussion. Rahner asserted, "The 'economic' Trinity is the 'immanent' Trinity and the 'immanent' Trinity is the 'economic' Trinity."[5] Rahner was reacting against the traditional division of Trinitarian dogma into two separate treatises, which

---

[3] "It is primarily God's causative action in us, and secondarily our corresponding response to him, the former being logically prior to the latter. The chief motive of worship is grace—that the God who initiates his movement toward us in order to make worship through the Son in the Spirit possible is the same one who draws us into the heavenly sanctuary through the Son in the Spirit." Dennis Ngien, *Gifted Response: The Triune God as the Causative Agency of Our Responsive Worship* (Colorado Springs, CO: Paternoster, 2008), xv.

[4] Theologians who prefer to avoid language that carries a philosophical load often use the language of immanence or internal relations rather than of ontology.

[5] Karl Rahner, *The Trinity*, trans. Joseph Donceel (repr., New York: Crossroad Herder, 2004), 22.

subsequently turned theology in a more abstract and reductionist direction. He wished to restore an outlook that was more holistic, biblical, and salvation oriented. This author affirms Rahner's axiom but in a modified way, as we shall see in chapter 7.

Regarding this second portrait, we continue our discussion of who God the Trinity is by focusing on a passage (2 Cor 13:14) that indicates how God works and how we are commanded to respond to him in worship. The text, which is given in the form of a benedictory prayer by Paul, divides itself into four major parts: first, "the grace of the Lord Jesus Christ"; second, "and the love of God"; third, "and the fellowship of the Holy Spirit"; and finally, Paul's particular request that this one God who works as three "be with you all." The apostle's prayer for Trinitarian grace, love, and fellowship indicates that this is a doxological text, a text authoritatively used in Christian worship. Harry Austryn Wolfson, a Jewish philosopher, noting that first-century synagogues dismissed worship with the threefold benediction of Numbers 6:24–26, speculated this was the background for the Pauline benediction.[6] If so, there would have been a resonance established in Jewish-Christian minds between the thrice-mentioned "Yahweh" of the Numbers benediction on the one hand and the three subjects of the Corinthian benediction on the other hand.

"The Grace of the Lord Jesus Christ"

Grace

The Greek term often translated as "grace" is χάρις. Paul uses χάρις as a central expression for his doctrine of Christian salvation: Grace originates in the freedom of God; grace is focused through Jesus Christ; grace becomes personal in faith alone; grace is behind the total experience of salvation but especially justification; grace is correlated with the gospel and its proclamation; and the presence of divine grace should display itself in a person's life. Especially interesting here is that grace is not correlated with the Father primarily but with the

---

[6] H. A. Wolfson, *The Philosophy of the Church Fathers*, 3rd ed. (Cambridge, MA: Harvard University Press, 1970), 149.

Son. Hans Conzelmann, a well-known New Testament theologian, makes the jarring claim, "Paul orientates himself, not to the question of the nature of God, but to the historical manifestation of salvation in Christ."[7] The apostle's emphasis on the historical display of grace in Jesus Christ, in this text and elsewhere, should therefore give theologians pause before they attempt to craft a theology of grace grounded in the inscrutable decrees of God the Father. Grace is theologically substantiated in the historical work of the Son.

"The grace of the Lord Jesus Christ." So, what exactly is the grace of Christ? In our exposition of this benediction, we shall have recourse primarily to what Paul's second epistle to the Corinthians reveals about this final verse in that letter. The best way to understand what Paul means is to read this final verse in the context of the letter in which it was written. When evaluated in light of the teaching of the whole book, it becomes clear that the capstone verse of 2 Corinthians is a remarkable summary of the living theological affirmations of the whole letter. The Christology of grace in the second Corinthian epistle is articulated with four references.

The first discussion of grace in its relation to God the Son begins in 5:21 and concludes with 6:1. Immediately prior to this passage, Paul was extolling the ministry of reconciliation that God assigned to Christ principally and the church derivatively. The grace that God gives is focused on his Son's sacrificial ministry on the cross. There is an unequivocal affinity of substitution with the atoning work of Jesus Christ. The Son was without sin, but the Father made the Son bear human sin "for our sake." The Father placed our sin on the Son "so that we might become the righteousness of God in him." In a short space "the grace of God" is seen as deriving from the Father and progressing toward sinful humanity through the mediation of the Son. God reconciles with sinful humanity by substituting his sinless Son for sinful humanity. God reconciles with humanity not on the basis of our righteousness but through giving us his Son's righteousness.

---

[7] Hans Conzelmann and Walther Zimmerli, "Χάρις, [etc.]," in *Theological Dictionary of the New Testament*, vol. 9, ed. Gerhard Friedrich, trans. Geoffrey W. Bromiley (Grand Rapids, MI: Eerdmans, 1974), 393–98.

The second discussion of grace in relation to the Son is found in 8:9, where, again, vicarious substitution is evident. This time, however, the exchange encompasses also the movement of eternity into time. Christ "was rich," replete in his deity and regal glory, but "he became poor." The eternal king of all kings entered his temporal realm as the impoverished son of a woman betrothed to an itinerant carpenter, beginning his earthly sojourn not in a palace but in an animal shelter. Why did the Son of the Creator endure such humiliation? He did this, says Paul, "for your sake." There is an unequal trade at work here. To begin with, Christ is rich and humanity is poor, but in the incarnation "he became poor." The proposed beneficiaries of his actions are the impoverished in spirit, who are nevertheless now offered riches because "by his poverty you might become rich." The gifting of salvation's riches is due entirely to God's inner freedom, for there is nothing intrinsically valuable in humanity itself that is prompting this exchange.

The third text relating grace to Christ again indicates a movement that originates in God and progresses toward humanity. "But He said to me, 'My grace is sufficient for you, for power is perfected in weakness'" (2 Cor 12:9). Because of his torments, Paul had asked the Lord Jesus to remove a weakness in his life. However, Christ indicated to Paul that his grace was sufficient for Paul. Indeed, divine power is perfected in human weakness. Christ's grace is "for you"—it is a divine power that comes from and through him to rest upon humanity. Moreover, it is a grace that takes human weakness and miraculously transforms that defect into perfection. Such a grace is "sufficient" for all of humanity's needs. Grace in Christ is enough; nothing else is required.

The fourth text (13:3) builds on the previous discussions of human sin and human weakness to point to Christ as the one who overcomes weakness with his powerful grace. What is significant about this particular text is that it identifies the movement of divine grace with the ministry of the apostle. Grace is a divine working that comes through the apostle to the church at Corinth. It is "Christ who speaks through me," and the proof of his divine condescension is to use a fallible human. Christ uses Paul as a means, working powerfully through the apostle in order to bring about the transformation of the weak.

The Indivisible Operations of the Trinity

The movement of grace is not simply, however, from Christ to the church through the apostle. Grace moves both internally within God and externally to humanity. The Father, the Son, and the Holy Spirit are each identified with the movement of grace in 2 Corinthians. We have seen above that the primary focus is on the Son. However, the Father is also in view at times. First, grace comes "from God our Father" as well as the Lord Jesus Christ (1:2; cf. 1 Cor 1:3). Second, the grace that is available through the atonement of Jesus Christ is specifically identified with "God," θεός typically being a reference to the Father, as we shall see (cf. 2 Cor 6:1). Third, the grace that is "of God" is made known through the preaching of the apostles (8:1).

Moreover, alongside the Son and the Father, grace is also identified with the work of the Holy Spirit. Again in 2 Corinthians, we read that the Spirit is the one who "gives life" (3:6). Moreover, the Lord is closely identified with the Spirit in 3:16.[8] The Spirit is the divine agent who works with the Son to transform the broken image of humanity "from glory to glory" (3:17). This indicates that the grace of the Holy Spirit concerns the personal application to the believer of what the Father has ordained from eternity and what the Son has accomplished through the cross. At the fourth-century council of Constantinople, which bequeathed to Christian posterity its widely revered version of the "Nicene Creed," the Holy Spirit is concluded to be "the Lord and Giver of life." While the premiere orthodox theologian at the council wanted to make even stronger assertions about the deity of the Holy Spirit, the council wanted to hew as closely as possible to biblical language in order to avoid offending others. It was from such

---

[8] On the modern scholarship regarding the exact relationship between the Son and the Spirit in Paul, see Malcolm B. Yarnell III, "The Person and Work of the Holy Spirit," in *A Theology for the Church*, rev. ed., ed. Daniel L. Akin (Nashville, TN: B&H, 2014), 496–97.

texts as 2 Corinthians 3 that these early biblical theologians learned that grace was a work of the Spirit as well as the Son and the Father.[9]

A general picture of how grace develops within God on the basis of these texts appears thus: Grace begins "from" the Father (1:2), and continues "in" the Son (5:21), which is then applied to the believer by the Holy Spirit (3:18). The divine movement of grace originates in the dynamic yet orderly relations between the three divine persons. Grace begins within God in the Father, whose love generates grace within the Son, and this same divine grace courses through the giving reality of the Holy Spirit. Distinct from, though reflective of, this internal dynamic within the Godhead, God also works graciously in the world as three and one.

The orthodox patristic theologians of both East and West spoke of the unity of operations between the three members of the Trinity. Basil of Caesarea, the leading Cappadocian Father in the East, argued that the Father is "the original cause," the Son is "the creative cause," and the Holy Spirit is "the perfecting cause."[10] Augustine of Hippo, who stands at the headwaters of Western theology, in his famous work on the Trinity similarly concluded that all the external works of the Father, the Son, and the Holy Spirit are indivisible, *omnia opera Trinitatis ad extra indivisa sunt.*[11] Basil's statement concerned God's work in Creation, and Augustine was speaking about God's work in the incarnation, but we have noticed here from 2 Corinthians a similar unity of operations in the whole movement of divine grace. The indivisible operations of God as Trinity, which the early Fathers

---

[9] Gregory of Nazianzus was the first theologian to clearly say that the Spirit is God and *homoousion* with the Father. His primary objection to the resulting creed from the Council of Constantinople was that it was too cautious, but the creed is universally interpreted through his exegesis. John McGuckin, *Saint Gregory of Nazianzus: An Intellectual Biography* (Crestwood, NY: St. Vladimir's Seminary Press, 2001), 272, 305, 355, 367–68.

[10] "For the first principle of existing things is One [God the Father], creating through the Son and perfecting through the Spirit." Basil of Caesarea, *On the Spirit*, 16:38, in *Nicene and Post-Nicene Fathers*, 2nd Series, vol. 8, ed. Philip Schaff and Henry Wace, trans. Blomfield Jackson (repr., Peabody, MA: Hendrickson, 1994), 23.

[11] Augustine, *The Trinity*, trans. Edmund Hill (Brooklyn, NY: New City, 1991), 103.

discovered through their reading of the biblical text, can and will be repeatedly witnessed in the biblical texts exposited in this book.

Who Is the Son?

While there is a unity of the Trinity in the origination and dispersion of divine grace, that grace is particularly affiliated, as we have seen, with the work of the Son. But who is this Son? Our focal passage uses the genitival construction of three names to describe him: τοῦ κυρίου Ἰησοῦ Χριστοῦ, "of the Lord Jesus Christ." To identify the Son, it will be helpful to consider each of these names in turn.

Κύριος. The Greek term translated as "Lord" has both Hebrew and Hellenistic roots. The Old Testament covenant name for God, Yahweh, as well as the more common name, Adonai, were translated into Greek as κύριος. The Greek-speaking Jew would have heard "the Lord" as a way to speak of the one true God.[12] Gentile Greeks would have used κύριος either as a formal reference to a noble person or as the indication of a deity.[13] The oriental ascription of deity to human rulers was transmitted through the Greeks to the Romans. From the time of the Emperor Nero, there was a steady increase of ascription of κύριος alongside growing claims of deity. When Christians were confronted by the demands of the state to proclaim Caesar as κύριος and sacrifice to his genius, they refused and were thus martyred because of their foundational belief in Jesus as κύριος.[14] "Lord" is a common New Testament term that is applied repeatedly to Jesus Christ. The basic Christian confession is Κύριος Ἰησοῦς, "Jesus is Lord," and its use indicates identity with God (cf. 1 Cor 12:3; Phil 2:6–11).[15] In

---

[12] Werner Foerster and Gottfried Quell, "Κύριος, [etc.]," in *Theological Dictionary of the New Testament*, vol. 3, ed. Gerhard Kittel, trans. Geoffrey W. Bromiley (Grand Rapids, MI: Eerdmans, 1965), 1058–62.

[13] Leon Morris, *New Testament Theology* (Grand Rapids, MI: Zondervan, 1986), 40.

[14] Foerster and Quell, "Κύριος," 1039–58.

[15] "Paul, then, does not make any distinction between θεός and κύριος as though κύριος were an intermediary god. . . . For Christians there is only one God with whom they have to reckon and from and to whom are all things (cf. 1 Cor 15:28). Again, there is only one Lord on whom they are dependent and through whom are all things, through whom they have their very being as Christians." Ibid., 1091.

other words, to claim Κύριος Ἰησοῦς is to confess that this person is God, thus Christ alone among men is to be worshipped and obeyed. We shall see in the next chapter how Jesus came to be included within monotheistic worship.

Ἰησοῦς. The typical Pauline construction is to place the name "Christ" before the name "Jesus," except when the name "Lord" is added, in which case he prefers the order of Lord Jesus Christ.[16] This is a general indication that Paul's Christology, his doctrine of Christ, more often functions as a "Christology from above" than a "Christology from below." Paul, like the apostle John, tends to start with Christ's deity and proceed to a consideration of his humanity; Peter and the synoptic Gospel writers, on the other hand, tend to start with Christ's humanity and proceed to a discovery of his deity. Subsequent theologians have offered various reasons for taking either of these approaches, with Daniel Akin recently advocating a "Christology from behind," by which he means starting with the Old Testament.[17]

Whatever the particular Christological approach one chooses to follow, it seems necessary that both his humanity and his deity be affirmed. "Jesus" is derived from the Old Testament name of "Joshua," which means "the Lord is salvation." By repeatedly referring to our Lord's human name, even as they are proclaiming his deity, Paul and the other apostolic writers are indicating that he is fully human. Jesus is the human name of the Son of God, reminding us that he was born as a human being, that he died as a human being, and that our humanity was raised with him from the dead. This human being, Jesus, now sits at the right hand of the Father in glory, and Christians eagerly await their own resurrection in order to join his exalted humanity.

Χριστός. "Christ" is the transliteration of a Greek word that means "anointed one," and its Hebrew equivalent is the word "Messiah." In the Old Testament oil was poured over kings, priests, and prophets in order to set them apart for ministry. The external ceremony of

---

[16] Morris, *New Testament Theology*, 40.
[17] Wolfhart Pannenberg, *Jesus—God and Man*, 2nd ed., trans. Lewis L. Wilkins and Duane A. Priebe (Philadelphia, PA: Westminster, 1977), 33–37; Daniel L. Akin, "The Person of Christ," in *A Theology for the Church*, 391.

anointing with oil indicates the invisible gift of the power of the Holy Spirit upon a person's life. "In each case the action signified that the person in question was solemnly set apart for the service of God."[18] The Jews during the time of Jesus learned from their reading of such prophecies as Daniel 9:25–26 to expect the coming of the Messiah from God to establish just rule. However, Jesus pointed to Psalm 110 and asked how the Christ could be both David's son and the Lord (Mark 12:35–37). The Lord thereby alluded to the mystery of the Messiah's contemporaneous humanity and deity. At his trial Jesus affirmed that he indeed was "the Christ, the Son of the Blessed" (Mark 14:61–62).[19] Jesus is the Christ, the one expected to enter history with a mission from God to establish the kingdom of God, and in him all of history comes and will come to its intended end.

Theological Summary

The eternal dynamic movement of grace within the Trinity has entered time through divine willing. God's grace comes to the world through the ministry of the Son, primarily, but also through the ministry of the Holy Spirit. The Son of God, the Lord Jesus Christ, fully God and fully man, the promised Messiah and the end of history, has brought divine grace into the world. First, this grace originates with the Father in the Son through the Spirit. Second, God's grace has come into the world in the ministry of the Son. Third, God's grace is still coming into the world through the perfecting work of the Holy Spirit.

God has chosen to use the church as a continuing means of his grace. This occurred primarily with the apostles and subsequently with the church. The apostles, whose writings were canonized in the New Testament, were the means by which God worked grace to bring salvation to the next generation of believers. These early Christians were gathered, thus becoming the church, and the church

---

[18] Morris, *New Testament Theology*, 40.

[19] While there is a secrecy motif in the Gospels surrounding Jesus as the Christ, it seems to be more a question of a proper understanding of what the Messiah entails rather than whether Jesus is the Messiah. This contradicts the destructive criticism of Wilhelm Wrede. Cf. ibid., 103–6.

itself is commissioned to repeat the apostolic message, Christ's message, to the world. When the gospel, the message of Jesus Christ, is proclaimed, the Spirit of God applies God's grace to those who hear through faith. The circuit is completed as God's grace brings the church into communion with God through Christ in the Spirit.

"And the Love of God"

The Trinitarian Implications of Καί

The Greek conjunction καί is most often used as a "connective" or "copulative" that places words or phrases in an accumulation or list. Καί, "and," carries with it a sense of qualitative or quantitative correlation.[20] For original Greek-speaking theologians, such as Basil of Caesarea, the conjunctions here (2 Cor 13:13) and in the baptismal formula of the Great Commission (Matt 28:19) led them to teach their flocks to worship the Father "with" the Son "together with" the Holy Spirit.[21] The "co-ordination" of the names in the Corinthian doxology and in the Matthean baptismal formula required Basil to conclude, "The relation of the Spirit to the Son is the same as that of the Son to the Father." While Basil is careful to hold in check "heathen" arithmetic linguistic definitions, he demonstrates that the conjunctions require a "connumeration" rather than a "subnumeration" of the Son and the Spirit in relation to the Father.[22] The equalitarian nature of the conjunction in this passage prompted the well-known New Testament theologian, A. T. Robertson, to exclaim, "It presents the persons of the Trinity in full form."[23] The fullness of the Trinity is extant in three consequences from these passages.

First, building on the arguments developed in chapter 1 above, from a simple linguistic perspective, the use of καί in Matthew 28

---

[20] "Καί," in *A Greek-English Lexicon of the New Testament and Other Early Christian Literature*, 2nd ed., ed. Walter Bauer, William F. Arndt, and F. Wilbur Gingrich (Chicago, IL: University of Chicago Press, 1979), 391–93.

[21] Basil, *On the Holy Spirit*, 1:3.

[22] Ibid., 17:42–43.

[23] Archibald Thomas Robertson, *Word Pictures in the New Testament*, vol. 4 (Nashville, TN: Broadman, 1931), 271.

and 2 Corinthians 13 to connect the Father and the Son and the Holy Spirit is perhaps the strongest indication of equality among the three. These three are treated as one God. In Matthew 28, the three are named and connected directly as divine subjects, while in 2 Corinthians 13, the three are connected as subjects through divine operations. In both of these biblical passages, the Father and the Son and the Holy Spirit are treated coequally and coextensively as God. The language of "person" has been historically applied to the three subjects in such passages as shorthand to identify the reality of each subject.[24]

Second, the doxological context of these two passages requires the treatment of the three as one object of human worship. Second Corinthians 13:13 is a prayer of blessing that calls upon the threefold God to bless the church, and Matthew 28:19 is a formal act of worship required by the Lord of his church and its new disciples. The equality and extension of identity to the three in the context of worship carries enormous implications. On the one hand, Scripture is clear that worship is to be given to the one God alone, who jealously requires the first and unique place in his people's hearts (cf. Deut 5:7–11; Matt 22:37–38). On the other hand, the reception of that unique worship in these passages is shared among three. Exclusive worship and, therefore, exclusive deity are thereby granted in these texts to all three persons at one and the same time.

Third, when the unitive description of the Trinity's relations in these two key passages, which is required by the use of καί, is placed alongside other biblical passages that affirm distinct relations between the three, the Cappadocian Fathers were compelled to speak of the different "modes of God's being." The word "mode" here indicates the variety of relationships between the persons. The use of such language is not to be confused with the heresy of Modalism, wherein the three are pictured by Sabellius as apparent modes of one divine person. For the orthodox fathers the relational ways of God's existence are not merely for the sake of appearances; they represent eternal realities. As we shall see, the Cappadocians read the New Testament carefully and, through especially the Gospel of John, concluded that there are

---

[24] For more on "person," see chaps. 4–6 below.

distinct relations between the three: The Father is defined through his relation with the Son—the Father is "ingenerate." The Son is defined through his relation with the Father—the Son is "begotten" or "generate." The Holy Spirit is defined through his relation with the Father (and, I would argue, through the Son)—the Holy Spirit is "proceeding."[25]

Love

According to 1 John 4:8 and 16, a principle attribute of God is his *agape*, "love." The adamancy with which John describes God as love in his first epistle has prompted some theologians to assert that divine love is the essential attribute of God. Scripture presents a rounded picture of God's character, a presentation of God that is so full that it can and does prompt some theologians to resolve inappropriately the tensions between such of God's attributes as power, judgment, and love. These tensions often revolve around the apparently paradoxical divine characteristics of holiness and love. According to Gustaf Aulén, while God's holiness is "the background and the atmosphere of the conception of God," love is "the governing center of the Christian conception of God."[26] He also describes love as "the dominant center" and "the inmost character" of God, a character that is "decisively defined by Christ and his work" on the cross.[27]

Aulén is critical of both the scholastic and the liberal interpretations of divine love[28] and refers back to John's conception for a proper glimpse of the heart of God:

> The Johannine statement, "God is agape," summarizes
> not only that which is essential in the New Testament, but
> also everything that can be said about the character of the

---

[25] J. Warren Smith, "The Trinity in the Fourth-Century Fathers," in *The Oxford Handbook of the Trinity*, ed. Gilles Emery and Matthew Levering (New York: Oxford University Press, 2011), 116. See discussion in chaps. 4–6 below.

[26] Gustaf Aulén, *The Faith of the Christian Church*, trans. Eric H. Wahlstrom and G. Everett Arden (Philadelphia, PA: Muhlenberg, 1948), 121, 125.

[27] Ibid., 130–31.

[28] Ibid., 126–29.

THE GOD WE WORSHIP: META

Christian idea of God. No other divine "attributes" can be co-ordinated with love, nor can these express something that would cancel love. Nothing more decisive can be stated about the Christian conception of God than the affirmation: "God is agape."[29]

We would agree with Aulén's large place for divine love but would not want to downplay the other attributes of God, which James Leo Garrett Jr. has organized around the major centers of holiness, love, and righteousness.[30] Love is essential to the being of God because that is what Scripture teaches about God. God possesses glory and holiness, and God exercises power and knowledge, but God "is" (ἐστιν) love. Thus, when Paul speaks of "the love of God," he is sounding an echo to John's claim about God's fundamental nature. God's love is spontaneous and self-giving, originating from within God and coming forth in the Son and the Spirit. God's love is active, overcoming evil through the divine power displayed in the atoning cross of Jesus Christ.

The Father

If God is Trinity, then which one of the persons is in view, assuming any particular person is in view, when the New Testament refers to θεός, "God"? In scholastic theology the word θεός could refer to any of the three subjects of the Trinity. Θεός might also refer to all three together considered as one. However, in New Testament theology, except where the context demands the inclusion of another divine person, θεός properly refers to God the Father. Karl Rahner states the case strongly:

> We maintain that in the New Testament ὁ θεός signifies the
> First Person of the Trinity, and does not merely stand for
> him often; and this applies to every case in which another
> meaning of ὁ θεός does not become clearly evident from

---

[29] Ibid., 131.
[30] James Leo Garrett Jr., *Systematic Theology: Biblical, Historical, and Evangelical*, 2nd ed., vol. 1 (North Richland Hills, TX: Bibal, 2000), chaps. 14–19.

the context. These few exceptions in no way support the opinion that ὁ θεός merely stands for the Father without actually signifying him.[31]

God's love thus has its principle in the Father. The Father is the source of love within the Trinity, and love proceeds from the Father through the Son and the Spirit to creation. According to Paul in 2 Corinthians, love is particularly identified with God the Father: "the love of God." According to Aulén, "What has been said about love applies also to the word Father when it is used about God."[32] God the Father loves the Son and the Holy Spirit. God the Father creates by reason of his love. God the Father redeems by reason of his love. God the Father judges and consummates all things by reason of his love. Love originates exclusively within the character of God, but love moves outwardly from God. On the one hand, to speak of divine love is to speak of the love that flows immediately from the Father to the Son and the Spirit and vice versa. On the other hand, to speak of divine love is also to speak of the Father's orientation *ad extra*, outside himself toward creation.

A few verses before the conclusion of his second letter to the Corinthians, Paul indicated that "the God of love and peace" resides with Christians, who demonstrate their union with the God of love through rejoicing, comforting, being of like minds, and demonstrating their completion in God (13:11). Doubtless, the role of the Father in giving comfort, which Paul expounded at the beginning of the epistle (1:2–4), was intentionally rehearsed at the end of the epistle. The same could be said of the Father's role in bringing joy (2:14), a particular concern in chapter 2, now brought into view again at the end of the letter. In addition, there is the sufficiency of the Father's work, which was introduced in 3:5 and is now echoed in the appeal to completion. Because the work of God the Father is

---

[31] Karl Rahner, *Theological Investigations*, vol. 1, trans. Cornelius Ernst (Baltimore, MD: Helicon, 1961), 126–27. Ethelbert Stauffer notes, however, that while θεός typically refers to the Father, there are a few instances in which θεός also refers to the Son, such as in John 1:1 and 20:28. "Θεός, [etc.]," in *Theological Dictionary of the New Testament*, 3:92 and 92n.

[32] Aulén, *The Faith of the Christian Church*, 135.

taught throughout the letter, highlights regarding the Father's working in love are summarized toward its denouement.

The Unity of Divine Love

Divine love has its principle in the Father, but divine love also characterizes the Son and the Holy Spirit. The Father shares all things, including love, with the Son and the Holy Spirit. As *grace* was seen above to be a demonstration of the unity of operations among the three, likewise *love* is a united work of all three subjects of the Trinity. In 2 Corinthians 5:14–15, we learn that God's love has particularly manifested itself in his Son on the cross. "The love of Christ" is so powerful in the Christian that it constrains us to die with Christ and live with Christ. Rahner argues the "genuinely personal love" of God is not the result of an abstract nature. "Love is not the emanation of a nature but the free bestowal of a person, who possesses himself, who can therefore refuse himself, whose surrender therefore is always a wonder and a grace." The love of God is manifested toward humanity "in the Sending and Incarnation, in the Cross and Glorification, of his only begotten Son."[33]

Because the unity of operations includes the love of both the Father and the Son, one would expect that it extend also to the love of the Holy Spirit. This was verified above with the indivisible operations regarding grace, and now in 2 Corinthians 6:6 we see that the Holy Spirit also participates in the divine work of love. The location of the Holy Spirit is here preceded by ἐν χρηστότητι, a concept closely related to love and translated as "goodness" or "kindness" and followed by ἐν αγάπη ἀνθποκρίτς, "sincere love." Rahner identifies the executor of the love of God as "the Pneuma of God, who pours forth upon us his love for us; and in this Spirit God's most intimate personal life is unfolded to us."[34] In summary, we can say that love is particularly identified with God the Father, who is the source of the Trinitarian life, but love is manifested to creation in the cooperative divine work of the Father, the Son, and the Holy Spirit.

---

[33] Rahner, *Theological Investigations*, 1:123.
[34] Ibid., 124.

"And the Fellowship of the Holy Spirit"

Subjective Genitive or Objective Genitive?

Most commentators agree that the genitives translated "of the Lord Jesus Christ" and "of God" should be taken as subjective genitives. In other words, grace comes from the atoning work of the Lord Jesus, and love comes from the agency of God the Father as the source of love. Scholars are divided, however, with regard to whether the third genitival construction is objective or subjective. There seem to be two possibilities: Does fellowship with God come from the Holy Spirit, the genitive functioning as a subject? Or do we enter fellowship with God through communion with the Holy Spirit, the genitive functioning as an object? The theological implications of this translation decision can be significant.

The interpretive decision may be reduced to a theological query. Is the Holy Spirit a divine agent, operating from within the Godhead? If so, then a subjective genitive is an appropriate possibility. If not, then only an objective genitive is possible, relegating the Spirit to a mere instrument rather than a divine participant. Recent commentators have sensed the dilemma and concluded that it is best to see the genitive here as possessing both subjective and objective properties. Paul Barnett, David E. Garland, and Ralph P. Martin have separately concurred in interpreting the Holy Spirit as both the initiator of fellowship and as the instrument of fellowship. Garland even uses the term *plenary genitive* to convey this truth. Martin argues that the clauses maintain their parallel nature if all three are interpreted as subjective genitives, a move that correlates with the full participation of the Holy Spirit within the Trinity.[35]

---

[35] Paul Barnett, *The Second Epistle to the Corinthians*, The New International Commentary on the New Testament (Grand Rapids, MI: Eerdmans, 1997), 618n14; David E. Garland, *2 Corinthians*, The New American Commentary (Nashville, TN: B&H, 1999), 556; Ralph P. Martin, *2 Corinthians*, Word Biblical Commentary (Waco, TX: Word, 1986), 495–96.

Κοινωνία

Into what is the Holy Spirit introducing Christians? The Greek word κοινωνία may be translated in three primary ways. John Webster prefers "fellowship" to "communion," for he is concerned that human beings not be interpreted as contributing something substantive to the life of the perfect God. His point is that we ought not add to or subtract from the perfection of the divine life. Webster's Barthian theological commitments demand the preservation of divine transcendence. He believes that the terminology of "fellowship" is less likely to detract from the intimacy of fellowship with God while maintaining the unbridgeable ontological gap between God and man.[36]

An evangelical theologian, Robert Letham, and a Roman Catholic cardinal, Avery Dulles, prefer the translation of "participation" or "communion" for κοινωνία. For Letham, "fellowship" is too weak, since Scripture teaches that we participate "in the nature" of God. Citing 2 Peter 1:3–4, Letham concludes that "we become sharers of the divine nature." "This is more than mere fellowship."[37] Avery Dulles agrees that the church is "much more than a society of friends. It is also a participation in the communion of the divine persons."[38]

Daniel Keating prefers to use the patristic terminology of "deification" to describe the theology of κοινωνία. Keating summarizes various arguments and points his own teacher (and mine), John Webster, to the fact that the Creator-creature distinction may be maintained, even with the language of "deification." "We share in the divine life (and so are deified), not by nature, but by grace." A careful but ready inclusion of such passages as 2 Peter 1:4 into evangelical soteriology, alongside a review of what the church fathers intended with the language of θέωσις, would seem to affirm Keating's point. The

---

[36] John Webster, "God's Perfect Life," in *God's Life in Trinity*, ed. Miroslav Volf and Michael Welker (Minneapolis, MN: Fortress, 2006), 150.

[37] Robert Letham, *The Holy Trinity: In Scripture, History, Theology, and Worship* (Phillipsburg, NJ: P&R, 2004), 468–69.

[38] Avery Cardinal Dulles, S. J., "The Trinity and Christian Unity," in *God the Holy Trinity: Reflections on Christian Faith and Practice*, ed. Timothy George (Grand Rapids, MI: Baker Academic, 2004), 74.

distinction between the Creator and his redeemed creatures seems to be retained through the deification of creatures being of grace rather than nature.

> Ours is a "participation" in the divine nature, but this participation is dependent on the utter difference between Creator and creature remaining intact. We remain the human beings we are, sharing in the divine life of the Father, Son, and Spirit as creaturely sons and daughters.[39]

The Holy Spirit is the agent who grants a believer communion with the Father, the Son, and the Holy Spirit. This is a communion for which we were originally created and for which the Father elected the Son to redeem us. Salvation is not merely from the horrors of a real place called hell nor even merely also to the joys of a place called heaven. Salvation is gained supremely through acceptance of the invitation to enter into an eternal relation with the Triune God!

As with the divine works of *grace* and *love*, so there is a unity of operations within the Trinity to bring about *fellowship*, as indicated in a cursory review of the second letter to the Corinthians. The Father, the Son, and the Holy Spirit are each included in the Trinitarian movement of salvation in 2 Corinthians 1:21–22: "Now He who establishes us with you in Christ and anointed us is God, who also sealed us and gave us the Spirit in our hearts as a pledge." The impetus is with the Father, but the Son is the point of contact with humanity, and the Spirit is the internal seal to Christian communion with God. The work of the Father in communion is indicated also in 1:3–4; 5:1–5; and 6:16. The work of the Son in communion is indicated also in 1:5 and 13:5. Finally, the work of the Holy Spirit in communion is repeated in 2 Corinthians 5:5 and in other Pauline sources, such as Romans 5:5. To borrow a metaphor from Irenaeus, who saw the Son and the Spirit as the two hands of God,[40] God loves

---

[39] Daniel A. Keating, "Trinity and Salvation: Christian Life as an Existence in the Trinity," in *The Oxford Handbook of the Trinity*, 451–52.

[40] Stephen M. Hildebrand, "The Trinity in the Ante-Nicene Fathers," in *The Oxford Handbook of the Trinity*, 101. While it is popular to use Irenaeus's anthropological analogy of the Trinity, it should be recognized that his economic Trinity is more evident and his immanent Trinity is less clear, especially with regard to the

redeemed human beings by wrapping his arms of grace in Jesus Christ and fellowship in the Holy Spirit around them.

"Be with You All"

Biblical Language Matters

Ἔσται. The threeness of God in this passage is clear, especially in its structure—the Father and the Son and the Holy Spirit—but his oneness is also evident. The word "be" is provided in English translations due to the presence of ἔσομαι, "will be," in verse 11, which verb is implied in verse 13. The verb ἔσομαι is the future indicative form of εἰμί, "to be," and it is, significantly, given in the third person singular, ἔσται, rather than in the third person plural. Paul did not need to switch from the singular to the plural because the God of which he speaks is one with three. It is the One "God of love and peace" in verse 11, whom Paul says will be with you. It is, likewise, the three persons of the one God who will be with you as a result of Paul's prayer in verse 13.

Μετά. The Greek preposition μετά does not carry quite the intimacy of ἐν or the closeness of σύν, two related prepositions. Yet there is a familiarity represented by μετά, a "with-ness" that carries a sense of "after-ness." This provides a subtle reminder that human participation in the Trinity is derivative—by grace, not by essence. And in spite of our created status, we are nevertheless granted a place with God, in relationship with all three subjects of the Trinity. For love he created us—Father, Son, and Holy Spirit. By grace he redeems us—Son, Father, and Holy Spirit. For communion he communes with us—Holy Spirit, Son, and Father. We are intended for life "with" and "after" him.

Spirit. In an insightful article Stephen O. Presley also argues that Irenaeus carefully separates his own prosopological exegesis from the insertion of extrabiblical narratives and multiple deities into the text as practiced by the Gnostics. Stephen O. Presley, "Irenaeus and the Exegetical Roots of Trinitarian Theology," in *Irenaeus: Life, Scripture, Legacy*, ed. Sara Parvis and Paul Foster (Minneapolis, MN: Fortress, 2012), 165–71.

Πάντων ὑμῶν. This literally means "all of you." In the south of the United States, a common colloquial expression of the second person plural is spoken as "y'all." In some ways it is a superior statement, for it preserves the distinction of the plural as opposed to the singular usage of "you." Paul wrote this letter not to a single individual but to the entire Corinthian church, among whose members were many he had previously expressed doubt about their salvation. However, he was convinced that this salvation was for "all," not merely for a secret "few" in the church.

How is the Trinitarian movement of God intended for us all? Within 2 Corinthians one finds that grace, love, and fellowship are to characterize the lives of the church, beginning with the apostle. In chapter 11, the apostle is for grace (v. 7), fellowship (v. 9), and love (v. 11). Through the avenue of Paul's preaching, God sends grace, fellowship, and love to the entire church. Grace is evident in the apostolic service in 8:19; 9:8; and 9:14. Fellowship is evident in his ministry in 1:7 and 6:14. And love is mediated in 8:7–8 and 8:24. The Trinity works as a unity through the apostle to bring about the unity of the church in grace, love, and fellowship.

Conclusion

So, *who* is this God we worship? According to the Corinthian benediction, he is Father, Son, and Holy Spirit—one God, three persons—who comes to humanity in grace, from love, with fellowship. This is the God who invites us into his life, empowering our worship of him. This is salvation—life with the one who is yet three—eternally ingenerate Father, eternally begotten Son, eternally proceeding Holy Spirit. This is the God who works diversely—one person stepping forward to lead in divine action—the Father in election, the Son in redemption, the Holy Spirit in perfection. Yet his works of diversity show a unity of operations—in grace, love, and fellowship—and this unity extends by grace toward the church. This is the God whose symmetrical beauty is simple in his perfect unity and dynamic in his perfect diversity. This is *who* we worship: God the Trinity.

So, *how* then are we to worship him: God the Trinity? The Trinity is for our contemplation, an exercise in which this essay has been summarily engaged. But the theology of the Trinity is also for this life in all its facets. Scripture portrays the Trinity as making an impact not only on abstract theology but also on ethics, mission, and Christian unity, as on all of our thoughts, attitudes, and actions. The early church fathers understood all of life as a theological program focused on the Trinity. One of them, Evagrius Ponticus, believed the spiritual life of the Christian was composed of practice, knowledge, and theology, with theology representing the vision of God. Counterintuitive to some polemical theologies within contemporary evangelicalism, he stated at one point that faith issues forth in love, which issues forth in knowing God. But in an accurate way, he argued that the whole Christian life is wrapped up in a theological movement toward God the Trinity. Theology and worship are inextricable. "If you are a theologian, you will pray truly; and if you pray truly, you will be a theologian."[41] To worship God correctly is to worship him as three-and-one with our whole mind, indeed with our whole being.

---

[41] Evagrius Ponticus, *De Oratione*, 60; cited in Frances M. Young with Andrew Teal, *From Nicaea to Chalcedon: A Guide to the Literature and Its Background*, 2nd ed. (London: SCM, 2010), 113–14.

THE ONLY GOD: שמע

Listen [שמע], Israel: The LORD our God, the LORD is One.
Love the LORD your God with all your heart, with all your
soul, and with all your strength. These words that I am
giving you today are to be in your heart. Repeat them to
your children.

Deuteronomy 6:4–7a (HCSB)

During the last chapter we learned that Paul presents the true
God as one yet three. God relates to humanity in this way, and
humanity must worship him correspondingly. To worship God truly
is to engage the unified life of the Father, the Son, and the Holy
Spirit. In this chapter we must look more closely at how Christians
speak of the three as one. And the best place to begin is where their
Bible put its emphasis—worshipping the one God alone. The earliest
Christians considered themselves to be fully committed to the God of
Scripture, and their Bible was that which Christians now call the Old
Testament. Their God was the God of Abraham, Isaac, and Jacob,
and of Moses, David, and the Prophets, as well as the God of Jesus
Christ. This chapter will examine the roots of Christian monotheism
and its earliest development in a Trinitarian direction.

The Devotional Confession of Israel

The ancient Jewish and early Christian emphasis on the exclusive worship of God is centered in a text known as the Shema. The Shema has
been approached as a symbol of worship and as a theological statement about the nature of God. Both of these approaches, the devotional approach and the confessional approach, possess validity and
are best treated together.

First, the Shema "has a liturgical aura about it, the feel of having
been shaped through long usage in the cult."[1] While its origin may
be debated among historical critics, it is doubtless that the Shema
became the center of Jewish devotional practices, including during
the Second Temple period, and has remained central in Jewish worship to this day. Duane Christensen said, "The words of 6:4 are in fact
the most familiar words of the entire Bible to the observant Jew, since
they are repeated daily."[2] Daniel Block notes the repetitive practice
remains: "To this day, orthodox Jews recite the Shema' twice daily as
part of their prayers in the morning when they wake up, and at night
before they fall asleep."[3]

Second, Deuteronomy 6:4 has been referred to as "the fundamental truth of Israel's religion,"[4] and as the *Grunddogma*, "basic
dogma," of the Old Testament.[5] It is called the Shema in Hebrew,

[1] S. Dean McBride, "The Yoke of the Kingdom: An Exposition of Deuteronomy
6:4–5," *Interpretation* 27 (1973): 297. Quell agrees that the Shema "has a hymnic character." Gottfried Quell, "The Old Testament Name for God," in "Κύριος,
[etc.]," in *Theological Dictionary of the New Testament*, vol. 3, ed. by Gerhard Kittel,
trans. by Geoffrey W. Bromiley (Grand Rapids, MI: Eerdmans, 1965), 1080. N. T.
Wright sees the Shema as an act of prayer and devotional commitment. N. T. Wright,
"One God, One Lord: How Paul Redefines Monotheism," *Christian Century* (27
November 2013), 22.

[2] Duane L. Christensen, *Deuteronomy 1–11*, Word Biblical Commentary (Dallas,
TX: Word, 1991), 137.

[3] Daniel I. Block, "How Many Is God? An Investigation into the Meaning of
Deuteronomy 6:4–5," *Journal of the Evangelical Theological Society* 47, no. 2 (2004):
194–95.

[4] Samuel R. Driver, *Deuteronomy*, 3rd ed., International Critical Commentary
(Edinburgh: T&T Clark, 2000), 89.

[5] W. Rupprecht, cited in Peter C. Craigie, *The Book of Deuteronomy*, 2nd ed., New
International Commentary on the Old Testament (Grand Rapids, MI: Eerdmans,
1976), 169n.

due to the first word in the text, שׁמע. In a philosophical vein the first sentence, verse 4, has sometimes been taken as an abstract, stand-alone creed: "Listen, Israel, the Lord our God, the Lord is one." However, the Shema, as we shall see, is primarily oriented in a relational and devotional direction. As a frequently cited devotional text, it is difficult to overestimate how important this text became in defining the faith of the people of Israel. Because of its repetition and its strict claim about the identity of God, it also functioned as the Jews' "central confession of faith."[6] "The Shema' is as close as early Judaism came to the formulation of a creed."[7]

The Shema is at the root of the Old Testament faith and is, therefore, foundational to New Testament Christianity, too. Christopher Seitz refers to the Old Testament as "the precondition of Trinitarian reflection" and argues, moreover, that the Israelites' "peculiar kind of monotheism" gave rise to Christianity's "Trinitarian convictions about the character of God."[8] As we shall see, the New Testament view of God as Trinity does not depart from the Israelite confession of God but is in harmony with it and develops thence. The Shema proclaims that the God of Scripture is uniquely God, yet relatedly, for he is "our God." This text certainly determines that all biblical religion is monotheistic (and at the least henotheistic), but biblical monotheism must be distinguished from the monotheism of Islam. Neither should biblical monotheism be conflated with the monotheism of later Judaism, nor that of Sabellianism, nor that of an Enlightenment unity that results in a reductionist and abstract mathematical definition of God. Scripture's writers declare emphatically that this unique, relational God is alone to be the object of worship. And human worship of God must be entire and singular in its devotedness. We begin with the immediate literary context of the first part of Deuteronomy 6, proceed to an exposition of the Shema, and conclude with a consideration of its early Christian reception.

---

[6] J. A. Thompson, *Deuteronomy: An Introduction and Commentary*, Tyndale Old Testament Commentaries (Downers Grove, IL: InterVarsity, 1974), 121.

[7] Block, "How Many Is God?," 195.

[8] Christopher Seitz, "The Trinity in the Old Testament," in *The Oxford Handbook of the Trinity*, ed. Gilles Emery and Matthew Levering (New York: Oxford University Press, 2011), 31.

The Law That Blesses (Deuteronomy 6:1–3)

Deuteronomy literally means "second law" and reveals the contours of the covenantal law between God and Israel. In spite of its focus on law, however, Walther Eichrodt warns that we should not approach it with a legalistic mind-set. "Its language is not that of the law, but that of the heart and conscience."[9] When we compare the law of the Old Testament with the laws of the nations that surround Israel in the ancient Near East, we discover that the pagan codes embody arbitrary justice, the dehumanization of lower classes, and gross brutality.[10] In contrast to the pagan nations, God's covenant with Israel raises the status of humanity by transforming law into a blessing.

Because the old covenant law is directly commanded by Yahweh, it "acquires a majesty" that places it above merely human laws. In other words, the law of Scripture is not a human innovation, which can be shifted according to human whim. It is divine law given to humanity for its benefit. Eichrodt describes Israel's law as "a spiritual achievement" that brings the whole of human life into devotional relation to God.[11] In doing so, it also places a higher value on human life and inculcates "a deepened moral sensibility."[12] The covenantal law's "humanitarian spirit," uniquely for the age, negates class distinctions in its applicability.[13] This enhanced moral sensibility for humans is ultimately based on the revelation of "the moral personality of God."[14] He explains further the theological underpinning of the blessing that God's law grants to Israel:

> There is evidence here of a genuinely noble humanity and
> a deepened feeling for equity as traits of Israelite law. This
> can hardly be explained except in terms of the knowledge
> of God—that God who created man after his own image
> and therefore protects him, even when he is liable to

---

[9] Walther Eichrodt, *Theology of the Old Testament*, vol. 1, trans. J. A. Baker (Philadelphia, PA: Westminster, 1961), 91.

[10] Ibid., 74–82.

[11] Ibid., 75.

[12] Ibid., 77.

[13] Ibid., 79.

[14] Ibid., 82.

punishment, because of the value and the right to life that
pertain to him as a human being.[15]

Because it is a law, the law of God binds the human being; but
as God's law it also blesses the human being. It blesses because God,
in love, uses his law to transform the human conscience and raise it
above itself. The law of God, as expounded in Deuteronomy 6:1–3,
has positive benefits. This is seen in at least seven different ways. First,
the law provides a standard for morality. The divine law contains commands that are to be performed, either negatively or positively, by all
human beings. And the law promises that, while there are intermediary judges within history, God himself will uphold that standard
eternally. Human actions have divine accountability.

The second way the law blesses is that it requires education.
The commands God gives are to be taught to the younger generations. The young are not left to make their own way but are raised
to know ethical excellence through the instructional efforts of their
elders. Education is key to moral advancement, but the secondary and
tertiary effects of education on the health and economic and political welfare of human beings are also extremely profound. Third, the
commands of the law are intended to cause the human being to "fear
the LORD your God all the days of your life" (v. 2), in other words, to
worship him. The law encourages human beings to direct their hearts
in devotion toward their Creator. We are reminded of the source of
our existence, its continuance, and its final consummation through
means of the law.

The fourth way in which the law brings a blessing is that it offers
life. We are to obey God's law, not in order to deprive us of vitality
but to preserve our vitality. Too often human beings view the law as
a means of burdening life, but it is intended to be a means of grace.
"Do this . . . so that you may have a long life" (v. 2c). The law's intent
is to instruct and prepare for life, an abundant life. The fifth way the
law blesses is that it establishes that God is interested in a personal
relationship with each human being. The law is not merely for the
leaders among the people. It is for all of the people. God is concerned

---

[15] Ibid., 79.

to relate to each human person on an individual basis. His law is for
"you, your son, and your grandson" (v. 2b).

The sixth thing we note about God's law is that it demands that the
individual human being consider all of his ways with meticulous concern. The Israelite must "be careful to follow" (v. 3a). This requires a
person to look constantly toward God's revelation and evaluate one's
own attitudes and actions, noting where he or she requires forgiveness and improvement. The human person is reminded of priorities
through careful consideration of God's Word. The seventh and final
blessing of God's law is that it really is intended to benefit the covenant community. God wants his covenant people to follow the law
"so that you may prosper and multiply greatly" (v. 3b).

In the grand sweep of Scripture,[16] we recognize, of course, that
the law is insufficient to bring about the final blessing of humanity
on its own. This is why the exhortation to receive, to remember, and
to retell the law concludes with a reference to a promise. While the
law cannot redeem human beings from the consequences of the law,
which all have broken, the law does contain the indication of a future
divine intervention (v. 3b). The prophets reminded later Israelites of
the law and the judgment that was to come or had already come due
to their disobedience. The people were removed from the land of
promise because of their defiance against God. But the same prophets also pledged that a wonderful change was coming. Both Jeremiah
and Ezekiel promised the Israelites that a new covenant would come
from God to transform their hearts, a transformation the law itself
was unable to provide (Jer 31:31–34; Ezek 37:14, 26).[17] In summary,
the law is firstly a means of blessing, but it secondly brings a curse on
the disobedient, and the people have disobeyed. Providentially, the
law is thirdly not the last word, for there is also the promise, which in
the New Testament is known as the gospel.

In these ways we see that God's law is intended to bless. By
departing from the law, people choose to depart from its blessing
and to enter lawlessness, which is under God's curse. Like the people
of Israel, we have all sinned. God's law came to bind humanity so

[16] For more detail on the divine οἰκονομία, see chaps. 5–8 below.
[17] Eichrodt, *Theology of the Old Testament*, 1:58–61.

that it might bless humanity. Human sin, in seeking an inappropriate freedom from God, actually bound humanity to a curse. God's gospel in Jesus Christ came to satisfy the necessary demands of God's law and set us free from the curse and to God. However, we have proceeded far beyond the immediate canonical context and must return to Deuteronomy's Shema.

The God Who Is (Deuteronomy 6:4–9)

The two primary sentences in our focal text from Deuteronomy 6 are verses 4–5. These two verses demonstrate, first, who God is, and, second, of what the human response to God ought to consist. Neither verse should be treated in isolation from the other. Modern theological scholarship tends to use verse 4 as a distinct propositional statement separable from and primary within the Shema. However, Gerald Janzen reminds us that while Mark places both verses 4 and 5 on the lips of Jesus, Matthew and Luke actually omit verse 4.[18] It seems best, therefore, to consider both verses 4 and 5, the descriptive and the hortatory aspects of the Israelite confession, as inextricably intertwined. First, the God of Israel is the Lord who is our God alone (v. 4). And without diminution in importance, second, we are to be totally devoted to him with every ounce of our being (v. 5). The remaining verses in this foundational passage in the Jewish religion consider how this truth is to be relayed to others (vv. 6–9).

The Lord Who Is Our God Alone

שמע ישראל יהוה אלהינו יהוה אחד. "Listen, Israel, the Lord our God, the Lord is One." Each Hebrew term from Deuteronomy 6:4 requires attention. Patrick Miller referred to the entire Shema as "the most important word," because Jesus considered it the first or greatest commandment. The Shema "is the primary link between Christianity and Judaism." Moreover, it is "the center of Deuteronomic theology,"

---

[18] J. Gerald Janzen, "Yahweh Our God, Yahweh Is One," *Encounter* 48 (1987): 53.

and Deuteronomy is "the center of OT theology." For these reasons Miller concludes that the Shema is "the cornerstone of biblical faith."[19] The Lord and his earliest disciples would agree that this text is important for the Christian understanding of who God is and how he must be worshipped.

שׁמע. Block commented on the delimiting function of the beginning command, "Listen!" The same word is repeated in 5:1; 6:4; and 9:1. The first instance introduces the Ten Commandments; the second occurrence, here in 6:4, introduces "a profound exposition of the essence of Israel's covenant relationship with Yahweh"; and the third marks the beginning of a new address by Moses.[20] Besides serving as a major transitional marker, the word שׁמע, "listen," is used to issue an alert. Something important is about to be proclaimed. By using this attention-gaining term, the Lord indicates that he is the God who speaks perspicuously to humanity. He is the God who clearly reveals himself in unambiguous terms to his beloved creature, thereby signifying that a relationship with God is possible. Because the one true God is speaking, it behooves the people to "listen!"

ישׂראל. The Hebrew means literally, "O Israel!" Through covenant God called the nation of Israel into existence. Because Israel came into existence as the result of divine election, the nation was put on notice that its existence is a divine work. God established the nation of Israel and always stood above it. The covenant provided Israel with a sense of God's transcendence, yet also of God's immanent presence to the nation. The covenant thus gave meaning to Israel's part in the flow of human history, even when that history involved horrific circumstances, which Israel brought on herself through disobedience.[21] In the book of Deuteronomy, the law served as the means of God's benevolence toward Israel, a benefit entirely due to God. "The majesty of divine love shows itself in this, that God alone has the power to dissolve the relationship, yet never makes use of it."[22] The covenant God gave to Israel reminds the people that

[19] Patrick D. Miller Jr., "The Most Important Word: The Yoke of the Kingdom," *The Illiff Review* 41 (1984): 15.

[20] Block, "How Many Is God?," 193.

[21] Eichrodt, *Theology of the Old Testament*, 1:36–45.

[22] Ibid., 54.

God is "the Father who loves his son Israel" and does not come as a mere judge, though he is a judge.[23] Through originally giving a name to Israel (Gen 32:28) and here covenanting with the people called by that name, God indicates that he both established and desires a deepening relationship with them.

יהוה. For the possibility of a relationship between persons to exist and to grow in intimacy, the identity of both must be known to one another. One of the primary ways persons identify one another is through naming. Moses queried the God who revealed himself at the burning bush regarding his name. The biblical idea of "the name of God" carries with it four "decisive elements," according to a neoorthodox Swiss theologian, Emil Brunner, and an evangelical American theologian, James Leo Garrett Jr. These four elements indicate that divine revelation has a relational character.[24]

In response to Moses, God disclosed his name as אהיה אשר אהיה (Exod 3:14a). This name may be translated in a number of ways, but most scholars agree that it is some derivation of the Hebrew verb, היה, "to be." The most common translation is "I am who I am,"[25] but "I will be who I will be," "I will be who I am," and "I am because I am" are also candidates. God then shortened the name to יהוה, "Yahweh" (Exodus 3:14b–15), which became a common name for the God of Israel in the Old Testament. In form Yahweh may have been the third person of "to be," so some scholars interpret it as "he causes to be," but others conclude it may be rendered "he is." As a form of self-address, it then becomes, "I am." Commentators typically point out

---

[23] Ibid., 55.

[24] The decisive elements, the first three provided by Brunner and the fourth provided by Garrett, are:

The name of God means the possibility of divine revelation. . . .

The name of God manifests the nature of God as Person. . . .

The naming of God is designed to lead human beings into communion or fellowship with God. . . .

The name of God intensifies the seriousness of blasphemy and cursing.

Emil Brunner, *The Christian Doctrine of God*, trans. by Olive Wyon (London: Lutterworth, 1949), 120–24; James Leo Garrett Jr., *Systematic Theology: Biblical, Historical, and Evangelical*, 2nd ed., 2 vols. (North Richland Hills, TX: Bibal, 2000), 1:219.

[25] This is the translation that was chosen for the Greek translation of the Hebrew, the Septuagint (LXX). Quell, "The Old Testament Name for God," 1072.

that such a name "is meant to express something like existence."[26] Whatever the exact meaning of the name, יהוה, which is often and not inappropriately interpreted as a verification of divine ontology, its covenantal context determines that God's name is, however, "no abstract concept or euphemeristic idea."[27]

Because of its holiness, as displayed for instance in the context it was given to Moses, the Jews refused to pronounce the name and substituted אדני (*Adonai*), "Lord," in its place. Adonai, which was translated into the Greek as κύριος, thus became "an expository equivalent for the divine name."[28] Adonai seems to have been deemed an appropriate substitute because of the contours of the relationship of God with his people. The ways in which the name of God is used in the Old Testament suggest that God is a personal God who invites Israel into a particular type of relationship. First, "it denotes, not just any deity, but an unequivocally distinct divine person."[29] Second, Yahweh is more than a god. Yahweh is the God who exercises universal sovereignty over his entire creation. Third, by this name Yahweh has entered a covenantal relationship with Israel, as detailed in the law of Moses, a relationship that helps Israel discern the nature of God. "The nature of God is thus compressed in the name of God. The name is both the quintessence of His person and the vehicle of His power. To name His name is to give concrete form to all that is perceptible in God."[30]

And what is perceived by Israel, who is given knowledge of the name? Israel learns that Yahweh is holy, which engenders awareness of an uncontrollable and demanding power. "Thus the name of God is a numinous force; it is נכבד, 'fraught with might,' and נורא, 'feared' (Deut 28:58), as is God Himself."[31] So, while God's name is given to

---

[26] Ibid. Quell, however, opines that the explanation of the name in Exod 3:14 indicates "a refusal to take up the question of the name of God," and thus the explanation has been interposed in the original. Ibid., 1073.

[27] Ibid., 1075.

[28] Ibid., 1058.

[29] Ibid., 1062.

[30] Ibid., 1070.

[31] Ibid.

establish a relationship, it also reveals the contours of that relationship to be one of submission to Yahweh as Lord.

אלהינו. This is actually a contraction of אלהים (*'Elohim*) and נו (*enu*). אלהים is the plural of אל (*'El*) the generic name for God, which would have been understood as a reference to deity in common with all the Semitic languages. The plural aspect of אלהים has been interpreted as indicating majesty, eminence, or greatness. The idea of such divine fullness correlates with the description of the God of the Old Testament according to a number of glorious attributes, such as 'El-Shaddai, almighty God; 'El-Elyon, most high God; and 'El-Hai, living God.[32] Then again, perhaps the plurality of אלהים; who nevertheless acts in a singular way in the biblical context, provides a linguistic hint toward a vital multiplicity within the unity of God.[33]

Scripture seems to teach that everyone, through general revelation, is innately aware of the existence of deity (Psalms 8; 19). However, we have replaced him with our own idols. The pagan nations surrounding Israel had their idols, their gods, often in a wide variety; but Israel understood that their God is unique. He is unique in relation to the other gods, and he is unique in relation to Israel. Yahweh is, indeed, the God who is alone to be worshipped because he alone is sovereign over the universe (Exod 20:3), for he alone created everything and has always existed (Neh 9:6; Ps 148:1–5; Isa 43:10; 44:6–8). These other gods cannot compare to him (Deut 4:35, 39; 32:17, 29; Isa 44:6; 45:5–6).

But in the Shema, rather than making a claim regarding his uniqueness among the gods, this God is clarified as being unique in relation to this nation. Yahweh is נו, "our" God. This most high God gave to the nations their inheritance, "but the Lord's portion is his people, Jacob his allotted heritage" (Deut 32:9). Again, in focus is the relational nature of God.

אחד. To this point each of the Hebrew terms in the Shema has reinforced the intimate nature of this most fundamental of doctrinal confessions. Proper hermeneutics indicates that words must be

---

[32] Garrett, *Systematic Theology*, 1:219–20.

[33] Aubrey R. Johnson, *The One and the Many in the Israelite Conception of God* (Cardiff, Wales: University of Wales Press, 1961), 23–28.

interpreted within the context in which they are used. There is no reason to believe this new term should not also serve a relational function. Indeed, it would be an unexpected and jarring shift to suggest that the word אחד (*'echad*) was to be taken as indicative of an austere monotheism, as if an arid and aloof God were comprised of a unitarian nature. And yet, because אחד means "one," the term has often been taken to mean that the Bible's Yahweh is a strictly monotheistic God.

Nathan MacDonald has carefully documented that the term *monotheism* is itself a relatively recent innovation, spawned in the debates of the European Enlightenment. Henry More, a Cambridge Platonist with Cartesian sensibilities, sought to refute pantheistic atheism. While apologetically useful, More's paradigmatic coining of the term, *monotheism*, nonetheless too easily pigeonholed theistic religions in binary terms.[34] The truth of religion was reduced to a function of static propositions rather than maintaining those propositions as expressions of a dynamic relationship. While Christianity has long used (and must use) propositions to clarify its proclamation, in the late seventeenth century religious discourse downplayed piety in favor of intellectualization. Truth was identified with materialistic precisionism in lieu of personal adherence. This terminology was thence brought into Old Testament studies at the university level.[35] The debates between personalists and propositionalists continue to exercise biblical and systematic theologians.[36]

Scholars as diverse as the neoorthodox Gottfried Quell, on the one hand, and evangelicals, such as Daniel Block and Gerald Janzen, on the other hand, have argued that the problem with the translation of אחד as "one" is that it too easily slips into Enlightenment-tainted monotheism. However, some of the suggested alternatives do not translate well into English. This is the case, for instance, with Janzen's proposal that אחד might be best understood as "integrity," "loyalty,"

---

[34] Nathan MacDonald, *Deuteronomy and the Meaning of "Monotheism"* (Tübingen: Mohr Siebeck, 2003), 6–20.

[35] Ibid., 21–51.

[36] Cf. the correlation of propositions with discipleship, and the twentieth-century debate over the New Testament's κήρυγμα. Malcolm B. Yarnell III, *The Formation of Christian Doctrine* (Nashville, TN: B&H Academic, 2007), 138–39, 142.

or "moral unity." While Janzen builds a strong linguistic and canonical case for his rendering of the term,[37] it does not roll off the tongue in a translation of the Shema very well. Ultimately, Janzen seems to be happy with the transliterated term, *'echad*. Although Gottfried Quell recognizes the problem with the tendency toward an abstract understanding of "one," he retains the term, explaining that it indicates not a speculative definition of the divine nature but exclusive worship.[38]

Rather than retaining "one" or moving toward a transliteration, other scholars have offered a fresh translation. MacDonald[39] and Block[40] enumerate and examine each of the alternative translations. MacDonald works through the first three alternatives, each of which uses "one" for אחד, and finds them lacking on an exegetical basis. He concludes that the fourth alternative, "YHWH is our God, YHWH alone," carries the "fitting sense."[41] Similarly, Block states that the "unitary interpretation" is weak and thus dismisses the first four translations, all of which emphasize "one." In their place he opts for the following: "Yahweh our God! Yahweh alone!" is best, if the confession is taken as a cryptic utterance. And for those preferring a nominal sentence, Block offers, "Our God is Yahweh, Yahweh alone!"[42]

To cement his argument, MacDonald finds an illuminating parallel of אחד in the beloved's exclusive devotion in Song of Songs 6:8–9.

---

[37] J. Gerald Janzen, "The Most Important Word in the Shema (Deuteronomy 4:4–5)," *Vetus Testamentum* 37, no. 3 (1987): 280–300.

[38] Quell says the Shema on the whole has "a hymnic character." Quell, "The Old Testament Name for God," 1080–81.

[39] MacDonald, *Deuteronomy and the Meaning of "Monotheism,"* 62–70.
YHWH is our God, YHWH is one
YHWH, our God, YHWH is one
YHWH, our God, is one YHWH
YHWH is our God, YHWH alone
Other Alternative Translations

[40] Block, "How Many Is God?," 196. For the sake of quick comparison with MacDonald's list, we have removed Block's repetition of "Hear, O Israel."
Yahweh our God, Yahweh is one
Yahweh our God is one Yahweh
Yahweh is our God; Yahweh is one
Yahweh is our God; Yahweh is One/Unique
Yahweh is our God; Yahweh alone

[41] MacDonald, *Deuteronomy and the Meaning of "Monotheism,"* 68.

[42] Block, "How Many Is God?," 201.

Mankind is similarly called to be single in its devotion to Yahweh.[43] Block finds support for his translation in the immediate context of the Shema, in the broader context of Deuteronomy where he discerns a profound parallel in Deuteronomy 6:14–15,[44] and in the "scriptural afterlife" of the Shema.[45] While not settling on the translation of אחד as "alone" in his earlier article, Janzen comes to compatible conclusions through a broad-ranging review of the Old Testament's use of אחד.[46]

When interpreted in the context of the Old Testament rather than with the apologetic demands of the early Enlightenment in mind, the more propositional portion of the Shema (Deut 6:4) appears to interpreters like Janzen, MacDonald, and Block to indicate a demand for the moral activity of "monolatry" rather than the mental category of "monotheism." The term "monolatry," which means literally "worship of one" when applied to the religion of the Bible, indicates that the Lord God is alone the object of human worship. As we use the term *monolatry*, it leaves to the side the ideas that pagan polytheism and patriarchal henotheism necessarily precede the development of monotheism.[47]

Similarly, as we use the term *monotheism*, it leaves to the side any expectation that the nature of God is reducible to a mathematical property. Arithmetic logic cannot comprehend the eternal God. God has established the laws by which creation functions, including mathematical laws, and such laws certainly reflect back on the nature of the deity who fostered them. However, such laws do not explain him sufficiently, nor do they delimit him. As biblical theologians continue to argue, the post-Enlightenment understanding of how unity and plurality correlate with deity in the Old Testament is due for fresh examination.[48]

---

[43] MacDonald, *Deuteronomy and the Meaning of "Monotheism,"* 74.

[44] Block, "How Many Is God?," 205–7.

[45] Ibid., 208–11.

[46] Janzen, "On the Most Important Word in the Shema," 282–300. Cf. Janzen, "Yahweh Our God, Yahweh Is One," 53–60.

[47] Michael S. Heiser, "Monotheism, Polytheism, Monolatry, or Henotheism? Toward an Assessment of Divine Plurality in the Hebrew Bible," *Bulletin for Biblical Research* 18, no. 1 (2008): 1–30.

[48] One of the earliest contributions in this regard is Aubrey Johnson's extension of H. Wheeler Robinson's discovery of the Hebrew idea of corporate personality from anthropology into theology proper. Johnson, *The One and the Many in the Israelite Conception of God*, 1–13.

The God Who Is Our Only Devotion

The Shema has sometimes been identified exclusively with Deuteronomy 6:4, but Richard Bauckham asserts that the Shema necessarily continues into 6:5.[49] Dean McBride provides a more subtle account, noting that in classical and modern Jewish usage, the Shema could be a reference to verse 4 alone, to verses 4–5, to verses 4–9, or to "a catena of biblical passages and accompanying benedictions."[50] From the perspective of Jesus Christ and his contemporary Jewish interlocutors, the Shema seems to have included both verses 4 and 5, at least according to the recounting of Mark 12:29–30. However, in the Gospels of Matthew and Luke, the theological conversation focused on verse 5, while verse 4 was silently omitted (Matt 22:37; Luke 10:27).[51] Moreover, Christianity's incarnate Lord referred to the Shema's demand for utter devotion to God as "most important" and to the related command of love toward humanity in Leviticus 19:18 as "second" (Mark 12:29–30). Finally, it should be noted that both Jesus and the Jewish legal experts with whom he engaged agreed that the emphasis must fall on the attitude of the heart toward God, while abstract definitions are conspicuous in their absence.

It could be argued that from either an ancient or a contemporary Jewish perspective, as well as from the New Testament perspective, the Shema may concern the truth of who God is, but even more important is the human heart's response to God. Verse 4, "Listen, Israel: The Lord our God, the Lord alone," is immediately followed by verse 5, "Love the Lord your God with all your heart, with all your soul, and with all your strength." In the Synoptic Gospels as a whole, the emphasis is given to verse 5, as noted previously. This should not be taken as an argument against a philosophico-theological approach to the Shema, but emphasis must be placed on religious devotion to God. What has been called "the fundamental truth" of the Old Testament must be completed in what has been called

---

[49] Richard Bauckham, *God Crucified: Monotheism and Christology in the New Testament* (Grand Rapids, MI: Eerdmans, 1998), 6.

[50] McBride, "The Yoke of the Kingdom," 275–76.

[51] Mark and Matthew place the Shema directly on the lips of Jesus, while Luke has a legal expert repeating the Shema.

"the fundamental duty."[52] It is instructive that Judaism only came to interpret verse 4 of the Shema in a radically monotheistic way in the third century after the rise of Christianity.[53] This raises the question of exactly how the Jewish milieu from which developed the earliest Christian churches understood itself as a "monotheistic" faith.[54]

Larry Hurtado has argued that the Jews in the period in which the Christian churches began had a "rather strict monotheistic stand—indeed, offensively strict in the eyes of virtually all pagans."[55] The Judaism of the New Testament era, which Hurtado calls "ancient Judaism," was not merely monotheistic but radically so. However, he also argues it "could stretch to accommodate reverence for additional figures without breaking." The elasticity of ancient Judaism's strict monotheism was due to the presence of "divine agents" within the Hebrew Bible and other ancient Jewish sources.[56] Among these divine agents were personified divine attributes and powers, such as Wisdom, Word, and Spirit;[57] exalted patriarchs, such as Enoch, Jacob, and Moses;[58] and principal angels, such as Michael, Yahoel, and Qumran's version of Melchizedek.[59] Jewish monotheism was not threatened with these divine agents because the personifications were understood metaphorically and the angels and patriarchs were never allowed any type of worship. The Christian "mutation"

---

[52] Driver, *Deuteronomy*, 89.

[53] McBride, "The Yoke of the Kingdom," 277, 287.

[54] It has been argued that Judaism in the second temple period did not develop a theory of monotheism because it was not compelled to acquire the abstract terms necessary for cross-cultural evangelism. Christians, on the other hand, acquired such out of the desire to disciple the nations. "Jews saw little need to explain their faith to outsiders, and their leaders were more concerned with the practice of worshiping God than with developing a theory of monotheism." Gerald Bray, *God Has Spoken: A History of Christian Theology* (Wheaton, IL: Crossway, 2014), 32.

[55] Larry W. Hurtado, *One God, One Lord: Early Christian Devotion and Ancient Jewish Monotheism*, 2nd ed. (New York: T&T Clark, 1998), 1.

[56] Ibid., 14.

[57] Ibid., 41–50.

[58] Ibid., 51–69.

[59] Ibid., 71–92.

of monotheism in a "binitarian" direction did not compromise this unrelenting Jewish monotheism.[60]

Hurtado's solution, however, is not without its detractors. Richard Bauckham divides prior approaches to the monotheism of ancient Judaism, which many scholars now call "Second Temple Judaism," into two main types. First is the "strict" monotheism of Hurtado and others. Second is the "flexible" monotheism offered by scholars interacting with Rudolf Bultmann's "Gnostic redeemer myth" theory. These scholars surmise that intermediary figures, including those to which Hurtado assigns "divine agency," at least blurred the lines of monotheism.[61] Bauckham puts forward a third thesis. The monotheism of Second Temple Judaism was indeed "strict." However, this strict monotheism was combined with a high Christology among the early Christians. On the one hand, "they drew the line of distinction between the one God and all other reality clearly." On the other hand, the New Testament uses strict monotheism in ways that allow "including Jesus in the unique identity of the one God as commonly understood in Second Temple Judaism."[62] Bauckham later coins the term, "Christological monotheism," to describe his third and favored theory of first-century Jewish monotheism. He also departs from Hutardo in asserting that the personified attributes are more than metaphorical; Word and Wisdom "participate in the creative work of God and in his sovereignty, and so belong intrinsically to God's unique identity."[63]

Whether one accepts the "strict" monotheism theory, the "flexible" monotheism theory, or Bauckham's strict-but-inclusive theory of ancient Judaism is thus disputable. What seems indisputable, however, is that the God thus worshipped was to receive exclusive

---

[60] Ibid., 93, 126. Johnson, writing a half century earlier, argued against too quickly moving into a metaphorical or other mode of interpretation in order to secure a "logical coherence often foreign to Israelite thinking." Johnson, *The One and the Many in the Israelite Conception of God*, 12, 31.

[61] Bauckham, *God Crucified*, 2–3. E.g., James D. G. Dunn, "Was Christianity a Monotheistic Faith from the Beginning?," *Scottish Journal of Theology* 35 (1982): 303–36.

[62] Bauckham, *God Crucified*, 3–4.

[63] Ibid., 25–27.

and entire devotion. Hutado refers to the monotheistic worship of both Jews and Christians in this early period with the synonyms of "devotion," "piety," "religious practice," and "religious life." In early Christianity, "we have a significantly new but essentially internal development within the Jewish monotheistic tradition, a mutation within that species of religious devotion."[64] Bauckham concurs. The early Christian church was "fully continuous with early Jewish monotheism but distinctive in the way it sees Jesus Christ as intrinsic to the identity of the unique God." And "the exalted Christ's participation in the unique divine sovereignty is recognized by worship."[65] Block, MacDonald, and McBride, among many other commentators, would not disagree with this emphasis: the Shema requires exclusive and entire worship of God the Lord, and this requirement applies to Christians as well as to Jews (indeed to all creatures).

Any consideration of the divine command in Deuteronomy 6:5, the "most important" command according to Jesus, must begin with the single imperatival verb, אהב (*'aheb*). There are two common Hebrew words in the Bible for the activity of "love," the verb אהב along with its cognate noun, אהבה (*'ahabah*), and the noun, חסד (*chesed*). Theologically, אהבה indicates electing love, requiring a prior divine movement, and חסד indicates subsequent covenant love made possible through election.[66] The Shema uses the verb אהב but applies it to humanity rather than God, which presents the theological problem of interpreting exactly how man's love for God is initiated.

According to McBride, God in his electing love chose Israel through the patriarchs. "The love of God toward Israel is hence synonymous with the acts of gracious election upon which the covenant is grounded."[67] Man's אהב toward God is, therefore, a "reciprocal love." "It is, indeed, the zealous allegiance to Yahweh's exclusive, divine kingship that underlies the manifold decrees, statutes, and

---

[64] Hutardo, *One God, One Lord*, 99–100.

[65] Bauckham, *God Crucified*, 26–27, 34.

[66] "*'Ahabah* is the cause of the covenant; *chesed* is the means of its continuance. Thus *'ahabah* is God's Election-Love, whilst *chesed* is His Covenant-Love." Norman Snaith, *The Distinctive Ideas of the Old Testament* (London: Epworth, 1944), 131–33; cited in Garrett, *Systematic Theology*, 1:275.

[67] McBride, "The Yoke of the Kingdom," 299–300.

ordinances in the Deuteronomic torah."[68] Loving God in this way indicates a totality of the heart and of the actions that proceed thence. Man's loving response to God's electing love is "motivated out of gratitude" and results in "personal," "intimate," and "particular" covenantal action.[69] Block says that "*'ahab* denotes the fundamental disposition of commitment within a covenant relationship that seeks the well-being and the pleasure of one's covenant partner, often without regard for oneself."[70]

In a chapter subtitled "'Monotheism' as Devoted Love," MacDonald reviews the various ways in which the language of אהבה, election love, was used in Scripture. אהבה was used within a number of intimate relationships, most of which involved exclusive and life-long attachments: husband and wife, father and son, king and subject, and master and slave.[71] In the immediate passage after the Shema, a number of verbs are used to express how Israel's love for God was to display itself. These included verbs of remembrance, fear, service, devotion, oath taking, jealousy, not testing, and keeping commands.[72] Deuteronomy 7 contains the violent חרם (*cherem*) legislation that has caused no small amount of concern for Christian exegetes, especially in the more tolerant modern period. According to MacDonald, it is best to understand the חרם of the land and its peoples to the Lord as "a metaphor of devotion to YHWH." Through חרם the cultic apparatus associated with pagan deities was to be dismantled entirely so that the hearts of the Israelites might be entirely given to the Lord.[73]

McBride points out that the threefold adverbial modification of the command to love has resulted in a variety of interpretations. Israel is to love God with לבב (*lebab*) heart, נפש (*nephesh*) soul, and מאד (*me'od*) strength. Rabbinic midrash said the reference to the heart concerned the will, the reference to the soul indicated commitment even to death, and strength obligated one's property. Early Christian exegetes viewed the terms as descriptive of internal anthropology,

---

[68] Ibid., 300.
[69] Ibid., 301.
[70] Block, "How Many Is God?," 201.
[71] MacDonald, *Deuteronomy and the Meaning of "Monotheism,"* 100–104.
[72] Ibid., 104–8.
[73] Ibid., 108–23, esp. 111–12.

respectively the mind, the soul, and spiritual power. McBride disagrees with both the Jewish rabbis and the Christian fathers. The three terms "were not meant to specify distinct acts, spheres of life, attributes, or the like." Rather, the adverbial qualifications are to be taken together to call the hearer to an "absolute singularity of personal devotion to God."[74] Block agrees with McBride and provides graphics to illustrate the holistic and concentric understanding as opposed to the partition understanding of the adverbial qualification of love toward God. Block concludes, "Covenant commitment must be rooted in the heart, but then extend to every level of one's being and existence."[75]

The commitment of the Israelites' hearts to the Lord was not, however, confined to that first generation. While the negative aspect of חרם removed alternative forms of educating the human heart regarding the divine (Deuteronomy 7), the positive aspect of אהבה toward the Lord God alone was to be transmitted to subsequent generations through a detailed and rigorous educational program (Deuteronomy 6). After the fundamental doctrine of "biblical monotheism"[76] is given in 6:4 and the fundamental duty is emphasized in 6:5, the Israelite's personal internal incorporation of the Shema is reemphasized in 6:6, and the education of subsequent generations is elaborated in 6:7ff.

"The book of Deuteronomy attaches a special importance to this task of teaching the family. But the demands of Yahweh's covenant are to be the subject of conversation at all times in the home, by the way, by night and by day. . . . God's love and His covenant demands were to be the central and absorbing interest of a man's whole life."[77] I have elaborated on the educational aspects and implications of this

---

[74] "While syntactically the three phrases are coordinate, semantically they are concentric, forming a sort of (prosaic) climactic parallelism. Thus, as noted above, לבב (*lebab*) alone designates the intentionality of the whole man; נפש (*nepesh*) similarly means the whole 'self,' [and] מאד (*me'od*) evokes the fullest 'capacity' of loving obedience to Yahweh which the whole person can muster." McBride, "The Yoke of the Kingdom," 303–4. At the same time that this devotion is personal, it is also communal. Ibid., 304.

[75] Block, "How Many Is God?," 202–4.

[76] J. A. Thompson, *Deuteronomy: An Introduction and Commentary*, Tyndale Old Testament Commentaries (Downers Grove, IL: InterVarsity, 1974), 122.

[77] Ibid., 123.

passage for the Christian family elsewhere.[78] But how did Christians come to incorporate the "radical," "strict," or "biblical" monotheism of the Shema into their fundamental dogmatic identity? More particularly, how did they incorporate worship of Christ Jesus with worship of God alone, much less the Holy Spirit?

Toward a Trinitarian Monotheism

It should be abundantly clear by now that while the Lord commonly advocated in both ancient Judaism and early Christianity is worshipped as God alone, the ascription of "monotheism" to the shared theological belief of that period is not without difficulty. Moreover, Judaism and Christianity soon diverged from each other, even as they both retained a commitment to worship exclusively the God of the Hebrew Bible, which Christians began to call the Old Testament. Gerald Bray evaluates the similarities and differences between the commonly founded yet increasingly divergent Jewish and early Christian beliefs about God. Both the ancient Jews and the early Christians believed that God alone was to be worshipped. They also agreed that this God was eternal, sovereign, personal, spiritual, holy, and good. He is the Creator who is simultaneously transcendent above his creatures yet intimately involved with their history. The crux of the Jewish-Christian disagreement about their common God concerned the place of the Messiah in relation to God.[79] The Christians, whether Jewish or Gentile, believed the Messiah was Jesus, that Jesus was exalted to the throne of God, and thus he must be worshipped. Non-Christian Jews were still awaiting the Messiah's arrival, did not place him on the throne with God, and considered the self-placement of Jesus on the throne of God blasphemous enough to deserve death (Matt 26:59–66).

But how did the Christian church come to the view that Jesus Christ was to be included with God in worship? A number of studies

---

[78] Yarnell, "'My Son, Be Strong in the Grace That Is in Christ Jesus': The Baptist Family at Worship," *Southwestern Journal of Theology* 49 (2006): 49–64.

[79] Gerald Bray, *God Has Spoken: A History of Christian Theology* (Wheaton, IL: Crossway, 2014), 69–96.

have investigated the development of this phenomenon in the New Testament documents. Many have focused on the titles ascribed to Jesus, such as "Son of Man," "Christ," "Lord," and "Son of God." Others have looked at Christological concepts such as his preexistence and his work in creation, redemption, and consummation. Hurtado decided to approach the matter from the perspective of how Jesus became the object of worship, believing the apostles' profound "visionary-prophetic experiences" of the exalted Christ were the source for the titles ascribed to him. When the apostles saw Christ exalted to the sovereign throne of the Father, this "produced the firm conviction that Jesus had been made to share so fully in divine prerogatives and heavenly glory that he was to be included in the devotional life of the elect and given the sort of veneration in their groups previously appropriate only for God."[80]

Hurtado discerned six features of the Christian inclusion of Jesus in divine worship: their hymns, prayers, use of his name, the Lord's Supper, confessions of faith, and prophetic pronouncements of his resurrection.[81] Unfortunately, Hurtado's treatment of Christ only from a "Christology from below" perspective brings intimations of adoptionism and subordinationism. He omits any discussion of Christ's divine preexistence, even with such significant "Christology from above" passages as the early Christological hymn in Philippians 2.[82] Moreover, while Hurtado affirms the "mutation" of Christian devotion of the one God into a "binitarian" shape, since it includes Jesus alongside his Father, he fails to consider a "Trinitarian" inclusion of the Holy Spirit.

Bauckham builds on the work of Hurtado, the two New Testament theologians serving as colleagues at premier Scottish universities. However, Bauckham goes beyond the "prophetic-visionary" experience thesis of Hurtado, saying Christians included Jesus within their exclusive worship of the one God in four ways. "First, the texts frequently refer to Jesus' exaltation or sovereignty over 'all things.'"[83]

---

[80] Hurtado, *One God, One Lord*, 120. Cf. ibid., 117–22.
[81] Ibid., 100–114.
[82] Ibid., 93–99.
[83] Bauckham, *God Crucified*, 31.

Only God was seen as sovereign over all creation, so Christ's inclusion in that sovereignty was without parallel and indicative of a shared divine identity. "Secondly, many of the texts emphasize Jesus' exaltation and sovereignty over all angelic powers, sometimes with an emphatic use of the potent Jewish imagery of height."[84] "Thirdly, the exalted Jesus is given the divine name, the Tetragrammaton יהוה (YHWH), the name that names the unique identity of the one God in a way that the sometimes ambiguous word 'god' does not."[85] "Fourthly, the exalted Christ's participation in the unique divine sovereignty is recognized by worship."[86]

While these and other biblical indicators of the deity of Christ Jesus have been considered in numerous monographs, biblical commentaries, New Testament theologies, and systematic theologies, we shall focus on the divine title ascribed to Jesus from the Shema.[87] Among the titles that at the least imply the divine identity of Jesus Christ, the Greek κύριος (Lord) is one of the most significant. Theologians in the higher critical tradition once argued that the ascription of "Lord" to Jesus is a later Hellenistic imposition.[88] But the early and widespread acceptance of *Maranatha*, the Aramaic cry of "The Lord has come," argues otherwise. The use of *Maranatha* within the early church has been one among many factors that have turned the acidic use of the historical critical method against its own conclusions.[89]

In the Synoptic Gospels, κύριε, the vocative use, may have been an honorific title, but Jesus's reference to himself as "Lord" points to something more significant (Mark 2:28; 11:3; 12:37). In the final

---

[84] Ibid., 32.

[85] Ibid., 34.

[86] Ibid.

[87] A summary of this research may be found in Leon Morris, *New Testament Theology* (Grand Rapids, MI: Zondervan, 1986), 39–55. A fuller compilation of research regarding the divine titles of Jesus may be found in Garrett, *Systematic Theology*, 1:665–710. The human titles are delineated in Garrett, *Systematic Theology*, 1:607–64.

[88] Rudolf Bultmann, *Theology of the New Testament*, trans. Kendrick Grobel, 2 vols. (New York: Scribner, 1951, 1955), 1:51, 124–28.

[89] The prayer of Maranatha as it appears in 1 Cor 16:22 was the "Achilles' heel" to this theory of evolving Christology. George Eldon Ladd, *A Theology of the New Testament* (Grand Rapids, MI: Eerdmans, 1974), 340.

passage listed, Jesus cites Psalm 110, a royal psalm ascribed to David. Psalm 110 is "the Old Testament text to which the New Testament most often alludes"[90] and is "the basis of the apostles' teaching on the exaltation, heavenly session and royal priesthood of Christ." In using it, Jesus challenged the contemporary Jewish expectation of the Messiah.[91]

In applying the royal psalms to the Messiah in this manner, Jesus also set the early church on a trajectory of interpretation that resulted in his inclusion with God on the divine throne. If the "my Lord" to which "the Lord" referred in the psalm of David was the Messiah, as Jesus argued, then the Messiah is worthy of worship. The Christ expected in the teaching of Jesus is thereby exalted to the throne of God and rules with God. Other royal psalms that indicate an intimate positioning of the Lord alongside the Lord, of the Son with the Father, include Psalm 2:7, which is cited accordingly in Acts 13:33 and Hebrews 1:5 and 5:5 and Psalm 45:6–7, which is used similarly in Hebrews 1:8–9. Psalm 8:6 is often used alongside Psalm 110 in the New Testament to indicate the gift of universal divine sovereignty to the Messiah, too: "You made him ruler over the works of your hands, and placed all things under his feet."[92]

The earliest κήρυγμα proclaimed by the apostles in the book of Acts makes much of Jesus as κύριος (cf. Acts 2:36). Acts also uses κύριος "simultaneously for God and for the exalted Jesus."[93] And as for the author of half of the New Testament books, "the heart of the Pauline proclamation is the Lordship of Christ" (2 Cor 4:5).[94] Salvation begins with an internal belief and an external confession that Jesus is Lord (Rom 10:9). Only those are Christians who actually receive Jesus as their Lord (Col 2:6). Nobody can confess Jesus as κύριος apart from the sovereign work of the Holy Spirit (1 Cor 12:3).

---

[90] There are 21 quotations or allusions. Bauckham, *God Crucified*, 29.

[91] Derek Kidner, *Psalms 73–150: A Commentary on Books 3–5 of the Psalms*, Tyndale Old Testament Commentaries (Downers Grove, IL: InterVarsity, 1975), 392.

[92] Cf. Matt 22:44; Mark 12:36; 1 Cor 15:25–28; Eph 1:20–22; 1 Pet 3:22.

[93] Ladd, *A Theology of the New Testament*, 338–39. Ladd argues that the turning point for the common Christian ascription of κύριος to Jesus came after his resurrection. Ibid., 172, 339.

[94] Ibid., 415.

God the Father has given the name of "Lord" to Christ Jesus and, at the end of all things, every knee shall bow and every tongue shall confess that Jesus is κύριος (Phil 2:9–10). The apostolic use of κύριος, as exemplified in Acts and in the Pauline epistles, is simultaneously monotheistic and inclusive of the Father and the Son. This is a profound and novel innovation from the perspective of both the Hebrews and the Greeks. "Paul, then, does not make any distinction between θεός and κύριος as though κύριος were an intermediary god; there are no instances of any such usage in the world contemporary with primitive Christianity."[95]

In reinforcing this novel move, Paul also dealt with the Shema. In 1 Corinthians 8:5, Paul dismisses the existence of multiple gods and multiple lords. In the next verse he provides a formula that retains yet advances the Shema. Note the structure of 1 Corinthians 8:6, which develops from the Shema's structure:[96]

There is one God, the Father,
    from whom are all things and we for him,
And one Lord, Jesus Christ,
    Through whom are all things and we through him.

When this passage is compared with Deuteronomy 6:4's identification of "God" and "Lord," it becomes clear, according to N. T. Wright, that the Shema has been "revised" and "robust[ly] redefined" with a "revolution[ary]" result.[97] "The real shock of the passage, though, is simply the inclusion of Jesus within the Shema."[98] Bauckham agrees, "It should be quite clear that Paul is including the Lord Jesus Christ in the unique divine identity. He is redefining monotheism as christological monotheism."[99] With his characteristic irenic restraint, Anthony Thiselton agrees with those who argue that

---

[95] Werner Foerster, "Κύριος in the New Testament," in *Theological Dictionary of the New Testament*, 3:1091.

[96] Both Bauckham and Wright delineate the fourfold structure. We have offset the modifying clauses further. Bauckham, *God Crucified*, 37; Wright, "One God, One Lord," 23.

[97] Ibid., 24.

[98] Ibid., 23.

[99] Bauckham, *God Crucified*, 38.

the Shema is the basis of 1 Corinthians 8:6. "Nevertheless, these discussions call attention to the placing together of God and Christ, of
creation and redemption, in a way that is both Pauline and yet draws
upon pre-Pauline credal traditions."[100] Hurtado also thinks it is prob-
able that Paul is alluding to and modifying "the traditional Jewish
confession of the uniqueness of the one God, the Shema."[101]

Wright, Thiselton, and Bauckham have commented on the various prepositions that describe the church's relationship with God and
the Lord. The church is "from" and "to" God the Father, indicating
both creation and eschatology. The church is, however, "through"
the Lord Jesus Christ, indicating sustenance. In Romans 11:36, all of
creation is said to be "from," "through," and "to" God the Father.
God the Father is thus the "efficient cause," the "instrumental cause,"
and the "final cause" of creation. However, in 1 Corinthians 8:6,
while the efficient cause and the final cause are the Father, the instrumental cause is Jesus Christ. "Paul's reformulation in 1 Corinthians
8:6 includes Christ in this exclusively divine work of creation."[102]

Extending the discussion into historical theology, Craig Blaising
concluded that the formation of the Nicene Creed was a "hermeneutical development" based on 1 Corinthians 8:6 and Deuteronomy
6:4. "This use of 1 Cor 8:6 is obviously intentional, and it reveals
to us the ultimate origin of the Nicene Creed. Its origins lie in the
New Testament restatement/interpretation of the *Shema*." Blaising
goes on to assert that the addition of the Holy Spirit was due to the
influence of the triune formula of Matthew 28:19, "but the primary
text is 1 Cor 8:6."[103] While I have argued (and still maintain) that
Matthew 28 provides the primary structure for the early Trinitarian
creeds,[104] Blaising has delineated the profound theological connection between the central confessions of the Old Testament, the New

---

[100] Anthony C. Thiselton, *The First Epistle to the Corinthians: A Commentary
on the Greek Text*, The New International Greek Testament Commentary (Grand
Rapids, MI: Eerdmans, 2000), 636–37.

[101] Hurtado, *One God, One Lord*, 97.

[102] Bauckham, *God Crucified*, 39.

[103] Craig A. Blaising, "Creedal Formation as Hermeneutical Development: A
Reexamination of Nicaea," *Pro Ecclesia* 19, no. 4 (2010): 384.

[104] Yarnell, *The Formation of Christian Doctrine*, 187–92.

Testament, and the postapostolic church. The New Testament theologian, George Eldon Ladd, made a similar suggestion. "The early church worshipped God; it also worshipped Jesus as the exalted *Kyrios.* Here in the earliest Christology of the primitive church are the beginnings of trinitarian theology."[105] The seamless transition from the exclusive worship of God the Lord in ancient Israel to the Christological monotheism of the New Testament to the Trinitarian monotheism of the early church is well on its way to being demonstrated.

The Challenge of Contemporary "Monotheism"

Much of this chapter has been concerned with exactly what monotheism is and whether, or (perhaps it could be stated better) in what way Christianity is monotheistic. Much of the difficulty present in the ascription of monotheism to the God of the Bible comes because theologians and philosophers appear to be using mathematics in inappropriate ways to describe God. Μόνος is the Greek adjective for "only" or "alone." (Interestingly, the Septuagint used the Greek numeral εἷς, or "one," rather than μόνος to translate the Hebrew אחד in Deuteronomy 6:4.) In spite of what, therefore, could have been a refocus on exclusive worship of God, the term "monotheism," as typically used in modern Western theological literature, has emphasized an abstract unity rather than a devotional exclusivity.

Perhaps at the root of this Western tendency toward a fundamental abstract unity in God, as opposed to exclusive worship, is the fact that the Latin Vulgate uses the numeral *unus* ("one") rather than *solus* ("only" or "alone") to translate the Hebrew אחד. The Latin choice may have made it easier for those in the Western traditions of Christianity to tend toward some form of Unitarianism. Theodore de Régnon's remarks that Greek Christianity began with the Trinity while Latin Christianity began with the divine unity have come under scrutiny in recent years, but most scholars recognize that the

---

[105] Ladd, *A Theology of the New Testament*, 341.

tendencies are there. The debate regarding Eastern versus Western trends continues among both Roman Catholics[106] and evangelicals.[107]

Perhaps the acerbic wit of Malcolm Muggeridge may help modern Western Christians question whether they have sometimes used mathematics inappropriately to define God. At the end of a broad-ranging critical evaluation of English culture, including its politics and religion, Muggeridge characterized the popular theology of the twentieth century: "God is mathematics, crieth the preacher. In the name of Algebra, the Son, Trigonometry, the Father, and Thermodynamics, the Holy Ghost, Amen."[108] The pious Christian may bristle at Muggeridge's impish humor, but his sarcasm should prompt serious reflection. A simplistic ascription of arithmetic's finite measures to the infinite God of the Bible, who is simply one at the same time that he is complexly three, will ultimately fail to capture who God is. "Who God is" according to the rich ontology of the apostle John is the subject of our next three chapters.

---

[106] Karl Rahner helped ignite the twentieth-century revival of concern for the Trinity using de Régnon's thesis. Vincent Holzer, "Karl Rahner, Hans Urs von Balthasar, and Twentieth-Century Catholic Current on the Trinity," in *The Oxford Handbook of the Trinity*, 319. But Lewis Ayres vehemently rejects this use of de Régnon. Ayres, "Augustine on the Trinity," in ibid., 123.

[107] Colin Gunton adopted the paradigm as part of his withering critique of Augustine, but his student, Stephen Holmes, recently sought to undermine that thesis and reclaim Augustine. Colin E. Gunton, *The Promise of Trinitarian Theology*, 2nd ed. (Edinburgh: T&T Clark, 1997), 30–55; Stephen R. Holmes, *The Quest for the Trinity: The Doctrine of God in Scripture, History and Modernity* (Downers Grove, IL: IVP Academic, 2012), 129–30, 144–46.

[108] Malcolm Muggeridge, *The Most of Malcolm Muggeridge* (New York: Simon & Schuster, 1966), 9.

4

GOD INTERPRETING GOD:
ΈΞΗΓΕΟΜΑΙ

> Nobody has ever seen God. The only begotten God, who
> is in the lap of the Father, has interpreted [ἐξηγήσατο] him.
> John 1:18

The difficulty of discerning "who God is," such as whether he
is Unitarian or Trinitarian or someone else entirely, has been
complicated by the knowledge that God is simply not visible to the
human eye. Because God is spiritual, or immaterial, he is not subject
to measurement in the physical realm. In the era that began with
modernity, the experimental method, which requires the manipula-
bility of matter, became the dominant means of perceiving truth and
testing alternative claims about truth. While the realm of materiality
has taken a prominent lead in modern science, human philosophy has
since ancient times recognized the epistemological limits of immaterial claims. The conclusion of the prologue to John's Gospel recapitu-
lates this problem with the incontestable claim that no one has ever
actually laid eyes on God. Human beings do not have the authority
to peel back the curtain that separates their historical bondage from
God's eternal freedom. Human beings do not have the ability to peer
at will into things divine.

However, according to John, while man cannot see God, God has the ability to open the curtain and reveal his eternal self to humanity within history. God has interpreted his mysterious existence to human beings through his Son, his begotten self. (We consider in the next chapter the interpretation of μονογενής, "begotten," and κόλπος, "lap" or "himself.") The final verb in John's prologue, ἐξηγήσατο, which is literally "to lead out," has been translated in a number of ways. It could mean "declare" (KJV, ASV), "make known" (NIV, ESV), "explain" (NASB), "reveal" (HCSB, NLT), "draw out" (Thayer), or even in its fullest metaphorical usage, "interpret." We have chosen to translate ἐξηγέομαι as "interpret" as a means of reminding contemporary exegetes, or interpreters, that the proper exegesis of God begins with the interpretation God himself gives.

The Gospel of Luke also ascribes to Jesus the role of theological exegete. The disciples on the road to Emmaus, slow and unwise, were given a Christological interpretation (διερμηνεία) and explanation (διάνοια) of the Hebrew Bible (Luke 24:25–27, 32). The risen Lord went on to explain the same hermeneutical method to the gathered disciples in Jerusalem (24:44–45).[1] Coming alongside John and Luke, who highlighted the role of the Son (cf. John 1:18), the apostles Peter and Paul point to the Holy Spirit as also necessarily involved in interpretation (ἐπίλυσις in 2 Pet 1:21; ἐγγράφω in 2 Cor 3:3; cf. John 14:26; 16:13). Exegesis is, in apostolic terms, a work of theological grace. However, within Protestant Christianity, theological exegesis has become largely suspect. Moreover, appeal to prior attempts at theological exegesis, such as that practiced among the early church fathers, has been largely dismissed.

The "Superiority" of Precritical Exegesis?

It may seem shocking that a contemporary theology text dedicated to evaluating the biblical portraits of God as a Trinity includes extensive

---

[1] For an insightful treatment of Jesus's view of the extent, truthfulness, and proper interpretation of the Hebrew Bible, see E. Earle Ellis, *The Old Testament in Early Christianity: Canon and Interpretation in the Light of Modern Research* (Grand Rapids, MI: Baker, 1991), 123–38.

interaction with commentators from the patristic era. The alienation that many contemporary scholars may feel when reading especially the next two chapters arises because the modern guilds of biblical theologians and systematic theologians have often ignored or denigrated the earliest Christian theologians. In a singularly provocative essay, originally written in 1980 but subsequently republished and widely cited, David Steinmetz challenged the modern exegetical *Zeitgeist*, particularly with regard to recognizing only the human author's original intent. "The medieval theory of levels of meaning in the biblical text, with all its undoubted defects, flourished because it is true, while the modern theory of a single meaning, with all its demonstrable virtues, struggles because it is false."[2]

Steinmetz made the claim, preposterous from a modernist perspective, that the early and medieval interpreters of the Bible might actually teach modern exegetes something substantive and beneficial. Steinmetz did not reject the historical critical method in its entirety, but he called for the judicious employment of both precritical and critical methods. He also called for the self-evaluation of the modern hermeneutical method in light of its own history.

> Until the historical critical method becomes critical of its
> own theoretical foundations and develops a hermeneutical
> theory adequate to the nature of the text that it is
> interpreting, it will remain restricted, as it deserves to be, to
> the guild and the academy, where the question of truth can
> endlessly be deferred.[3]

The difficulty of using the early church fathers in biblical commentary began with the Reformation and intensified with the Enlightenment. While Steinmetz considered the progress of precritical exegesis from Origen in the third century through Nicholas of Lyra in the fourteenth century, a review of the historical context in which contemporary exegesis has been pursued since the Middle

---

[2] David C. Steinmetz, *Memory and Mission: Theological Reflections on the Christian Past* (Nashville, TN: Abingdon, 1988), 163. The author must disclose that he appreciates Steinmetz's influence in the supervision of his 1996 master's thesis at Duke University.
[3] Ibid.

Ages is also required. In this chapter we begin with a review of of the progress of exegesis since the Reformation period, paying special attention to the problems introduced in modernity. It is hoped that biblical exegetes in the fields of biblical theology and systematic theology will be encouraged not only to place the biblical text properly but also to criticize their own method of perceiving and construing that biblical text. In this way a more chaste and objective interpretation of Scripture may be possible.

Patristic Exegesis and Evangelical[4] Exegesis

During the Reformation, Martin Luther became famous for his willingness to set aside the vast authority of patristic exegesis and elevate his conscience's understanding of the Bible. What good is it "to rely on the venerable old Fathers"? "Were not they too all equally blind, or rather, did they not simply overlook the clearest and most explicit statements of Paul?"[5] Of course, Luther's view was more nuanced than a mere rejection of all patristic contributions. On the one hand, he held patristic theology worthy of condemnation. "Even under the judgment of that whole choir of saints that you invoke, or rather of the whole world, we dare to say, and we glory in saying, that it is our duty not to admit something that is nothing and the nature of which cannot with certainty be shown."[6] Luther was ready to oppose the

---

[4] The term *evangelical* is used herein in three broad senses: first, to refer to all those who stem from the various Reformation traditions; second, to refer to the scions of the pietistic and evangelical revivals of the seventeenth and eighteenth centuries; and third, to refer most peculiarly to the twentieth-century American post-fundamentalist movement. The context will manifest its particular usage. For more on the meaning of "evangelicalism," and its distinction from the free church tradition, see my *The Formation of Christian Doctrine* (Nashville, TN: B&H, 2007), xiii–xvi and *passim*. For a more detailed taxonomy, see Roger E. Olson, *The Westminster Handbook to Evangelical Theology* (Louisville, KY: Westminster John Knox, 2004), 3–8.

[5] Cited in Christopher A. Hall, *Reading Scripture with the Church Fathers* (Downers Grove, IL: InterVarsity, 1998), 12.

[6] Martin Luther, *De Servo Arbitrio*, in *Luther and Erasmus: Free Will and Salvation*, ed. E. Gordon Rupp and Philip S. Watson, Library of Christian Classics (Philadelphia, PA: Westminster, 1969), 152.

"numerous body of most learned men, who have found approval in so many centuries," even if on his side were "only Wyclif and one other, Laurentius Valla."[7]

On the other hand, more positively, he did believe the fathers should be consulted in biblical interpretation. According to Paul Althaus, Luther "did not absolutize the Bible in opposition to tradition. . . . The Holy Spirit led not only the apostles but also Christendom since the time of the apostles."[8] Luther was willing to speak of the fathers with "praises."[9] For instance, he believed the early councils could be helpful, especially with the doctrines of the Trinity and the person of Christ.[10] But the tradition of the fathers cannot be accepted haphazardly because not all of them were saints and their writings have been misused.[11] Patristic doctrine must be subjected to the test of Scripture: "We are commanded not to admit any dogma that is not first proved by divine attestation."[12] The fathers may be used but primarily as a prompt for biblical exegesis. "The writings of all the holy fathers should be read only for a time, in order that through them we may be led to the Holy Scriptures."[13] After the Council of Trent advocated a two-source theory of tradition, oral and written, Protestant intellectuals coalesced around the critique that Scripture alone remains authoritative. The oral apostolic tradition, also known simply as tradition, was treated with suspicion, though again it was not summarily rejected.[14]

During the Enlightenment, the selective appropriation of patristic exegesis was replaced with a firm denunciation of the fathers' contributions, especially when extrabiblical and metaphysical language regarding "natures" and "persons" is involved. The Enlightenment view of

---

[7] Ibid., 144–45.

[8] Paul Althaus, *The Theology of Martin Luther*, trans. Robert C. Schulz (Philadelphia, PA: Fortress, 1966), 335.

[9] Luther, *De Servo Arbitrio*, 145.

[10] *A Compend of Luther's Theology*, ed. Hugh Thomson Kerr Jr. (1943; repr., Philadelphia, PA: Westminster, 1980), 15.

[11] Luther, *De Servo Arbitrio*, 146, 151–52.

[12] Ibid., 147.

[13] *A Compend of Luther's Theology*, 13.

[14] Martin Chemnitz, *Examination of the Council of Trent*, trans. Fred Kramer, 4 vols. (St Louis, MO: Concordia, 1971–1986).

history entailed the dismissal of Europe's triumphant Christian centuries as "dark ages," as well as of all theological explanations of history and its meaning. It also entailed the applause of contemporary modernity for lifting up the human light that had flashed momentarily first in classical paganism then in the Renaissance.[15] The Enlightenment philosophers saw themselves as "inhabiting a climate of criticism" that took them beyond the superstitions of the Christian religion. The philosopher was self-conceived as omnicompetent in his critical capacity, as missionary in his zeal for truth, as autonomous in his relation to theology, and as aggressive in his approach to competing claims for rationality.[16] The premier standards of truth were mathematical and experiential while all religious claims, especially the miraculous, were dismissed as superstitious and farcical.[17] David Hume was "the purest, most modern specimen" of the Enlightenment, and he was convinced that Christianity, in its orthodox and heterodox forms, was irrational. The only proper response for an orthodox Christian involved in the philosophical conversation, which uses autonomous reason as the standard of truth, is to depart.[18]

The reception of the Enlightenment within European and American Christianity has been told in various ways, but what is sometimes forgotten is how thorough the success of the Enlightenment, including its critique of Trinitarianism, has been even within the more conservative sectors of evangelical Christianity. Paul C. H. Lim details the rise of anti-Trinitarianism within seventeenth-century Protestant England, often among rationalist evangelicals who were seeking to be more strictly "biblical."[19] Maurice Wiles provides a sympathetic

---

[15] Hugh Trevor-Roper, *History and the Enlightenment* (New Haven, CT: Yale University Press, 2010), 1–16, 129–43.

[16] Peter Gay, *The Enlightenment: An Interpretation: The Rise of Modern Paganism* (London: Norton, 1966), 127–32.

[17] Ibid., 139, 145–50. Enlightenment philosophy typically arose among those who rejected the Calvinist milieu that had temporarily sheltered them against the even more intolerant Roman church. Hugh Trevor-Roper, *The Crisis of the Seventeenth Century: Religion, the Reformation and Social Change* (New York: Harper & Row, 1968), 179–218.

[18] Gay, *The Enlightenment*, 417–18.

[19] Paul C. H. Lim, *Mystery Unveiled: The Crisis of the Trinity in Early Modern England*, Oxford Studies in Historical Theology (New York: Oxford University

and nuanced reading of both Arianism and Socinianism within the Church of England and among Presbyterians well into the eighteenth century.[20] Russell E. Richey noted the rise of anti-Trinitarianism from within the English Puritan movement. Richey demonstrates how the important term of *candour* shifted in four phases, from indicating purity of character, to sweetness of temper, to openness of mind, and finally to outspokenness. Within the third phase the Rational Dissenters went from "rejecting a creedal basis of unity" to making "a dogma of rejecting creeds." During the fourth phase of meaning, Joseph Priestley was influential in helping many dissenters to make a "fearless and open avowal" of Unitarianism.[21]

Stephen Neill extends the narrative of the Christian academy's reception of the Enlightenment critique of Scripture into the nineteenth and twentieth centuries, outlining advances within both the German and British centers of this activity.[22] James K. Mead presents the development of the discipline of biblical theology as a series of increasing fractures between the academy and the church: history versus theology, individual authors versus the whole canon, the Old Testament versus the New Testament, the meaning of the text versus the text itself, pure description versus normative truth claims, the Hebraic versus the Hellenistic, the event of revelation versus its record, religion versus theology, and history versus myth.[23] The basic division seems to be, however, the conflict between verifiable history and revealed theology.

For conservative evangelicals, the theological problem was located in the inspiration of the Holy Spirit. If a scholar accepted the biblical testimony as inspired, then he tended to accept its metaphysical

---

Press, 2012). See my review of Lim's book in *Anglican and Episcopal History* 83, no. 3 (2014): 341–43.

[20] Wiles correctly noted that the two heresies must be distinguished. Arianism maintained an inferior deity of the Son, while Socinianism removed his deity altogether. Maurice Wiles, *Archetypal Heresy: Arianism Through the Centuries* (New York: Oxford University Press, 1996).

[21] Russell E. Richey, "From Puritanism to Unitarianism in England: A Study in Candour," *Journal of the American Academy of Religion* 41, no. 3 (1973): 382–83.

[22] Stephen Neill, *The Interpretation of the New Testament 1861–1961: The Firth Lectures*, 1962 (New York: Oxford University Press, 1964).

[23] James K. Mead, *Biblical Theology: Issues, Methods, and Themes* (Louisville, KY: Westminster John Knox, 2007), 24–48.

claims, such as that Jesus reveals the invisible God. If not, then he was left with the pieces of the biblical testimony and no divinely granted means of comprehending them. As a result of the loss of this authoritative metanarrative, biblical theologians were tempted to offer various and often conflicting alternatives to correlate the multitude of biblical data. In a highly perceptive work, Hans Frei argued that the historical critical method left theologians in the modern period with only the symbols or the history behind the text. The realist narrative of the Bible itself was forsaken.[24]

During the twentieth century the rejection of Scripture's inspiration by the Spirit and the integrity of its revelation of Jesus as the eternal Son of God reached its high point in the assertive historical theology of Adolf von Harnack. The great German liberal decried the replacement of the ethical call of Jesus to brotherly love with "Hellenistic" speculations focused on the nature of God and the person of Jesus.[25] Among biblical scholars the twentieth century reached its high point of doubt about the patristic contribution with the equivocal existential theology of Rudolf Bultmann, whose influential project was the demythologization of the New Testament. Like Harnack, Bultmann declaimed the Hellenistic attempt to speak of Jesus as possessing a divine nature, but he also rejected the liberal solution of an ethical gospel. For Bultmann, New Testament Christology is about the appropriation of Jesus as eschatological Messiah for the sake of personal transformation.[26] Along with the rejection of the Bible as an inspired text came the downgrading of Jesus as the Son of God incarnate through the Enlightenment's presupposition that the miraculous is mythical, even irrational.

Neill agrees with our claim that biblical studies since the Enlightenment have been dominated by the application of methods derived particularly for the physical sciences.[27] While he delivers a

---

[24] Hans W. Frei, *The Eclipse of Biblical Narrative: A Study in Eighteenth and Nineteenth Century Hermeneutics*, new ed. (New Haven, CT: Yale University Press, 1980).

[25] Adolf Harnack, *What Is Christianity?*, trans. Thomas Bailey Saunders (New York: Harper, 1957), 51, 217–45.

[26] Summarized well in Rudolf Bultmann, *Faith and Understanding*, ed. Robert W. Funk, trans. Louise Pettibone Smith (London: SCM Press, 1969), 262–85.

[27] Neill, *The Interpretation of the New Testament*, 7.

nuanced account of especially New Testament studies and offers a now-dated summary of the historical critical method's positive contributions and continuing challenges,[28] Neill does not challenge the pervasive direction of modern biblical studies. Another respected biblical theologian, Brevard S. Childs, however, suggested a way forward for the discipline of biblical theology. He advocated the continuing deep study of individual books and authors but within a canonical framework. Childs also called for biblical theologians and systematic theologians to overcome the divisions between their disciplines.[29] Voices from disciplines other than biblical theology have offered similar proposals. We now turn to their evaluations.

Criticizing Enlightenment Exegesis

In a strong rebuttal to modern biblical scholars' rejection of the doctrine of the Trinity, Francis Watson argues that there are reasons modern scholars' "anti-trinitarianism" must be resisted. First and foremost, Watson points especially to the influence of John Locke's *The Reasonableness of Christianity as Delivered in the Scriptures* (1695), which he argues was "developed under the influence of the Socinian tradition." He surmises, therefore, "that the anti-trinitarianism of modern scholarship is, as it were, built into the interpretive framework it employs, rather than stemming inductively from the texts."[30] Watson's second and third reasons deal with the historical myopia of modern scholars and recent improvements in understanding the biblical exegesis of the early fathers.

Coordinate critiques of modern scholarship have been offered in the works of David S. Yeago and Christoph Schwöbel. Schwöbel argues that the modern bias against the "Hellenization of Christianity"

---

[28] Ibid., 338–45.

[29] Brevard S. Childs, *Biblical Theology: A Proposal* (Minneapolis, MN: Fortress, 2002). For a summary evaluation of the biblical theology movement after the mid-twentieth century, cf. Mead, *Biblical Theology*, 48–59. John Collins offers a most intriguing concept, arguing that the metaphysical claims of the biblical writers must be given serious consideration. John J. Collins, *Encounters with Biblical Theology* (Minneapolis, MN: Fortress, 2005), 22.

[30] Francis Watson, "Trinity and Community: A Reading of John 17," *International Journal of Systematic Theology* 1, no. 2 (1999): 169.

did not result in "a corresponding positive evaluation of the roots of Christianity in Jerusalem and the Old Testament."[31] Schwöbel then proceeds to show how the triadic patterns of the New Testament result in "grammatical rules" that encourage Trinitarian theology. Moreover, this Trinitarian grammar is rooted nowhere else than in the Old Testament.[32] After engaging in detailed exegesis of the Bible in conversation with the fathers, Yeago concludes that although the "conceptual terms" employed by the early fathers are different from those of the New Testament, the "judgements" the fathers made were valid.[33] Contrary to the modern biblical scholars' preconceived bias, "the ancient theologians were right to hold that the Nicene *homoousion* is neither imposed on the New Testament texts, nor distantly deduced from the texts, but rather describes a pattern of judgements present in the texts."[34] Our own separate exegesis of the Gospels, especially of the Gospel of John, largely concurs with the conclusions of Schwöbel, Watson, and Yeago, as we shall see

In case contemporary evangelicals reading this book are tempted to see modernist bias as primarily a liberal or neoorthodox phenomenon, it must be recognized that the appropriation of the Enlightenment denigration of patristic exegesis has been true for evangelical scholars, too. In his groundbreaking jeremiad against contemporary evangelicalism, Mark Noll wrote of "The Evangelical Enlightenment." Through the intellectual appropriation of the Scottish Enlightenment, American fundamentalists also came to read the Bible according to modernist categories. The Bible was isolated from the tradition of its transmission and reception and placed in the hands of individual scholars, who considered their task to be reading it as a collection of facts, in exactly the same way as "the natural philosopher."[35] The Campbellite movement was especially keen to adopt such an isolated

---

[31] Christoph Schwöbel, "The Trinity Between Athens and Jerusalem," *Journal of Reformed Theology* 3 (2009): 22–23.

[32] Ibid., 28–37.

[33] David S. Yeago, "The New Testament and the Nicene Dogma: A Contribution to the Recovery of Theological Exegesis," *Pro Ecclesia* 3, no. 2 (1994): 159.

[34] Ibid., 153.

[35] Charles Hodge, *Systematic Theology*, vol. 1 (Grand Rapids, MI: Eerdmans, 1952), 10–11; cited in Mark Noll, *The Scandal of the Evangelical Mind* (Grand Rapids, MI: Eerdmans, 1994), 98.

rationalist reading,[36] but Craig Blaising has shown how the same method also extended into early Dispensationalism.[37]

More recently, however, many scholars have begun to push back programmatically against what Thomas C. Oden calls "modern chauvinism." "The label *modern chauvinism* refers to the attitude of those who assume the intrinsic inferiority of all premodern ideas and texts, and the intrinsic superiority of all modern methods of investigation."[38] For Oden, whose own personal journey from liberal scholarly rejection of biblical and patristic thought to open appropriation of classical orthodoxy has inspired many young scholars, the Enlightenment position toward the fathers may be dismissed with prejudice as proud, illusory, and impotent.[39] Evangelicals such as Robert Webber,[40] Stephen R. Holmes,[41] D. H. Williams,[42] and Michael A. G. Haykin[43] have since joined in the call for a more careful listening to the exegetical contributions of the early church fathers.

---

[36] Noll, *The Scandal of the Evangelical Mind*, 84–88, 98.

[37] Ibid., 129.

[38] Thomas C. Oden, *The Rebirth of Orthodoxy: Signs of New Life in Christianity* (New York: HarperCollins, 2003), 8.

[39] Ibid., 7–9. Oden's journey from modern chauvinism to classical appropriation is described in Hall, *Reading Scripture with the Church Fathers*, 15–18; Oden, *The Rebirth of Orthodoxy*, 82–96.

[40] Robert Webber, *Ancient-Future Faith: Rethinking Evangelicalism for a Postmodern World* (Grand Rapids, MI: Baker, 1999).

[41] Unfortunately, Holmes summarily characterizes the attitudes of the Anabaptists to patristic tradition as one of "escape," appealing to one text by one theologian. Stephen R. Holmes, *Listening to the Past: The Place of Tradition in Theology* (Grand Rapids, MI: Baker, 2002), 14–17. A more nuanced understanding of the Anabaptist appropriation of patristic contributions would have been served by a wider study, such as the thought of Marpeck, Sattler, Schiemer, or Riedemann. Robert Friedmann noted that in disputations the Anabaptists often began with the ancient creeds so as "to confirm their strict creedal orthodoxy. In brief, they accepted the *Apostolicum* as a whole without hesitation, since it did not in any way interfere with their own particular concern for discipleship and the building up of the kingdom." Robert Friedmann, *The Theology of Anabaptism: An Interpretation* (repr., Eugene, OR: Wipf & Stock, 1998), 53.

[42] D. H. Williams, *Evangelicals and Tradition: The Formative Influence of the Early Church*, Evangelical Ressourcement: Ancient Sources for the Church's Future (Grand Rapids, MI: Baker, 2005).

[43] Michael A. G. Haykin, *Rediscovering the Church Fathers: Who They Were and How They Shaped the Church* (Wheaton, IL: Crossway, 2011).

More than a mere help at times of dryness, these scholars would describe the "ressourcement" of evangelical theology through patristic exegesis as "a vital need for evangelicals." Patristic exegesis is necessary for the ongoing life of the churches for several reasons. Haykin provides a litany of such: "to aid in her liberation from the Zeitgeist of the twenty-first century; to provide a guide in her walk with Christ; to help her understand the basic witness to her faith, the New Testament; to refute bad histories of the ancient church; and to be a vehicle of spiritual nurture."[44] Williams warns, "If contemporary evangelicalism aims to be doctrinally orthodox and exegetically faithful to Scripture, it cannot do without recourse to and integration of the foundational tradition of the early church."[45] Hall concurs, stating the case eloquently from the assumption that every human culture has limited perspective: "The fathers tend to grasp facets of the gospel that modern sensibilities too often overlook. They hear music in the Scripture to which we remain tone-deaf."[46]

Reclaiming Patristic Exegesis

Once the need for appropriating patristic exegesis of the Bible is accepted as potentially beneficial, the difficulty for anyone that has picked up a patristic biblical commentary, or one of the fathers' occasional pieces, is in how to do so. Patristic exegesis can be densely packed with linguistic and historical analysis of the biblical text in one sentence, then suddenly offer a comprehensive metaphysical claim in the next. Frances M. Young provides a robust account of patristic hermeneutics. She demonstrates that the early fathers paid close attention to the linguistic aspects of the biblical text (μεθοδεία) as well as to the historical aspects of the biblical text (ἱστορία).[47] However, unlike modern exegetes, the fathers treated the Bible as a unitive text inspired by the one Holy Spirit.

---

[44] Ibid., 28–29.
[45] Williams, *Evangelicals and Tradition*, 18.
[46] Hall, *Reading Scripture with the Church Fathers*, 38.
[47] Frances M. Young, *Biblical Exegesis and the Formation of Christian Culture* (New York: Cambridge University Press, 1997), 76–89.

Moreover, the fathers, whether within the Alexandrian school or the Antiochene school, were convinced that there was a universal narrative sense (διάνοια) to Scripture. The Bible must be interpreted according to its intent (σκοπός), an intent encapsulated in the rule of faith or canon of truth. The intent of Scripture focused on the κήρυγμα or gospel of Jesus Christ, which was incorporated in a Trinitarian form in the creeds.[48]

Young argues strenuously and convincingly that the typical modern presentation of the methods of patristic exegesis, as divisible into the literal, the typological, and the allegorical, is flawed and misleading. Such terms as "literal," "history," "allegory," and "typology" must be understood within the patristic context and according to their emphases. When this is done, we are presented with a much more complex picture. The Antiochene reaction to Origen's allegory in particular was concerned with maintaining the comprehensive textual narrative, including the honoring of revealed history. However, like Alexandria, Antioch was not confined to the modern sense of history but looked through ἱστορία to the higher vision of divine movement, θεωρία.[49] Young refers to the dominant form of patristic exegesis as "figural," a form of interpretation that comes closest to the modern rendition of Christ-centered typology.[50] In an intriguing move, New Testament theologians from E. Earle Ellis to Richard B. Hays have embraced the terminology of "typological interpretation," "figural interpretation," or "figural reading" to describe how the New Testament writers handled their Bible, which we call the Old Testament.[51]

John J. O'Keefe and R. R. Reno provide a personal account of how the early church fathers may be read. They point out that their own journey proved difficult at first because we moderns have a different theory of hermeneutical reading than the early fathers. They describe their own journey to reading patristic exegesis of the Bible

---

[48] Ibid., 16–28, 29n–30n, 123–30.

[49] Ibid., 168–85.

[50] Ibid., 186–213.

[51] Ellis, *The Old Testament in Early Christianity*, 139–57; Richard B. Hays, *Reading Backwards: Figural Christology and the Fourfold Gospel Witness* (Waco, TX: Baylor University Press, 2014), 1–3.

as occurring in three stages. First, they had to understand that the historical critical method we are taught makes it difficult to read the fathers, because modernity operates from a "referential theory of meaning." Modern Christians assume that the meaning of the Bible is beyond the text and the interpreter must strip away the symbolic matter, through linguistic, historical, and social analyses. Second, they came to understand that even a theological reading of the Bible from a phenomenological perspective is not ultimately how the fathers read the Bible. While the fathers did read Scripture theologically, they did not seek to go beyond the text to independent theological principles but into the text. The third strategy they adopted was to read the Bible with the fathers as if they were reading into the text rather than looking behind it. Drawing on Origen, O'Keefe and Reno note that the fathers believed God spoke in the reading of the Bible.[52]

> If anyone ponders over the prophetic sayings with all the attention and reverence they deserve, it is certain that in the very act of reading and diligently studying them his mind and feelings will be touched by a divine breath and he will recognize that the words he is reading are not utterances of men but the language of God.[53]

O'Keefe and Reno demonstrate at length how the fathers followed three basic strategies in reading the Bible: intensive reading, which takes both linguistic analysis and historical location seriously, though

---

[52] John J. O'Keefe and R. R. Reno, *Sanctified Vision: An Introduction to Early Christian Interpretation of the Bible* (Baltimore, MD: The John Hopkins University Press, 2005), 7–13.

[53] Origen, *On First Principles*, Preface, trans. in ibid., 12. Origen believes Scripture cannot be properly understood apart from a work of the Spirit in the purified heart of the believer. "The Scriptures were written by the Spirit of God, and have a meaning, not such only as is apparent at first sight, but also another, which escapes the notice of most. For those (words) which are written are the forms of certain mysteries, and the images of divine things. Respecting which there is one opinion throughout the whole Church, that the whole law is indeed spiritual; but that the spiritual meaning which the law conveys is not known to all, but to those only on whom the grace of the Holy Spirit is bestowed in the word of wisdom and knowledge." Origen, *De Principiis*, Preface, 8, in *Origen*, trans. Frederick Crombie, in *Ante-Nicene Fathers*, ed. Philip Schaff, vol. 4 (repr., Peabody, MA: Hendrickson, 1994), 241.

the fathers tended to accept the historical accuracy of Scripture; typology, which allowed them to correlate the Old and New Testaments through Christological paradigms; and, allegory, which allowed them to range further in their ruminations and application of the biblical text. However, O'Keefe and Reno warn that the key hermeneutical terms of "literal" and "allegory" must not be understood according to modern definitions, but in the way that the fathers themselves used them. Ultimately, they argue that the *canon*, the "rule of faith," grounded patristic exegesis, that the patristic goal was worship, and that personal transformation was deemed necessary for proper interpretation of the Bible. It seems, then, that the best way to read the fathers is in the same way the fathers read the Bible, by "immersion"[54] in the texts themselves. We have attempted to do so herein, even as we maintain the Reformation call to critique the fathers. We also seek to be faithful to the Enlightenment call to take the biblical languages and history seriously, striving not to read a preferred outcome back into the biblical text.

Θεολογία and Οἰκονομία

One patristic exegetical distinction that many Christian scholars through the centuries have found helpful is the presupposition that there is a difference between θεολογία (theology) and οἰκονομία (economy). The distinction was promoted in a preliminary yet authoritative form by Athanasius of Alexandria but stated most eloquently by Gregory of Nazianzus. It was subsequently used, in transmuted forms, during the Christological debates as codified at Chalcedon, and it has been featured in more recent systematic presentations of the Trinity. This patristic distinction also provides the different themes for the current and following chapters. The general meaning of οἰκονομία is that which God has done, is doing, and will do with regard to creation and redemption. The general concern for θεολογία is who God is, conceptually different from his actions, though epistemologically available only through his actions.

For Athanasius, the distinction arises from basic grammatical principles. Any student should learn from his γραμματικός that a literary

---

[54] O'Keefe and Reno, *Sanctified Vision*, xi.

text is composed of at least a time (καιρός), a character (πρόσωπον), and a subject matter (πρᾶγμα). The aspect of "time" was important to Jesus and the disciples, for instance, in discussing the sign of Christ's return. The sense (διάνοια) of the biblical text demands that each of these aspects be properly identified. The time spoken of with regard to the Son of God is important, for it may refer, for example, to his earthly ministry, or to his subsequent return, or to before the incarnation. The temporal aspect is helpful for identifying the character as well, for references to Christ's character may either indicate he is acting as God or acting as a man.[55] The scope (σκοπός) of Scripture demands that we distinguish between whether a particular reference is to Christ as God or Christ as man: "There is in it [Scripture] a double account concerning the Savior."[56] This "partitive exegesis," to borrow John Behr's summary description, is encapsulated in the statement that "Christ is God become man." When speaking of Christ as God, this is θεολογία; when speaking of Christ becoming man, this is οἰκονομία.[57] Or, to state it more simply, theology refers to who God is, while economy refers to what he does. Theology is concerned with the timeless nature of God, while economy is concerned with the narrative presentation of redemption.[58]

Among the Cappadocian Fathers, Gregory of Nazianzus provides the most frequent examples of the distinction. For Gregory the interpreter must rise above "the earthbound carnality of your opinions" and "ascend" to that which is "exalted" and "nobler," "the more sublime expressions of the divinity." One must distinguish between "the expression of the nature" and "the expression of the economy." Coming from Oration 29, Behr calls this "the clearest statement of the principle of partitive exegesis in the fourth century."[59] Christopher A.

---

[55] John Behr, *Formation of Christian Theology*, vol. 2, *The Nicene Faith* (Crestwood, NY: St. Vladimir's Seminary Press, 2004), 208–10.

[56] Athanasius, *Arians* 3.29.1; cited in ibid., 211.

[57] Behr, *The Nicene Faith*, 212–13.

[58] Ibid., 214. Behr claims that Athanasius has introduced with this distinction an axiom, which itself cannot be demonstrated, only asserted. Ibid., 215. It could be argued, however, though it would take much more space than is available here, that Athanasius's principle is derived from the way Scripture presents Christ. That, of course, was Athanasius's lifelong project. Cf. Phil 2:5–11.

[59] Gregory of Nazianzus, *Oration* 29.18; cited in Behr, *The Nicene Faith*, 349.

Beeley argues, however, that Gregory's distinction has too often been misinterpreted in both the East and the West. θεολογία is Gregory's central concern, and θεολογία is "the confession of the divinity of the Son and the Spirit, or of the entire Trinity, as they are revealed in the divine economy." Yet θεολογία is not primarily concerned with crisp doctrinal formulation but with personal knowledge of the Trinitarian life, a *visio Trinitatis*, if you will. "In its most basic sense, 'theology' is the knowledge of the Divinity of the Father in the person of the divine Son by the indwelling of the Holy Spirit, who is also divine."[60] Moreover, Beeley says, over against such interpreters as Karl Holl, theology is not to be contrasted with economy, for theology is available only through economy. The Trinitarian connection between theology and economy is not an abstract doctrine but a living truth.[61]

Morwenna Ludlow summarizes the nature of Gregory's exegesis as a "profound belief that God's actions reflect his true essence, albeit in a refracted and indirect manner."[62] While Ludlow does not extend her summary to the modern discussion of the relationship between the economic Trinity and the immanent Trinity, her subtle statement is helpful in that regard (as we shall see more fully in chapter 7). Through the economy, in particular the redemptive work of the Savior, then, humanity may approach and know the divine life. And the divine economy, while prophesied in the writings of the Old Testament, is manifested to humanity in the earthly life of Jesus. The four Gospels, which provide the authoritative accounts of the earthly ministry, death, and resurrection of the Lord Jesus Christ, are therefore of supreme importance for coming to a knowledge of God.

While the Synoptic Gospels of Matthew, Mark, and Luke present the disciples' knowledge of God in Christ as arising in a progressive manner, the Gospel of John presents the knowledge of God in Christ from the beginning of its account. The explicitly theological nature of John's

---

[60] Christopher A. Beeley, *Gregory of Nazianzus on the Trinity and the Knowledge of God: In Your Light We Shall See Light,* Oxford Studies in Historical Theology (New York: Oxford University Press, 2008), 196–97.

[61] Ibid., 198–201.

[62] Morwenna Ludlow, "The Cappadocians," in *The First Christian Theologians: An Introduction to Theology in the Early Church,* ed. G. R. Evans (Malden, MA: Blackwell, 2004), 179.

Gospel is perhaps why the early church fathers spent more time with that Gospel than with any other.[63] In the words of Clement of Alexandria, John presents to the church "the spiritual gospel."[64] In comparison with the Synoptic writers, who track the earliest disciples' perception of the οἰκονομία before the dawning of a fuller understanding of θεολογία, John begins with θεολογία before proceeding to οἰκονομία. In his commentary on the Gospel of John, Cyril of Alexandria marks the breaking point in the narrative at 1:11, where John "little by little comes down from sheer theology to an explanation of the οἰκονομία with the flesh that the Son accomplished for us."[65] In the next chapter we will begin likewise with the θεολογία before proceeding to the οἰκονομία in the subsequent chapter, with the understanding that the practical οἰκονομία brings us again and again to glimpse the eternal θεολογία.

The ability of man to discern eternity, or what Immanuel Kant calls the "noumenal," the metaphysical reality typically received as a priori truth, was challenged strongly by this "most important European philosopher of modern times."[66] Kant's central concern in his "greatest masterpiece," the *Critique of Pure Reason*, was to account for the fact that man cannot know that which is beyond his experience. Therefore, such metaphysical claims as the existence of God, the immortality of the human soul, and the beginning and end of creation have been ruled unknowable for modern philosophers. This skepticism toward metaphysical matters, toward issues of eternity and time's relation to the eternal God, also made its way into biblical hermeneutics.[67]

The Enlightenment-inspired historical critical method, itself a historically bound movement, is thus primarily concerned with discerning the historical events behind the text. The biblical text is

---

[63] According to Francis Watson, "the Gospel of John was the single most important text in the construction of the patristic doctrine of the Trinity." Watson, "Trinity and Community," 168–69.

[64] Maurice F. Wiles, *The Spiritual Gospel: The Interpretation of the Fourth Gospel in the Early Church* (New York: Cambridge University Press, 2006), 8.

[65] Cyril of Alexandria, *Commentary on John*, vol. 1, trans. David R. Maxwell, ed. Joel C. Elowsky (Downers Grove, IL: IVP Academic, 2013), 59.

[66] Henry E. Allison, "Kant, Immanuel," in *The Oxford Companion to Philosophy*, ed. Ted Honderich (New York: Oxford University Press, 1995), 435–38.

[67] Cf. Sebastian Rehnman, "The Realist Conception of Revelation," in *The Trustworthiness of God: Perspectives on the Nature of Scripture*, ed. Paul Helm and Carl R. Trueman (Grand Rapids, MI: Eerdmans, 2002), 253–72.

deemed unreliable when it makes metaphysical claims. This way of reading the Bible stands in opposition to the precritical concern for the eternal within the text. It also makes the overarching structure of the Gospel of John immaterial, perhaps even impossible to discern. If Kant's anti-metaphysical bias is allowed to dominate the evangelical historical critical method, it makes theological exegesis like that pursued in this book difficult at the least and an impossibility at the worst.[68]

Problems in Theological Language

While the modern interpretation of Scripture is handicapped by its antimetaphysical bias, patristic interpretation (as well as medieval and Reformation forms of exegesis) assumes that the biblical language is capable of indicating the eternal. However, the earliest biblical interpreters were themselves divided over exactly how much Scripture can possibly relay about God. On the one extreme, theologians such as Eunomius believed that language could state exactly what God is. And for Eunomius, a leader among the later Arians, God's essence is that he is "unbegotten." Heavily influenced by both Aristotle and Neo-Platonist philosophy, Eunomius thus turned theology into "technology," according to Theodoret's evaluation. For Eunomius, because God is defined as "unbegotten" or "ingenerate," the Son of God, who is "begotten" according to Scripture, must necessarily be of a different nature from God.[69] If Kant is convinced that it is impossible

---

[68] Kant's philosophical claim that human beings cannot know God could be overcome through George Hegel's philosophy of history and Spirit. Hegel argued the knowledge of God is established through the coalescence of deity and humanity in Jesus. Because he offered a profound philosophical basis for knowing God, Hegel made idealism attractive for theologians in the German tradition. Hegel went further, however, arguing that God comes to know himself in human knowing. Moreover, God's activity defines his being. Hegel's influence also helps explain how German evangelicals have tended toward a more dynamic understanding of Trinitarian being. Bruce L. McCormack, "Introduction: On 'Modernity' as a Theological Concept," in *Mapping Modern Theology: A Thematic and Historical Introduction*, ed. Kelly M. Kapic and Bruce L. McCormack (Grand Rapids, MI: Baker Academic, 2012), 10–13.

[69] Johannes Quasten, *Patrology*, vol. 3 (repr., Allen, TX: Christian Classics, 1999), 306–9.

to speak of eternal matters, Eunomius is convinced that eternity is knowable absolutely. God is definable and apparently confined by language. Standing between these two extremes are most of the early theologians that later generations have come to know as orthodox.

Basil of Caesarea believed language was naturally handicapped in its portrayal of reality.[70] In an epistle to his friend, Gregory of Nazianzus, Basil wrote, "No theological term is adequate to the thought of the speaker, or the want of the questioner, because language is of natural necessity too weak to act in the service of the objects of thought."[71] Gregory of Nazianzus, responding to the Eunomian movement, took his discussion of the weakness of language in a more theological direction. The human mind cannot "comprehend" (λαμβάνειν) God, for God is infinite and cannot be measured. "He contains all of existence in himself without beginning or end, like an endless, boundless ocean of being. He extends beyond all our notions of time and nature, and is outlined by the mind alone, but only very dimly and in a limited way."[72] While our human words may point toward God in a relative manner, they may not speak absolutely of him. When we say God is great or God exists, we need to recognize that he is infinitely beyond even the concept of greatness or of existence. God's existence and sovereignty transcend the ideas that we have of these things. We can understand God to a limited extent but never entirely. The greatest theologian comprehends more of God but never completely.[73]

---

[70] We have not introduced Augustine's contribution into this particular discussion since Eastern developments throw excellent light on the balance needed between Eunomian presumption and Kantian denial. However, Augustine's emphasis on the divine gift of revelation through words is also helpful: "Yet although nothing can be spoken in a way worthy of God, he has sanctioned the homage of the human voice, and chosen that we should derive pleasure from our words in praise of him." Augustine, *On Christian Teaching*, trans. R. P. H. Green (New York: Oxford University Press, 1997), 1:14. Augustine's discussion of signs in books 2 and 3 in *De Doctrina Christiana* is *sine qua non* for exegetes of every era.

[71] Basil of Caesarea, epistle 7, in *Nicene and Post-Nicene Fathers*, 2nd Series, ed. Philip Schaff, vol. 8 (repr., Peabody, MA: Hendrickson, 1994), 115.

[72] Gregory of Nazianzus, *Oration* 38; cited in Beeley, *Gregory of Nazianzus on the Trinity and the Knowledge of God*, 102.

[73] Beeley, *Gregory of Nazianzus on the Trinity and the Knowledge of God*, 90–110. Gregory of Nyssa likewise considers the limits of language from a theological perspective. Eric Daryl Meyer, "Gregory of Nyssa on Language, Naming God's Creatures,

To put the problem of theological language in metaphysical terms, we may state that God has an essence, but we cannot speak of what his essence is. As Gregory of Nyssa said in reaction to Eunomius, we can biblically know God's attributes (such as "wisdom, power, life-giver, light, compassion, and love") through his actions and titles, but we cannot know God's nature or essence.[74] To put the problem of theological language in systematic terms, divine knowledge is thus apophatic, beyond human definition, even as human beings may also speak things about God positively, in a kataphatic manner. Kataphaticism, positive theology, argues that we may speak certainly, if haltingly, of who God is, while apophaticism, negative theology, reminds us that there must also be silence. Systematic theology requires the judicious employment of both kataphaticism and apophaticism, speaking of God with certainty where possible yet remaining judiciously silent about God.[75] This is because Jesus, God in the flesh according to John, has interpreted the invisible God to us, but he certainly has not told us everything about himself, for we may not comprehend him.[76] With our hermeneutical method somewhat clarified, we now turn to a summary exegesis of θεολογία according to the Gospel of John.

---

and the Desire of the Discursive Animal," in *Genesis and Christian Theology*, ed. Nathan MacDonald, Mark W. Elliott, and Grant Macaskill (Grand Rapids, MI: Eerdmans, 2012), 103–17. Cf. Young, *Biblical Exegesis and the Formation of Christian Culture*, 140–60.

[74] Nonna Verna Harrison, "Gregory of Nyssa on Knowing the Trinity," in *The Holy Trinity in the Life of the Church*, ed. Khaled Anatolios (Grand Rapids, MI: Baker Academic, 2014), 55–61.

[75] For further discussion of the apophatic and kataphatic ways of theology, see Vladimir Lossky, *Orthodox Theology: An Introduction* (Crestwood, NY: St. Vladimir's Seminary Press, 1989), 31–35. For a sublime yet provocative contemporary approach to theology from an apophatic perspective, tracing patterns from the silences in church history, see Diarmaid MacCulloch, *Silence: A Christian History* (New York: Viking, 2013).

[76] Gregory of Nyssa treated the knowledge of God as a matter of approach and wonder rather than as a matter of grasping and denuding. Anatolios, *Retrieving Nicaea*, 160–64.

5

THE GOD WHO IS:

ΘΕΟΛΟΓΙΑ

He [the Holy Spirit] will glorify me, for he will take of mine and will announce it to you. All things whatsoever the Father has are mine, therefore I said that he takes of mine and will announce it to you.

John 16:14–15

The Common Possession of Father and Son

It is an audacious claim for a human being to say that he shares everything with God, as the man Jesus does here. It complicates that claim to say there is still a third who acts as a willful agent with what belongs in common to both God the Father and this man. "Mine," the first person possessive pronoun, is a simple and much-used word in any language, indicating personal ownership. But it is a word, in the way used here, which carries utterly profound implications. In the Greek the longer oblique forms, ἐμέ and ἐμοῦ, are used in these verses rather than the typical enclitic forms, με and μου, a linguistic move that prompts attention. The reader's mind is thereby drawn to query what exactly the Father and the Son possess in common. The meaning of Jesus's use of the simple possessive pronoun becomes even more urgent when he soon addresses God in prayer and refers again to their common possession, now using both the first and second person pronouns

(John 17:10). What does it mean when the Son claims that everything the Father has is also his? Moreover, what does it mean that the Holy Spirit has equal privilege in disposing of this common possession?

In order to meet the overall goal of our attempt to evaluate whether and how Scripture reveals God as Trinity, it is incumbent to read the Bible with a broad range of the most thoughtful scholars. This sampling of previous scholarship must include not only modern commentators, who have dominated most of the contemporary discussion, but in an effort to listen to other voices, it must also include the witness of commentators throughout the history of biblical exegesis. In this chapter, which focuses upon a reading of the Trinity in the Gospels, in particular the Gospel of John, we will in part evaluate whether patristic exegesis and its chosen language adequately conveys the meaning of the Gospel writers and, behind them, the meaning of their Lord Jesus Christ. Among the early church fathers, Eastern and Western, the linguistic and canonical settings of the terms in this crucial passage from John 16 indicated a commonality of deity, alongside a procession of deity from the Father.

Standing near the end of the Trinitarian debates, receiving the fruit of a century of theological formulation, and near the beginning of the Christological debates in the East, Cyril of Alexandria (d. 444) interprets the words of Jesus in John 16:14–15 to mean not that the Son and the Father have "a mere likeness founded on similarity," as if they were "only moulded by adventitious graces." Instead, God the Father and his Son have "complete similarity and equality," or "complete and perfect essential equality and likeness," such that "their attributes are common, or rather identical." To speak of common attributes is to suggest a common ontology, a "consubstantiality," which the Spirit likewise shares with the Father and the Son.[1] The perfect commonality of the Father and the Son, however, does not indicate that they are entirely the same, for they are different in one way: the Son "is not Himself the Father." There is a relationship between the two that allows both the Father and the Son to share everything, a relation of generation. The Father's generation

---

[1] Cyril of Alexandria, *Commentary on the Gospel According to St. John by S. Cyril, Archbishop of Alexandria*, trans. P. E. Pusey and Thomas Randell, 2 vols. (Oxford: James Parker, 1874; London: Walter Smith, 1885), 11.2.1.

of the Son is the means by which they share in all things: "what He That begat hath, belongs also to Him that is begotten of Him."[2] In a similar though distinct way, "the Spirit receives of the Father and the Son the things that are theirs."[3] Cyril refers to the sharing of deity between the Father and the Spirit in two ways, expressing both a sense of equality and of order. "He [the Spirit] is in Him [God] essentially, and proceeds from Him inseparably and indivisibly."[4]

Standing at the headwaters of Western theological thought, Augustine of Hippo (354–430) interprets the Gospel of John in a similar way, though with an emphasis on the Holy Spirit's double procession from the Father and the Son. Regarding the relationship of the Father, the Son, and the Holy Spirit in John 16, Augustine says, "For the Son is born of the Father, and the Holy Spirit proceedeth from the Father; but the Father is neither born of, nor proceedeth from, another."[5] This is how the Father, the Son, and the Holy Spirit are distinguished from, and relate to one another: the Father is the source from which the Son is begotten and the Holy Spirit proceeds. The order of the processions for Augustine does not endanger their equality, however, for the processions are eternal: "to that immutable and ineffable nature, there is no proper application of Was and Will be, but only Is."[6] In John 17:10, a text that is primarily concerned with the economy of salvation, there is still enough light to make a claim about who God is within himself. "Where it is sufficiently apparent how it is that all that belongs to the Father belongs to the Son; in this way, namely, that He Himself is also God, and of the Father born, is the Father's equal." John 16:15, asserts Augustine, speaks explicitly of divine ontology. In describing the Father's possessions as "mine," the Son "referred to those things that concern the actual deity of the Father, and in which He is equal to Him, in having all that He has."[7]

---

[2] Ibid.

[3] Ibid., 11.2.2. Note that this and similar statements by Cyril are compatible with the *filioque* clause in the Western rendering of the Nicene Creed.

[4] Ibid., 11.2.1.

[5] Augustine, *Homilies on the Gospel of John*, trans. John Gibb and James Innes, in *Nicene and Post-Nicene Fathers*, First Series, ed. Philip Schaff, vol. 7 (repr., Peabody, MA: Hendrickson, 1994), 99.4.

[6] Ibid., 99.5.

[7] Ibid., 107.2.

The Eternal God Who Comes and Goes

The narrative genre dominates Scripture, especially in the Gospels, and this indicates the necessity of perceiving God through his acts, of discerning θεολογία through οἰκονομία. John's Gospel, in contrast with the Synoptic Gospels, places eternity and history, the realm of the noumenal and the realm of the phenomenal, in a deliberately dialectical relationship. The idea of descending and ascending is given paradigmatic status early and often in the Gospel's text, with a focus on Jesus Christ as the center of this movement.[8] "Jesus has become the nexus between heaven and earth."[9] For instance, in John 1:51, Nathanael is promised, "You will see the heavens opened and the angels of God ascending and descending on the Son of Man." Following on the heels of Jesus's invitation to two other disciples to "come and see" (1:39), this promise that human beings will be granted sight into the realm of the eternal is given a prominent literary arrangement. Along with this overarching pattern of God coming and going in the Son (and the Holy Spirit), still other patterns may be discerned, as we shall see.

Paul Berge has identified John 16:28 as providing the chiasmic structure to the whole Gospel. Note the movement between God and the world: "I came from the Father, and I have come into the world; again I am leaving the world, and going to the Father."[10] A

---

[8] From a parallel perspective, Karl Rahner identifies the New Testament at large, presumably focusing on the Pauline and Johannine literature as well as Hebrews, as teaching a "descent Christology [*Deszendenzchristologie*]," while the Synoptic Gospels and the Acts of the Apostles present us, presumably through the progress of their narratives, an "ascent Christology [*Aszendenzchristologie*]." Karl Rahner, *The Trinity*, trans. Joseph Donceel (repr., New York: Crossroad Herder, 2004), 65.

[9] Richard B. Hays, *Reading Backwards: Figural Christology and the Fourfold Gospel Witness* (Waco, TX: Baylor University Press, 2014), 86.

[10] John 16:28   Structure of the Gospel of John
     A I came from the *Father*   A John 1:1–18
       B and have come into the *world*   B John 1:19–12:50
       B¹ again I am leaving the *world*   B¹ John 13:1–17:26
     A¹ and going to the *Father*   A¹ John 18:1–21:25
Paul S. Berge, "Texts in Context: Easter to Trinity with the Gospel of John: Bearing Witness to the Father, Son, and Holy Spirit," *Word and World* 18, no. 2 (1998): 207.

number of other texts provide a similar outline of Jesus's movement from heaven to earth and back to heaven, some of which come from the lips of Jesus himself. "No one has ascended into heaven, but He who descended from heaven: the Son of Man" (3:13). "You are from below, I am from above; you are of this world, I am not of this world" (8:23). "I proceeded forth and have come from God, for I have not even come on my own initiative, but he sent me" (8:42), which may be paired with, "I go to him who sent me" (7:33). And at the crucial narrative point, between the coming of Christ through chapter 12 and the beginning of his return to the Father, the evangelist says Jesus knew that "he had come from God and was going to God" (13:3).

The location of Jesus as the one who moves between eternity and history is key to understanding the Gospel of John and its central character. This paradigm of movement provides not only the literary structure of the Gospel; it also helps human minds to navigate, with appropriate chasteness, the liminal boundary between Creator and creation. Through the revelation of Jesus Christ, human beings, who are bound within history, are allowed glimpses into the eternal habitation of God, the place of the One who is manifested as Father, and Son, and Holy Spirit. Andreas J. Köstenberger refers to the narrative of John's Gospel as a "cosmic drama" that "commences with God 'in the beginning' prior to creation" and "encompasses both heaven and earth."[11]

The structure of movement between heaven and earth is not finally, however, restricted to God alone. At the beginning and at the end of the Gospel is the command of Jesus to "follow me" (1:43; 21:19, 22). The promise that creatures will glimpse the movement between heaven and earth is paralleled by a command to enter a dynamic personal relationship with God. However, there is a significant problem with the command: even the disciples are singularly unable to obey the command to follow Christ, at least before his death and resurrection. "As I said to the Jews, I also say to you, 'Where I am going, you cannot come'" (13:33; cf. 7:34). This is the human dilemma: How

---

[11] Andreas J. Köstenberger, *A Theology of John's Gospel and Letters: Biblical Theology of the New Testament* (Grand Rapids, MI: Zondervan, 2009), 293. Köstenberger discerns the seams in the Gospel differently than Berge, but adopts a similar two-act pattern, the parts of which he refers to as a "Book of Signs" and a "Book of Exaltation." Ibid., 167–70.

can humanity follow Jesus to God when fallen humanity cannot arise to God? How may humans obey Christ when they cannot do so in their own power? The problem is restated, along with its solution, in another Johannine summary.

The one who has come from God transcends those who are from below, those who are so caught in the world that they will not receive his testimony (3:31–32). The solution to the human dilemma of inaccessibility to the divine is distinctly Trinitarian: First, Jesus is the one who "speaks the words of God" (3:34a). Second, Jesus "gives the Spirit without measure" (3:34b), presumably enabling an internal response to the words of God. Third, God the Father places all things in the Son's hands (3:35), presumably including those to whom he issues the call to follow him. The final verse of this summary concludes the Trinitarian movement toward humanity and offers the potential of human movement toward God, explaining that the key to entering eternity is faith, while lack of obedience results in divine wrath (3:36). The exact way in which God enables the internal human response of faith, which results in salvation, is not given definition here, except that God is said to move as a Trinity in doing so. From other texts in the same chapter, we learn that man can follow Jesus to God through being born again or born from above by the Holy Spirit, along with believing the Word, and repenting toward God.[12] Human beings cannot follow Jesus in their own power, but they may follow Jesus to the Father by the power of the Holy Spirit.

Perceiving Θεολογία in John's Prologue

We shall delve deeper into the divine οἰκονομία of redemption in the following chapters, but in this chapter θεολογία is the focus. The

---

[12] The third chapter of John is recognized as a premiere soteriological text. In verses 1–8, salvation comes through the sovereign work of the Spirit in regeneration. In verses 9–18, salvation is offered as a gracious gift through the Son, and human faith is required for its appropriation. In verses 19–21, repentance toward God is also discussed as a requirement. According to Beasley-Murray, the availability of eternal life "is epitomized in the famous John 3:16, and in the sentences that both follow and precede it." G[eorge] R. Beasley-Murray, *Gospel of Life: Theology in the Fourth Gospel* (Peabody, MA: Hendrickson, 1991), 4.

Gospel of John, as we noted with Cyril of Alexandria,[13] begins with
θεολογία and proceeds to οἰκονομία, or to put it another way, the
Godward side of the dialectic may be momentarily distinguished and
considered apart from its worldly side. While Cyril puts the transition
from theology to economy at verse 11, modern commentators typically consider the prologue or preamble of John's Gospel as extending
to verse 18.[14] The conceptual distinction of θεολογία and οἰκονομία
is ultimately overcome within the narrative. The prologue, characterized literarily by its "rhythmical prose,"[15] begins in the same way
as the book of Genesis. "In Gen 1:1 'In the beginning' introduces
the story of the old creation; here it introduces the story of the new
creation. In both works of creation the agent is the Word of God."[16]
Through the explicit orientation to Genesis 1:1, John takes the reader
back to the point where God in eternity and creation in history began
their association. But his discussion, with its prosaic progression and
its conceptual content, pushes the human mind beyond the bounds
of time back or beyond into eternity. The interrelated Johannine concepts of λόγος and θεός, or if we recognize the patristic neologism,
θεολογία, are key to this discussion.

Λόγος

The secondary literature regarding John's employment of λόγος indicates a complex association of meanings in both secular and religious
literature, suffusing the Greek and Hebrew worlds of thought. Λόγος
in the Hellenistic understanding focused on the word as reason, which
developed in philosophy into a bridge of understanding between man

---

[13] See the section on "Θεολογία and Οἰκονομία" in chap. 4 above.

[14] F. F. Bruce, *The Gospel of John: Introduction, Exposition and Notes* (Grand
Rapids, MI: Eerdmans, 1983), 28–46; George R. Beasley-Murray, *John*, Word Biblical
Commentary (Waco, TX: Word, 1987), 1–17; D. A. Carson, *The Gospel According
to John*, Pillar New Testament Commentary (Grand Rapids, MI: Eerdmans, 1991),
111–39; R. V. G. Tasker, *The Gospel According to St. John: An Introduction and
Commentary*, Tyndale New Testament Commentaries (Grand Rapids, MI: Eerdmans,
1980), 41–49; Köstenberger, *A Theology of John's Gospel and Letters*, 336–508.

[15] Bruce, *The Gospel of John*, 28.

[16] Ibid., 28–29.

and the world, in theology between God and man, and ultimately into a cosmic theological entity.[17] While Philo sought to synthesize the Hebrew and Greek understandings, the Hellenistic understanding is primarily "dianoetic" or intellectual, while the Hebrew understanding has a "dynamic" or creative emphasis. Both elements were taken into the Septuagintal version of the Old Testament.[18] Λόγος in the New Testament spans both divine and human speech and identity. Human words are variable and weak, but the divine Word and words convey truth and powerfully transform the human heart.[19]

In the Johannine literature the divine λόγος took on personal characteristics and became identified with the human Jesus (e.g., Rev 19:13). Jesus is never given, like the prophets, the words of God to speak, for he already is the Word of God. The "fundamental NT fact constantly described" is that "Jesus is not just the One who brings the Word but the One who incorporates it in His person, in the historical process of His speech and action, of his life and being."[20] In John 1:1–2, λόγος as preexistent Word is placed in the beginning with the Father, while in 1 John 1:1–2, he derives from the Father as the beginning.

Gerhard Kittel argues that commentary on the Johannine use must never treat λόγος abstractly but as personally active. He also argues that λόγος is never detachable from God.[21] George R. Beasley-Murray demonstrates that the Ancient Near Eastern peoples, Jewish and pagan, correlated Word with Wisdom.[22] (Proverbs 8:22–31 thus was treated as a primary Christological text in the early church.)[23]

---

[17] H. Kleinknecht, "The Logos in the Greek and Hellenistic World," in *Theological Dictionary of the New Testament*, vol. 4, ed. Gerhard Kittel, trans. Geoffrey W. Bromiley (Grand Rapids, MI: Eerdmans, 1967), 77–91.

[18] O. Procksch, "The Word of God in the Old Testament," in ibid., 91–100.

[19] Gerhard Kittel, "Word and Speech in the New Testament," in ibid., 100–122.

[20] Ibid., 126.

[21] Ibid., 130–32.

[22] Beasley-Murray, *John*, 8–9; Bruce, *The Gospel of John*, 30.

[23] As is well known, the early theologians, both Arian and Nicene, accepted the personification of Wisdom as identical with the Word who became flesh in Jesus. They disagreed, however, over when Wisdom came into existence. The Nicene theologians believed Wisdom was prior to creation, and creation is inclusive of time, and thus Wisdom is eternally God. The Arian theologians focused on the Septuagint's

Rather than trying to argue that John's use of λόγος should be taken with a primarily Hellenistic or a primarily Hebrew understanding, Beasley-Murray concludes there is a convergence of meaning in the New Testament application to Jesus. Both the Hebrew דבר (*dabar*) as God's creative act and the Hellenistic λόγος as God's divine nature ought to be incorporated in academic commentary on John 1. "The employment of the Logos concept in the prologue to the Fourth Gospel is the supreme example within Christian history of the communication of the gospel in terms understood and appreciated by the nations. . . . [T]he Word acted in the words and deeds of Jesus and brought about the redemption of the nations."[24]

Θεός

While the Johannine prologue's οἰκονομία indicates how God saves, its θεολογία indicates a close relationship of identity between God and the Word. Perceiving the exact relationship of God with his Word may not be glibly accomplished. The Word is said, on the one hand, to be God, and on the other hand, to be with God. These two ways of presenting the Word, as both "God" and "with God," provide the basic shape of the Christian perspective of the identity of Jesus Christ as divine. Καὶ ὁ λόγος ἦν πρὸς τὸν θεόν, "and the Word was with God,"[25] is immediately followed with καὶ θεὸς ἦν ὁ λόγος, "and the

---

translation of the Hebrew in Proverbs 8:22 as "created," arguing that Christ was subsequent to the eternal Father even if before the rest of creation. Nicene theologians typically argued the idea of creation here refers not to Christ's deity but to his humanity, even if that has to be taken in a preincarnate sense. The Nicenes pointed to Proverbs 8:25, which refers to Wisdom as "begotten" before creation, as the proper reference to Christ's deity. Cf. e.g., J. Warren Smith, "The Trinity in the Fourth-Century Fathers," in *The Oxford Handbook of the Trinity*, ed. Gilles Emery and Matthew Levering (New York: Oxford University Press, 2011), 117. Modern scholars almost universally argue the personification should be taken in a poetic sense and note that the better translation of the Hebrew in Proverbs 8:22 is "acquired" or "possessed" rather than "made" or "created." Bruce, *The Gospel of John*, 31, 64n7.

[24] Beasley-Murray, *John*, 10.

[25] The preposition πρός is typically translated as "to" or "toward," but "with" is not an inappropriate translation, as seen for instance in Mark 6:3.

Word was God."[26] The first statement posits a distinction between God and the Word; the second statement posits an identity between God and the Word. The first says the Word has a personal relationship with God; the second says the Word is God himself.

The first statement, καὶ ὁ λόγος ἦν πρὸς τὸν θεόν, indicates there are two persons who are facing one another, the Word toward God, the Word with God. The choice to use πρός in the first statement, which may be translated as "with" but is more commonly rendered "toward" or "to," may be intentional, for persons are properly placed relationally in the facing position. As Roger Scruton has argued eloquently, it is as individuals situate their faces toward each other that their distinct identities and readiness for personal relationship are made evident.[27] With the two persons placed with or toward each other in the first statement, the addition of the following statement indicates, in a way that begins to pull the mind above the ability of human language to convey divine meaning, that this person is also one with this other. Καὶ θεὸς ἦν ὁ λόγος indicates that the Word and God subsist not just in a personal relationship but also in a predicative relationship. To speak of the Word is also to speak of God. In other words, there is a shared possession as well as a relational distinction.

The orthodox Greek-speaking fathers ultimately agreed to refer to this shared possession of God as οὐσία, "essence" or "nature," and the distinctions between the Word and God (and the Holy Spirit) as ὑπόστασις, "persons." In the Latin the corresponding terms were *essentia* or *substantia* and *persona*. In the West, Augustine noted that

---

[26] The anarthrous construction in the second clause has caused some confusion for Greek novices. First, it has sometimes been argued that an indefinite article is required. In this way, "the Word was God" becomes "the Word was a God." However, the anarthrous construction is typical with a definite predicate noun. Moreover, the absence of a definite article does not automatically require the inclusion of an indefinite article. Second, it has sometimes been argued that θεός should be translated as "divine" rather than "God." Donald Carson disagrees. "This will not do. There is a perfectly serviceable word in Greek for 'divine' (namely *theios*)." Carson, *The Gospel According to John*, 117.

[27] Roger Scruton, "The Face of the Person," in idem, *The Face of God: The Gifford Lectures 2010* (New York: Continuum, 2012), 73–112.

exact translations between Greek and Latin could be confusing.[28] Moreover, within specific languages, the particular terms were subject to shift as the arguments developed. However, the exact terms were themselves less important than what was being attempted, "for the total transcendence of the godhead surpasses the capacity of ordinary speech. God can be thought about more truly than he can be talked about, and he is more truly than he can be thought about."[29] In the East, Athanasius recognized that the exact words, take ὑπόστασις for instance, could be variable. Khaled Anatolios says that at the Council of Alexandria in 362, Athanasius "is less concerned with terminological usage than he is with the substantive signification that such usage is meant to convey."[30] Words such as οὐσία and ὑπόστασις or πρόσωπον (the Greek word for "face," which was often treated synonymously with ὑπόστασις), whatever their prior meanings in the Hellenistic milieu and however philosophically complex, are not as important as the theological meaning derived from Scripture.[31] The terms function as placeholders that ought to be correlated with thought patterns generated in the encounter with the divine Scriptures. Human language was being used to paint the mysterious encounter between eternal Creator and human creature in a manner intentionally faithful to the revelation of Scripture.

On the basis of this twofold affirmation about the Word, that he is both God and with God, the Johannine prologue then makes clear that this Word was the agent of creation. He is not the object of creation but the subject of creation. A strong line is drawn between God

---

[28] Augustine, *The Trinity*, trans. Edmund Hill (Hyde Park, NY: New City, 1991), 196.

[29] Augustine, *The Trinity*, 224–25. Basil Studer, *Trinity and Incarnation: The Faith of the Early Church*, ed Andrew Louth, trans. Matthias Westerhoff (Collegeville, MN: Liturgical, 2002), 182–85.

[30] Khaled Anatolios, *Athanasius,* The Early Church Fathers (New York: Routledge, 2004), 31.

[31] "By way of a general warning, it is important to note that any attempt to define fourth-century theological terminologies by reference solely to their philological origins or to a history of non-Christian philosophical development runs the constant danger of resulting in an artificial clarity that is not reflected in actual theological usage." Lewis Ayres, *Nicaea and Its Legacy: An Approach to Fourth-Century Trinitarian Theology* (New York: Oxford University Press, 2004), 92.

and creation, and the Word is placed firmly and firstly on the divine side of that line: "He was in the beginning with God" (1:2). His indispensable and universal role in creation is stated both positively, "all things came into being through him," and negatively, "apart from him nothing came into being that has come into being" (1:3). Later, we are reminded, "the world was made through him" (1:10). John the Baptist similarly testifies to his ontological priority, saying, "He was before me," even though "he came after me" (1:15). That last phrase, which brings us back to consider the divine economy, must now receive an account.

Θεολογία *and* Οἰκονομία *in John's Prologue*

In the Johannine prologue, after the Word is brought into identity with (and distinction within) the deity, the Word is then pictured as being brought into an intimate relation with humanity. However, "intimate relation" is too weak as a theological description of what actually occurs. It is more appropriate to say that John represents God in Christ as being brought not merely into intimacy with humanity but into identity with humanity. In verse 14 we are confronted with a startling claim. The Word, who is God and with God, sharing deity and distinct within that deity—this divine Word "became flesh." From the perspective of linguistic convention, Cyril of Alexandria notes that the word "flesh" (σάρξ) does not restrict our consideration merely to the body, for John "takes the part for the whole and refers to humanity with the word flesh."[32] Moreover, "he does not say that the Word came into flesh but that the Word became flesh."[33] This allows us to see that the Word is not attached temporarily but permanently to our human nature. God has not merely come to humanity in Christ but has become one with humanity in Christ.

John often employs language of contrast (e.g., "light" and "darkness," "eternal" and "world," "life" and "death," "God" and "man"), but the significant and potentially permanent gaps between these confronting word pairs may be bridged through divine initiative. One

---

[32] Cyril of Alexandria, *Commentary on John*, 62.
[33] Ibid., 63.

of the contrasts John does not allow permanence is that of "flesh" and "spirit." He reacted to Gnosticism in its incipient form, which insisted on a sharp separation between "spirit" and "matter." The Gnostics taught a type of docetism, the early heresy that Christ only appeared (δοκέω) to take on human flesh. John, who personally saw and touched Jesus the human being, responded negatively to this idea and asserted that in Christ's incarnation, God has "come in the flesh" (1 John 4:2–3; 2 John 7). When John, therefore, states that "the Word became flesh" in John 1:14, he is putting God in a human being, presenting the eternal God as sharing life with time-bound humanity. "For the Gnostics, redemption consists of deliverance from matter, from time, from history. For John, on the other hand, redemption is a deliverance, that is, transformation, of matter and time and history."[34] The Gnostics keep time and eternity separate; the Gospel of John presents the eternal God as entering time in order to change humanity. The change in humanity does not mean the Word has brought a different humanity, but fallen humanity has been restored through the grace of the incarnation.[35]

John 1:14 goes on to describe Jesus as dwelling among us. Literally, "he pitched his tabernacle."[36] Christ as the fulfillment of the feasts, including the feast of tabernacles, becomes a major theme in John's Gospel, demonstrating how the God of the Old Testament is now present to Israel in the man Jesus.[37] According to E. Earle Ellis, the "incarnation principle" taught in John 1:14, when placed in tandem with the deity of the Word in 1:1, is "rightly regarded as the key to the whole of the gospel."[38] According to F. F. Bruce, moreover, "It is this scripture, more than anything else in the NT, that provided the foundation for the doctrine of the person of Christ formulated in the Creed of Nicaea (AD 325) and the Definition of Chalcedon (AD 451)."[39]

---

[34] E. Earle Ellis, *The World of St. John: The Gospel and the Epistles* (Grand Rapids, MI: Eerdmans, 1984), 36.

[35] Cyril of Alexandria, *Commentary on John*, 62–63.

[36] Bruce, *The Gospel of John*, 40.

[37] Hays, *Reading Backwards*, 87.

[38] Ellis, *The World of St. John*, 36.

[39] Bruce, *The Gospel of John*, 40.

Cyril of Alexandria, who was instrumental in fostering and defending the creedal definitions, would remind us that the purpose of Christ's incarnation was not for the sake of theological propositions, but "so that having everyone in himself he might reconcile everyone in one body with the Father."[40] Theological claims about the person and natures of Jesus Christ, who is God and with God, as well as a human being, express in human language the reality of God's work of salvation. In the process of bringing redemption to humanity, God has attached humanity to himself in the Word. The redemptive work of God, οἰκονομία, has thus transformed humanity through bringing humanity in the Word into θεολογία. Thus, in perceiving the Gospels' presentation of God coming to man as man, we may also speak of the Son as sharing the nature of God and the nature of man, even as he is one person.

John's prologue uses not only λόγος to describe the nature of Jesus Christ as God, who then became a human being, but other terms, too. These terms likewise place Christ with God according to his actions and attributes. We have already noted, first, that the Word, who later became flesh in Jesus, was the agent of divine creation (1:3, 10). He is, second, the agent of divine revelation, for he is φῶς, "light." Like λόγος, φῶς is used elsewhere in Scripture to describe God. God is the "Father of lights" and the source of all good grace (Jas 1:17), and Christ as sovereign Lord dwells within his unapproachable light (1 Tim 6:16). The early church fathers made much of the relation of Christ to God as "light of light."[41] Also like λόγος, which indicates reason, a reason that underlies all things and is perceptible to human beings, the light is said to enlighten every human being (John 1:9). This light is the true light that comes into the world, into the darkness of the world (1:5). But the darkness cannot comprehend the light, the word for "comprehend" indicating both understanding and authority.

---

[40] Cyril of Alexandria, *Commentary on John*, 64.

[41] Iain M. MacKenzie, *The "Obscurism" of Light: A Theological Study into the Nature of Light* (Norwich, UK: Canterbury, 1996), chaps. 8–10. MacKenzie distinguishes between God as uncreated light and his gift of created light.

Third, he is the agent of divine redemption, for he is ζωή, "life." According to John 5:26, the Father, who "has life in himself," has also "granted the Son to have life in himself." From a theological perspective, "That gift of the Father to the Son must be assumed to be prior to creation." From an economic perspective, "the Gospel is concerned to show how the life of the new creation has become possible for the world through the Son of God. It is none other than the life mediated through the Son."[42] This life is eternal life, life with the Father through his Son (John 3:16). Christ is λόγος, φῶς, and ζωή, and he has come into the world with them as his own. The Son of God, who possesses the attributes of God, creates humanity, reveals God to humanity, and redeems humanity for life with God.

The Rudimentary Triune Pattern in John's Gospel

The Gospel of John paints a portrait of the eternal God that takes a threefold form. This is accomplished not so much in direct propositional statement as in how the Father, the Son, and the Holy Spirit are placed in dynamic eternal relation to one another. The Trinitarian pattern discernible in John's Gospel may be seen in the ascription of monarchy to the Father, generation to the Son, and procession to the Holy Spirit. We begin with the Son, "the only begotten God."

The Only Begotten God

The concluding verse of the prologue is especially important because of its profound ascription to Jesus of the title, μονογενὴς θεὸς, "only begotten God." In the prologue, θεός, "God," is used eight times, six of which refer to the Father, while two refer to Jesus.[43] The Johannine prologue begins with a reference to Jesus as θεός (1:1) and concludes with a reference to Jesus as μονογενὴς θεὸς (1:18). Jesus is on the one hand directly granted deity, but on the other hand his deity is presented in a particular way. Μονογενής has been translated

---

[42] Beasley-Murray, *Gospel of Life*, 4.
[43] Köstenberger, *A Theology of John's Gospel and Letters*, 362.

as "only begotten" and as "one and only." Friedrich Büchsel prefers the former, arguing that in its context, μονογενής is "not just a predicate of value" but indicates "Jesus is in the closest intimacy with God," and "denotes the origin of Jesus." Succinctly, "it means 'only-begotten.'"[44] Köstenberger prefers "one-of-a-kind," arguing that the term indicates "a child particularly special to its parents" when used in the Septuagint.[45] Büchsel's translation assumes that Sonship naturally entails generation, while Köstenberger's translation is weakened by the need to add the word "Son" to the text and to place "God" in an appositional phrase.[46]

Both Büchsel and Köstenberger would agree that, however translated, the Son has a unique and valued relationship with the Father. Moreover, the weaker translation here does not hinder the doctrine of the Son's generation (i.e., being begotten), which is explicitly taught in Hebrews 1:5–6. There the literal term is γεγέννηκά, "begotten." Another important Johannine text for μονογενής in reference to the Son is John 1:14, where the Son shares the Father's glory. Other references include John 3:16 and 3:18, where the Son is sent and given in order to bring salvation into the world. Moreover, the Johannine prologue is not bereft of the explicit language of begetting (γεννάω), specifically with regard to humans being born by the activity of God through faith in Christ (1:13). Note also that the Son in 1:18 is said to be ὁ ὢν εἰς τὸν κόλπον τοῦ πατρὸς, "he who is in the bosom of the Father." Κόλπος refers to an extremely close intimacy, within the

---

[44] Friedrich Büchsel, "Μονογενής," in *Theological Dictionary of the New Testament*, vol. 4, 737–41.

[45] Köstenberger, *A Theology of John's Gospel and Letters*, 362. He also summarizes Pendrick, who argued from the high infant mortality rate that there were others begotten but dead, and cites Moody and Walker in support. Andreas J. Köstenberger and Scott R. Swain, *Father, Son and Spirit: The Trinity and John's Gospel*, New Studies in Biblical Theology (Downers Grove, IL: InterVarsity, 2008), 77n. Dale Moody argues that Jerome's translation of the Greek μονογενής into Latin as *unigenitus* (only begotten) rather than *unicus* (only) was a transposition fostered under the influence of Gregory of Nazianzus's argument regarding the Son's being γέννημα (begotten) and entered English translations in this way. Dale Moody, "God's Only Son: The Translation of John 3:16 in the Revised Standard Version," *Journal of Biblical Literature* 72, no. 4 (1953): 213–19.

[46] Köstenberger and Swain, *Father, Son and Spirit*, 76–78; Köstenberger, *A Theology of John's Gospel and Letters*, 381–82, 382n.

"bosom" or "lap." Another possible translation of κόλπος is, according to Köstenberger, even "himself."[47]

The early theologians agreed that the relation between Father and Son prompts consideration of the immaterial derivation of the Son from the Father. The so-called Logos theologians, such as Justin Martyr and Tertullian, drew upon an abstract concept of λόγος as "reason" and conceived of Christ as an extension of the divine mind. Origen of Alexandria, whose thought was influential on most subsequent theologians, disagreed. Origen said that λόγος is a title, which describes an important aspect of the Son, as all of his titles say something about him, but the title manifestly does not name the Son's nature. Moreover, through close attention to context, Origen noted the earlier Logos theologians' appeal to Psalm 45:1 as a precursor to John 1:1 was inappropriate, for the speaker in that psalm is the human David, not God. Origen was concerned that the Logos theologians were misusing Scripture and opening the door to making the Son a second God through placing his divine origin in time.[48]

Origen appealed instead to the name of the "Son." Applying logic to the Father and Son relation emphasized in the New Testament, Origen says that because the Father is eternal, he is always Father; likewise, the Son is necessarily eternal. To diminish the Son's eternality entails the necessary diminishing of the Father's eternality; to maintain the Father's eternality requires affirmation of the Son's eternal nature. Exegetically, again paying close attention to context and language, he noted that John 1:1 and 1:14 must be read in tandem. Verse 1 specifically says that the Word "was" God, but verse 14 then says that the Word "became" human. The use of "was" in verse 1 indicates that this was already the case "in the beginning," but the use of "became" in verse 14 indicates that the one who is eternally the Son entered history as a man. "The word 'became' refers to the flesh; the word 'was' refers to his divinity."[49] Philippians 2:5–8 similarly refers to the Son in his preexistent state as "being in

---

[47] Ibid., 382.

[48] Ronald E. Heine, *Classical Christian Doctrine: Introducing the Essentials of the Ancient Faith* (Grand Rapids, MI: Baker, 2013), 65–66.

[49] Origen, *Commentary on John*, fragment 2, translated in ibid., 61.

the form of God," but in his temporal incarnation he "took on the form of a servant."[50]

After Origen, both Nicene and Arian theologians agreed that the Son was begotten of the Father, for being a father necessarily entails the derivation of a son from the father through generation.[51] Origen and the leading theologians of the following generations noted that the Son's derivation is described with the verb, γεννάω (to beget or generate). This is according to the descriptions of the Son as begotten in Psalm 2:7, which was repeated in Hebrews 1:5–6 and 5:5–6 (cf. 7:3, 17), and according to the description of Wisdom as begotten in Proverbs 8:25 (LXX).[52] Generation or begetting is also implied in the Johannine contexts in which μονογενής is used (cf. 1:13, 18; 3:3–8, 16). So far the orthodox and the heretics agreed that generation was the means by which Christ received his being from God, but they fell into irreconcilable disagreement over what generation entailed regarding the relation between the nature(s) of God and Christ.

For the Nicene theologians, generation indicates that the Father gave his nature to the Son; for the Arian theologians, generation indicates that the Father gave a different nature to the Son. For Athanasius and the Nicene theologians, generation occurs before time—the Father's generation of the Son is emphatically eternal.[53] For the Arians, generation occurred in a timeless time (ἄχρονος) before

---

[50] Heine, *Origen: Scholarship in the Service of the Church* (New York: Oxford University Press, 2010), 93–103, 139–40; idem, *Classical Christian Doctrine*, 57–67.

[51] For a historical presentation of how Origen's exegesis shaped subsequent theological discourse, see for example, Ayres, *Nicaea and Its Legacy*, 20–30. Ayres argues that Origen was unclear in how the Son is both the same yet different from the Father, and subsequent theologians followed either a "sameness" trajectory (e.g., Athanasius) or a "diversity" trajectory (e.g., Arius). Ibid., 40–61.

[52] Origen argued that the term "today" does not place God in time itself, for God is timeless. History cannot restrict the eternal God. Ibid., 63.

[53] Later, during the first Christological crisis, Cyril of Alexandria argued there are two types of γέννησις, generation: eternally from God the Father and temporally according to the flesh from a woman. Nestorius, condemned as a heretic at the Council of Ephesus (431), argued there was only one generation, the eternal one. Neither of the leading agents in the primary Christological debate considered the generation of the Son to be only temporal. Frances Young, *From Nicaea to Chalcedon: A Guide to the Literature and its Background* (Philadelphia, PA: Fortress, 1983), 217–18.

the ages, but it is a generation that is created and is thus not actually eternal (ἀΐδιος). The Son, concluded Arius, emphatically does not share the Father's being.[54] Arius, a radically conservative biblical exegete, was attempting to preserve the divine monarchy from any taint of mutability or corruptibility; but in doing so, he created divisive theological categories for Christian exegetical practice that required answering.[55]

Athanasius responded to Arius with a sustained exegetical consideration of Scripture, diagraming its theological implications. While this is not the venue for analyzing Athanasius's theological exegesis, which is voluminous, a cursory summary from just a few pages of his *Orationes contra Arianos* provides the following: First, the Son performs actions that are reserved for God, such as giving life to others or giving the Holy Spirit.[56] Second, the Son possesses the attributes of God, such as incorruptibility, wisdom, and sovereignty.[57] Third, the Son receives titles that in their eternal sense are reserved for God, such as "Lord," "King," and "God."[58] Fourth, the Son is to be worshipped at the command of God.[59] He concludes by alluding to the text that began this chapter: "For He ever was and is, as Son, so also Lord and Sovereign of all, being like in all things to the Father, and having all that is the Father's, as He Himself has said."[60]

Logically, Athanasius pointed out that the Arians were the ones who introduced unscriptural terminological subtleties that contradicted the witness of Scripture and the logic of the terms themselves. Athanasius asked difficult questions: How can the Father be eternal yet not have an eternal Son? How can the Son be a mediator between

---

[54] "The statement of faith of Arius and his Alexandrian supporters," translated in Rowan Williams, *Arius: Heresy and Tradition*, 2nd ed. (Grand Rapids, MI: Eerdmans, 2001), 270–71.

[55] Ibid., 175–78.

[56] Athanasius, *Orationes contra Arianos*, in *Nicene and Post-Nicene Fathers*, Second Series, vol. 4, ed. Philip Schaff and Henry Wace, trans. A. Robertson (repr., Peabody, MA: Hendrickson, 1994), 2:16, 2:18.

[57] Ibid., 2:16.

[58] Ibid., 2:16–17.

[59] Ibid., 2:16.

[60] Ibid., 2:18.

humanity and God, if he himself is not also God?[61] How can the Son be worshipped as God, yet not be God, as the Arians claim? Athanasius was reluctant to go beyond scriptural language and embrace the language of οὐσία (essence), but Arius's explicit denial that the Son shared all things with the Father forced him to address that language, too. His defense of the clauses of the Nicene Creed, including ὁμοούσιος (that the Son is of the same essence as the Father), was necessary because they "contain the sense of the Scripture."[62]

Ultimately, Athanasius saw Arianism as posing a threefold danger. First, Arianism does not interpret Scripture according to Scripture's own scope of presenting Christ as both God and man. Second, Arianism makes impossible the redemption of fallen man. Humanity requires a mediator that is both man and God, and the Arians separate Christ from God. Third, Arianism diminishes the eternal glory and honor that Scripture accords to the Son of God. At the same time the Arians claim to worship the Son, they hypocritically deny him his honor as God. "If you had understood his love for us, you would not have estranged the Son from the Father and would not have made him who reconciled us to his Father a foreigner [to the divine essence]."[63] For Athanasius, the leading defender of Christian orthodoxy in the patristic period, the deity of the Son, a deity that the Father eternally shares with his Son through generation, must be affirmed. It must be central to our theology because it is scriptural, because it is necessary for salvation, and because it is necessary for worship. Jesus Christ, the Son of God, is generated eternally and ontologically from God the Father. He is the "begotten God."

The Divine Monarch

The Christian inheritance of the Old Testament, as we saw in chapter 3, required the correlation of the worship of the only true God with the inclusion of Jesus Christ within the identity of God. The biblical

---

[61] Williams, *Arius*, 240–41.

[62] Thomas G. Weinandy, *Athanasius: A Theological Introduction*, Great Theologians (Burlington, VT: Ashgate, 2007), 73–74.

[63] Athanasius, *Festal Letter* 10:9; Anatolios, *Athanasius*, 86.

necessity of maintaining the uniqueness of God the Father weighed heavily on the early church. Both orthodox and heretics agreed that the Father was μοναρχία, "the one source." Basil of Caesarea classified δόγμα as not subject to proclamation, like κήρυγμα, because of its general ecclesial acceptance. And Basil "the Great," named for his important defense of orthodoxy, believed the monarchy of the Father is a dogma that ought not be lost.[64] However, among earlier theologians were those who went so far in the direction of preserving the monarchy of the Father that they either endangered the identity of Jesus with God and turned the Holy Spirit into a mere power, or they nullified any distinction between the Father, his Son, and the Holy Spirit.

Historians have divided these early "Unitarian" theologians into two main branches, both of which emphasized the monarchy of God the Father and were active during the second and third centuries. First, the so-called Dynamic Monarchian theologians included, in the West, Theodotus the leatherworker and Theodotus the money-changer, and in the East, the Alogi of Asian Minor and Paul of Samosata, bishop of the highly prominent church of Antioch. The Alogi, literally "those against the Logos," preserved the monarchy of the Father through denying the Gospel of John, which they accused of being pseudony- mous, devoid of arrangement, and contradictory to the adoption- ist Christology they perceived in the Synoptic Gospels. They also attacked the Revelation of John for its fantastic contents. Harnack describes them as the first historical critical scholars.[65] The thought of Paul of Samosata is difficult to reconstruct from the sources, but he was condemned at the Council of Antioch in 268–69 for teaching that Christ was a "mere man" and the Holy Spirit was grace. It was

---

[64] Basil of Caesarea, *De Spiritu Sancto*, in *Nicene and Post-Nicene Fathers*, Second Series, vol. 8, ed. Philip Schaff and Henry Wace, trans. Blomfield Jackson (repr., Peabody, MA: Hendrickson, 1994), 18:47. The divine monarchy was broadly presumed by the time of the writing theologians, so much that it is difficult to recon- struct the term's origin in biblical commentary. First John 1:1–2 seems to be the most likely source. Cf. Origen, *De Principiis*, in *Ante-Nicene Fathers*, vol. 4, ed. Alexander Roberts and James Donaldson, trans. Frederick Crombie (repr., Peabody, MA: Hendrickson, 1994), 1:1:1–9.

[65] Adolf Harnack, *The History of Dogma*, trans. James Millar, vol. 3 (repr., Eugene, OR: Wipf & Stock, 1997), 14–19.

suggested that "Paul's motivation was to preserve the uniqueness of the Father as the one God of all."[66]

The so-called "Modalistic Monarchian" theologians included, in the West, Tertullian's *bête noire*, Praxeas, along with four bishops of Rome, and, in the East, the followers of Sabellius. The Modalistic Monarchians preserved the unity of God, not through having the Son adopted for a divine role as with the Dynamic Monarchians but through directly identifying the Father with his Son with the Holy Spirit. In other words, the Modalistic Monarchians denied there were any eternal distinctions between the Father, the Son, and the Holy Spirit. Tertullian, in the "oldest Christian work on the subject of the Trinity,"[67] thus condemned Praxeas for having crucified the Father, subjecting God to corruptibility. Corruptibility, which includes death, was contrary to incorruptibility, which correlates with the eternity of God and was one of the most important divine attributes in the early church. The eventually triumphant orthodox theologians appealed against Modalism to the rule of faith and within Scripture to the Johannine writings. The Gospel of John was especially helpful because of its λόγος doctrine.[68] These early orthodox theologians, the so-called Logos theologians, turned to the writings of John, because as we have seen they posit not just economic distinctions but also theological distinctions between the Father and the Son.[69]

In spite of the Logos theologians' success in maintaining both the unity and the distinctions between the Father and the Son, the person of the Holy Spirit was not given careful exegetical treatment. For instance, although Tertullian bequeathed to posterity the term *Trinitas*, and offered the widely accepted Latin terms of *substantia* and *persona* to describe the unity and distinctions within God,[70] his doctrine of the Spirit was problematic. In the midst of a careful review

---

[66] John Behr, *The Formation of Christian Theology*, vol. 1: *The Way to Nicaea* (Crestwood, NY: St. Vladimir's Seminary Press, 2001), 213.

[67] Gerald Bray, "Tertullian," in *Shapers of Christian Orthodoxy: Engaging with Early and Medieval Theologians*, ed. Bradley G. Green (Downers Grove, IL: InterVarsity, 2010), 68.

[68] Harnack, *History of Dogma*, 3, 71.

[69] Studer, *Trinity and Incarnation*, 70–75.

[70] Ibid., 71.

of the Johannine distinctions and unity of the Father and Son, for instance, he writes, "But the Word was formed by the Spirit, and if I may express myself like this, the Spirit is the body of the Word."[71] Origen noted that the word for "spirit" taken literally has a material meaning, but the word is used metaphorically in its context. Tertullian could have learned something from his fellow African regarding the immateriality of spirit as used in Scripture.[72] But both Tertullian and Origen could also have performed more careful exegesis, in the Gospel of John for instance, regarding the eternal distinctions between the Holy Spirit and the other two "persons" of the Trinity. That, however, was the work of the later Cappadocian theologians.

The Proceeding God

Through his careful reading of Scripture, Basil of Caesarea laid the exegetical groundwork upon which so much of the historic Christian doctrine of the Holy Spirit's membership within the divine Trinity has been constructed. Basil's book on the Holy Spirit was written in response to the accusation that he improperly worshipped God. Specifically, Basil was accused of praying to the persons of the Trinity in the manner of "connumeration" as well as "subnumeration." Connumeration "is appropriate to subjects of equal dignity," while subnumeration is assigned "to those that vary in the direction of inferiority."[73] The distinction, borrowed from heathen philosophy, is nevertheless instructive. Indeed, the problem of the Trinity is in large part reducible to the position one takes in answer to this question. If one is unwilling to worship the Son and the Holy Spirit as one worships the monarch, the Father, one has exclusively affirmed subnumeration. The tendency toward an exclusive subnumeration, the downgrading of the divine status of the Son and the Holy Spirit, informed all sorts of early heresies, from Dynamic Monarchianism to

---

[71] Tertullian, *Against Praxeas*, 8; Bray, "Tertullian," 82.

[72] Wiles, *The Spiritual Gospel*, 67.

[73] Basil did not necessarily like the terms, due perhaps to the way his opponents elevated them, but he maintained the logical distinction. Basil, *De Spiritu Sancto*, 17:42.

Arianism to Pneumatomachianism. It may properly be used to classify modern religious groups and tendencies, from Jehovah's Witnesses on the right to Universalist Unitarians on the left. Americans who believe the Holy Spirit is a force and not a person, which according to a 2014 poll characterizes many evangelicals,[74] have also embraced a strong form of subnumeration.

Basil's doxological practice included two forms of reference to the Trinity. He prayed to the Father "with the Son together with the Holy Ghost," and he prayed to the Father "through the Son in the Holy Ghost." The first form applies the category of connumeration or equality to the three persons of the Trinity, while the second form applies the category of subnumeration or inferiority to the Father, the Son, and the Holy Spirit. It must be recognized that the goal of Basil's most well-known opponent, Eunomius of Cyzicus, was to derive theology from proper biblical exegesis. When Eunomius's followers heard Basil refer to the Trinity in terms of equality, they sensed an implicit form of Sabellianism. Eunomius argued that the linguistic prepositions typically applied to the Father, the Son, and the Holy Spirit are important. He discovered that the Bible refers to the Father in terms of "of whom," while the Son is presented in terms of "through whom," and the Spirit is spoken of in terms of "in whom" or "in which."[75] According to Basil, the Eunomians then applied philosophical categories of causation, which appear to derive from Aristotle, to the biblical prepositions. These helped them conclude the Father is the Creator, the Son is a subordinate agent or instrument, and the Spirit is only in time or space.[76] Eunomius turned typical biblical prepositional ascriptions into a hermeneutical rule that required the Son and the Holy Spirit be conceptualized as possessing different natures. Eunomius's strict subnumeration preserved the uniqueness of the Father, but in doing so, he transformed the Son into a demigod and the Spirit into a power.[77]

---

[74] Ligonier Ministries and LifeWay Research, *The State of Theology: Theological Awareness Benchmark Study* (TheStateOfTheology.com, 2014), 11:12.

[75] Andrew Radde-Gallwitz, *Basil of Caesarea: A Guide to His Life and Doctrine* (Eugene, OR: Cascade, 2012), 50–57.

[76] Basil, *De Spiritu Sancto*, 2.4, 3.5.

[77] Stephen M. Hildebrand, *Basil of Caesarea*, Foundations of Theological Exegesis and Christian Spirituality (Grand Rapids, MI: Baker, 2014), 72–76.

Basil's response was to encourage his Eunomian opponents to reevaluate their way of reading the Bible. If we may soften his polemics, Basil said we should ask not, "How does biblical terminology reflect precise Hellenistic grammatical rules?" Rather, we should ask, "How does the biblical use of the Greek language create its own linguistic rules and thought patterns?" Basil wanted theology to be guided by scriptural paradigms (παραδείγματα or ὑποδείγματα), and this requires careful attention to all of the linguistic norms and linguistic peculiarities that arise within the biblical text.[78] Basil did not argue against the overarching Johannine tendency, for instance, to speak of the Son and the Spirit as coming "from" or "of" the Father. That John pictured the Father as the divine source with the use of such prepositions is indisputable, but that is not the only Johannine paradigm. First, "of" (ἐχ or ἀπό) is used, for example, of the Son (John 1:16; 16:15) and the Holy Spirit (John 3:6; Gal 6:8) as well as of the Father.[79] Second, "through" or "by" (διά) is used, for example, of the Father (1 Cor 1:9; Gal 4:7) and the Holy Spirit (1 Cor 12:8; 2 Tim 1:14) as well as the Son.[80] And third, "in" (ἐν) is used, for example, not just of the Spirit, but also of the Father (Eph 3:9; 2 Thess 1:1).[81]

For Basil, "Scripture varies its expressions as occasion requires," and our theology must be open to its paradigms rather than forcing alien laws upon it.[82] Basil was not arguing that the linguistic pattern Eunomius detected was false. Basil was arguing that it was not the only linguistic pattern. Multiple arrays within Scripture should be recognized. Alongside the prepositional paradigm of subnumeration, there is also a paradigm of connumeration. For instance, with regard to the placement of the Son and the Holy Spirit "with" the Father, Basil appeals to the Great Commission of Matthew 28:19. As we noted in chapter 1, the baptismal formula commanded by the Lord places the three in a pattern of equality, what the Greeks would classify as connumeration. The Lord Jesus, the so-called second person of the Trinity, "has delivered to us as a necessary and saving doctrine

---

[78] Radde-Gallwitz, *Basil of Caesarea*, 32–34.
[79] Basil, *De Spiritu Sancto*, 5.8–5.9.
[80] Ibid., 5.10, 5.12.
[81] Ibid., 5.11.
[82] Ibid., 4.6.

that the Holy Spirit is to be ranked with the Father." The Lord did "indeed conjoin the Spirit with the Father and Himself in baptism."[83]

The grammatico-theological rule Basil discerned includes both the subnumeration of the Three and the connumeration of the Three: "The Church recognizes both uses, and deprecates neither as subversive of the other." For instance, while we come to the Father "through" the Son in prayer, the eternal glory of the Father is "with" the Son.[84] One could perhaps argue that Basil was saying that theologically, the three are connumerative, while economically, the three are subnumerative, and in this illustration, he was. However, he soon reminds the reader that the Son is not ἄναρκος, without cause, in relation to the Father, the ἀρχῆς. Basil cites three Johannine passages to support his contention that the Son eternally derives his being from the Father, including "I live through the Father" (John 6:57) and "the Son can do nothing of himself" (5:19). The Son, according to Basil, is on the one hand not "without cause" (ἄναρκος) and on the other hand "self-existent" (αὐτοζωή).[85] For Basil, subnumeration and connumeration are both helpful when speaking theologically, that is of the eternal Trinity.

Where Basil's rule of interpretation, based on the two Trinitarian paradigms he discovered in the Bible, had its most important impact was in the development of the doctrine of the Holy Spirit. Basil argued that the Holy Spirit should be worshipped as fully God because of the way Scripture treated the Holy Spirit. The Spirit possesses titles proper to him as God, such as "Spirit of God" (Matt 12:28) and "Spirit of truth who proceedeth from the Father" (John 15:26),[86] along with "holy," "sanctifying," "good," "Paraclete,"[87] and "Lord."[88] The Spirit engages in activities that are performed by God alone, including redemption,[89] creation, and revelation,[90] as well as providence,

---

[83] Ibid., 10.24–10.25.
[84] Ibid., 7.16.
[85] Ibid., 8.19.
[86] Basil, *De Spiritu Sancto*, 9.22.
[87] Ibid., 19.48.
[88] Ibid., 21.52.
[89] Ibid., 15.36.
[90] Ibid., 16.38.

the ordering of the church,[91] and judgment.[92] The Spirit possesses the divine attributes, such as incomprehensibility, omnipresence, goodness, and glory.[93] The connumeration of the Spirit as God is most strongly proved by his inclusion alongside the Father and the Son in the dominical form of baptism.[94]

The Holy Spirit's subnumeration within the Trinity is identified with the particular language of John 15:26: The "Spirit of truth" is ὅ παρὰ τοῦ πατρὸς ἐκπορεύεται, "he who proceeds from the Father." Basil differentiates the Holy Spirit's eternal procession from the Son's eternal generation. The Holy Spirit "is moreover said to be 'of God;' not indeed in the sense in which all things are of God, but in the sense of proceeding out of God, not by generation, like the Son, but as Breath of His mouth."[95] The language of procession in its application to the eternal relation of the Holy Spirit to the Father comes from the Bible and on that strength was championed in the influential works of Gregory of Nazianzus and Gregory of Nyssa, and retained in Christian history.[96]

With the lineaments of John's portrait of God worked out in some exegetical detail, a summary description of the God discerned therein is now required. From a close examination of the Johannine view of God in this chapter, in the next we step back from his portrait to give our impression of what John has been attempting to convey through appeal to John's own use of analogy.

---

[91] Ibid., 16.39.

[92] Ibid., 16.40

[93] Ibid., 22.53–24.55.

[94] Ibid., 10.24–12.28.

[95] Ibid., 18.46.

[96] Origen earlier used the language of procession to distinguish the Spirit's origin from the Father, effectively if not systematically placing the Spirit's procession alongside but distinct from the Son's generation. In his systematic treatise, Origen did not provide John 15:26 as an explicit prooftext, but the allusion is definite. Origen, *De Principiis*, 1.2.13, 3.5.8.

6

EVEN AS GOD: ΚΑΘΩς

That they all may be one; even as [καθὼς] you, Father, are
in me and I am in you, that they also may be in us, so that
the world may believe that you sent me. The glory that you
have given me I have given to them, so that they may be
one, even as [καθὼς] we are one.

John 17:21–22

Metaphors

Κ αθὼς, which means "even as" or "just as," is a common adverb
in the Greek language and is used extensively in the New
Testament. The term is so common that its force in John's Trinitarian
narrative may slip the unwary exegete. The primary function of
this adverb is to establish a comparison.[1] The seventeenth chapter
of John's Gospel employs καθὼς eight times in the so-called high
priestly prayer of Jesus, making it the highest concentration of the
term within the Gospel of John and the Gospels generally (17:2, 11,
14, 16, 18, 21, 22, 23). With such extensive use, the author, who
places it on the lips of Jesus, is indicating the metaphorical nature of
Jesus' discourse.

---

[1] "Καθὼς," in *A Greek-English Lexicon of the New Testament and Other Early
Christian Literature*, 2nd ed., ed. Walter Bauer, William F. Arndt, and F. Wilbur
Gingrich (Chicago: University of Chicago Press, 1979), 391.

Metaphors use literal language in a figurative fashion to point to another reality. A "metaphor" has been defined as a "figure of speech whereby we speak about one thing in terms that are seen to be suggestive of another."[2] Academic philosophers use the example of "Achilles is a lion," which if taken in a literal manner becomes absurd. However, when taken as a figurative comparison, "Achilles is a lion," means, "Achilles is like a lion in respect of the following features." The point of a metaphor is to suggest certain aspects of one thing apply to another. The results can often be surprising because disparate things are brought into relation with one another, encouraging expansive forms of thought.[3] According to G. B. Caird, a metaphor is a lens. "[I]t is as though the speaker were saying, 'Look through this and see what I have seen, something you would never have noticed without the lens!'"[4]

It should not be surprising, therefore, that the theologian who wrote the Gospel of John uses metaphors to prompt us to think beyond the confines of this world and suggest dimensions of the eternal. Jesus often used figurative language, in just this way, for instance with his parables. What is surprising is that the Lord in John 17 uses figurative language to suggest, not a view of eternity according to a worldly metaphor, but a view of the way the world will become according to an eternal metaphor. The metaphors that Jesus employs in his high priestly prayer turn the human-to-divine direction of the metaphors and similes[5] that dominate the Synoptic Gospels in the other direction.[6] In John 17, Jesus does not say, "The kingdom of

---

[2] Janet Martin Soskice, *Metaphor and Religious Language* (New York: Oxford University Press, 1985), 15. "Metaphor" derives philologically from the Greek μεταφέρειν, "to bear along" or "to transfer." On figurative language in Scripture, see the still helpful introduction and notes of E. W. Bullinger, *Figures of Speech Used in the Bible Explained and Illustrated* (New York: Young, 1898), i–xvii.

[3] Robert A. Sharpe, "Metaphor," in *The Oxford Companion to Philosophy*, ed. Ted Honderich (New York: Oxford University Press, 1995), 555–56.

[4] G. B. Caird, *The Language and Imagery of the Bible* (Philadelphia, PA: Westminster, 1980), 152.

[5] The distinction between a metaphor and simile is that a simile makes an explicit comparison while a metaphor makes an implicit comparison. This distinction is not always maintained. Ibid., 144.

[6] Elaine M. Wainwright, dwelling on the use of metaphorical language in the Gospel of Matthew, notes that metaphors are necessary when speaking of God. This

heaven is like" this or that aspect of the world, but the church in the world should be like this or that aspect of God. The metaphors established by Jesus's use of καθὼς here thus tell us that God is a certain way, and the Son is praying to the Father that believers would be as he is in those ways. We are thus able to discern what God is like through Jesus's description of what believers should be like in relation to God, the world, and other believers.[7]

The significance of this move should not be missed. Jesus, even while using human language with its limits, is telling his disciples that this is who God is. God does not simply work like this. God is this! Jesus is telling us in his discourse that this is God's reality. On the basis of this structure of God's reality, believers are then to see this pattern become real in their own lives. More than saying that God is real, Jesus is teaching that God is real in this particular way. Jesus uses the language of unity and relationality to point to God's being. On the basis of divine ontology, he then provides an outline of the structure of the church's practice. The primary reality is provided with God, and the church's reality is represented as an extension of the divine reality. Who God is, as a unity and a relationship, is the basis for the structure of what the church ought to be. Divine ontology, if we may speak in this way, provides the structure of the church's economy. In a stunning reversal of the dominant contemporary paradigm that the Triune economy is our only access to the immanent Trinity, Jesus argued that the Trinity's economy for the church is accessible through an analogy with the immanent Trinity.

---

is because God is always beyond our ability to name him. "All such attempts will be like a finger pointing toward the one who is beyond all our imagining but whose naming in our theologizing is limited to human language. God is always beyond our naming and imaging." Wainwright, "Like a Finger Pointing to the Moon: Exploring the Trinity in/and the New Testament," in *The Cambridge Companion to the Trinity*, ed. Peter C. Phan (New York: Cambridge University Press, 2011), 34. While we agree with Wainwright's warnings regarding metaphor, we also note that Scripture does provide names for God. As the Cappadocians indicated, some of these names are more proper than other titles. These proper names include "Father," "Son," and "Holy Spirit."

[7] Caird says the "vehicle" is that which a word normally implies, but a "tenor" is that which bears a new meaning. Caird, *The Language and Imagery of the Bible*, 152.

For instance, in John 17:21–22, Jesus explains that there is both unity and intimate relationship in God. One aspect of the divine reality is that there is a unity between the Father and the Son. "We are one," Jesus said to the Father (v. 22). But this unity is not rigidly simple but complexly simple. The unity of God is a unity that involves, at the least, one person, a "you," the Father, addressing another person, a "me," the Son. The one God, composed of at least two persons, is thereby an "us" (v. 21). The shape of the complex unity of God is described according to a mutual indwelling. Jesus referred, in an act of prayer, to God the Father as "you," and he placed him in a certain relationship to himself. Σύ, πάτερ, ἐν ἐμοὶ κἀγὼ ἐν σοί: "You, Father, [are] in me and I [am] in you." The language of relationship between these two divine subjects is one of in-ness. John's intimate relation of the Father with the Son was detected by the early church fathers as including also the Holy Spirit, as we saw in the last chapter. The mutual indwelling of Word and Spirit is also a prominent feature in the eighth chapter of Paul's letter to the Romans.

This mutual indwelling of the three subjects in the one God has been described within church history with such terms as περιχώρησις, communion, and interpenetration. John of Damascus, systematizing the contributions of the Cappadocian fathers, coined the term περιχώρησις to describe the mutual indwelling of the three persons of the Trinity. Karl Barth, drawing on John's relational analogies—between God and God, God and believers, and believers with one another—employs a number of terms to describe the intimacy. Barth grounds the contours of church life in the being of God, and his discussion is instructive in its derivation from the writings of John.

> This one thing is therefore the divine, the θεῖον, the essence of God in the revelation of His name, which is the subject of our enquiry. That is to say, we shall find in God Himself, in His eternal being, nothing other than this one thing. As and before God seeks and creates fellowship with us, He wills and completes this fellowship in Himself. In Himself He does not will to exist for Himself, to exist alone. On the contrary, He is Father, Son and Holy Spirit and therefore

alive in His unique being with and for and in one another.
The unbroken unity of his being, knowledge and will
is at the same time an act of deliberation, decision and
intercourse. He does not exist in solitude, but in fellowship.
Therefore what He seeks and creates between Himself and
us is in fact nothing else but what He wills and completes
and therefore is in Himself.[8]

What allows Barth, among many others, to speak of the eternal relationships within God, in terms of simplicity and complexity, of unity and fellowship, are the highly suggestive theological metaphors originally employed by the Lord as relayed by John. The use of metaphoric language is helpful for taking the human mind beyond the limits of the cosmos in order to peer momentarily into the reality of God.

Of course, problems arise between interpreters, because metaphors according to their fruitful nature prompt different suggestions in human minds.[9] In order to discern the limits of metaphorical suggestion, most theologians would appeal to the work of the Holy Spirit in the close reading of the Word.[10] Applying our leading text to the theological task, we also note that the Spirit and the Word work within the community of believers in such a way that the scholar must interact humbly with the church and its biblical interpreters through the ages. On the basis of this caveat regarding the helpfulness, difficulty, and complexity of employing human language to describe God, and after extensive interaction with theologians through the ages, we turn now to my own description of the portrait of God suggested in the Gospel of John.

---

[8] Note Barth's emphasis on the freedom of God to be. The reference to θεῖον derives from Acts 17:29. Karl Barth, *Church Dogmatics*, vol. 2, *The Doctrine of God*, part 1, trans. T. H. L. Parker et al., ed. G. W. Bromiley and T. F. Torrance (Edinburgh: T&T Clark, 1957), 275.

[9] Sharpe, "Metaphor," 555.

[10] Francis Watson, "Authors, Readers, Hermeneutics," in *Reading Scripture with the Church: Toward a Hermeneutic for Theological Interpretation*, ed. A. K. M. Adam et al. (Grand Rapids, MI: Baker Academic, 2006), 119–23.

Trinitarian Patterns in the Gospel of John

Through years of reading the Gospel of John, it becomes apparent to many scholars, including the current writer, that the Trinity is woven into the text like a subtle yet dominant pattern woven into a colorful tapestry. This pattern becomes more evident, more detailed, and more startlingly beautiful with every careful examination of the text. Christoph Schwöbel, Udo Schnelle, and Keith Johnson have referred to "grammatical rules"[11] or "rules in exposition"[12] derived from the Gospel of John. These rules parallel what the early church fathers referred to as the *regulam fidei*, "the rule of faith." Similarly, Andreas Köstenberger and Scott Swain have discerned "tracks" that allow them to develop major "Trinitarian themes" from the Gospel of John.[13] The following patterns (cf. Basil's παραδείγματα) are the result of my own labor but have some commonalities with the writers just mentioned, along with many others. I tested their rules and the patristic "rule of faith" according to the patterns I have discerned in reading John and have concluded the basic outline of the orthodox Christian κανών regarding the divine identity is clearly discernible in the text. The reader is offered the following fivefold reflection upon the Johannine patterning of God and asked to read deeply and often that apostle's Gospel and letters to see whether they likewise discern a similar portrait of God.

God the Trinity Is Utterly Separate Above Creation

The κόσμος, "world," has an origin, but God is presented as without origin, as eternal, as above, beyond, or behind time and history and

---

[11] Schwöbel, "The Trinity Between Athens and Jerusalem," 28; Udo Schnelle, "Trinitarisches Denken im Johannesevangelium," in *Israel und seine Heilstraditionem im Johannesevangelium*, ed. M. Labahn, K. Scholtissek, and A. Strotmann (Paderborn: Schöningh, 2004), 367–86; cited in Schwöbel, "The Trinity Between Athens and Jerusalem," 29.

[12] Keith E. Johnson, "Augustine's 'Trinitarian' Reading of John 5: A Model for the Theological Interpretation of Scripture?," *Journal of the Evangelical Theological Society* 52, no. 4 (2009): 804–7.

[13] Andreas J. Köstenberger and Scott R. Swain, *Father, Son and Spirit: The Trinity and John's Gospel*, New Studies in Biblical Theology (Downers Grove, IL: InterVarsity, 2008), 23.

matter. God simply "was" "in the beginning" (John 1:1–2), while creation has a beginning due to his will and action. Or, to draw on a Pauline analogy borrowed from a pagan poet, we might say that creation and its history exists and progresses within God (Acts 17:28). The one God affirmed by both John and Paul created the world by his Word and his Spirit. Jesus described his own preexistence in John 17:5: "that glory I had with you before the world began." The apostle in almost poetic terms described the Son's subsequent relation to the world: "He was in the world, and the world was created through him, but the world did not recognize him" (1:10). Again, "He was with God in the beginning. Everything was created through him, and apart from him not one thing was created that has been created" (1:2–3). Regarding the creative work of the Holy Spirit, Jesus says, "The Spirit is the One who gives life" (6:63a). Along with the early church fathers, we must draw a bold line between the Creator and his creation; and the Son and the Holy Spirit are perceived as being on the Godward side of that line from eternity.[14]

During his high priestly prayer, Jesus said to the Father, "You loved me before the world's foundation" (17:25b). And at another time Jesus told the Pharisees, "Very truly I tell you, before Abraham was, I am" (8:58). The reference to Genesis is one his Jewish interlocutors perceived and were incensed about. Jesus was granting himself the status of preexistence, in reference to Abraham, and the status of deity, in reference to the covenant name, "I am."[15] Of the five (or six) major characters in John 14–16—the Father, the Son, the Holy Spirit, believers, and the world (along with its ruler)—the first three of them are permanently differentiated from the others. The Father, the Son, and the Holy Spirit desire restored fellowship with the world through

---

[14] "As a result of the Arian controversy, the hierarchy was destroyed and a radical distinction was established between the Creator and everything that derived its being from his creative activity." Frances Young, *From Nicaea to Chalcedon: A Guide to the Literature and Its Background* (Philadelphia, PA: Fortress, 1983), 178.

[15] The "Christological model of preexistence with regard to Genesis" may be found here in John, but Genesis is also used in Paul and the author of Hebrews to build the same case. Knut Backhaus, "'Before Abraham Was, I Am': The Book of Genesis and the Genesis of Christology," in *Genesis and Christian Theology*, ed. Nathan MacDonald, Mark W. Elliott, and Grant Macaskill (Grand Rapids, MI: Eerdmans, 2012), 74–84.

the divine work of redemption, and fellowship may be restored with them through faith, but they are eternally different from the world.

God the Father Is the Source, Continuance, and End of the Trinitarian Relations

The Son repeatedly says that he has come "from" the Father. Examples of all three Greek prepositions that indicate origin may be found in the text being used to describe the eternal Father-Son relation: ἐκ (8:42), παρά (6:46; 7:29; 9:33; 16:27–28; 17:8), and ἀπό (13:3). The Son also says he is returning πρός, "to," God the Father in the eternal heaven. The Father is the origin and end point of the Son, and the Son is always also "with" (πρός or μετά) and "in" (ἐν) the Father, indicating an eternal relation with contemporary effect. This language of indwelling suggests a shared existence. "I am in the Father and the Father is in me" (14:10; cf. 6:38–40; 8:24; 12:44–45, 49–50; 14:11; 16:32; 17:21).

The first epistle of John begins by referring to the Father as ἀρχῆς, the "source" of the Son (1 John 1:1–3). The Holy Spirit is "from" (παρὰ) the Father (John 15:26), and he is also "from" (ἀφ') the Son, though apparently in a derivative way (16:12–14). Jesus says that whatever the Father possesses is "mine," and the Holy Spirit also takes from this "mine" that is common to the Father and the Son (16:14–15).[16] Another indication that the Father, the Son, and the Spirit share a common existence with its basis in the Father is found in how the Gospel of John uses the possession of life. The Father has given of his "life" to the Son (5:26), so that the Son is also called "life" (1:4; 14:1), and the Spirit is one who can sovereignly give "life" to yet others (6:63a). The theological transition from speaking of "life" to speaking of "being" is not a difficult one to make.

---

[16] See chap. 5 above regarding "mine."

God Is One, and His Unity Extends Unhindered to the Son and the Holy Spirit

The unity of God is not altered (i.e., he remains without multiplication or division) when we learn, in the New Testament, that the Son and the Holy Spirit are included along with the Father in the identity of the only God, who was originally revealed in the Hebrew Bible. The Word was not only "with God," but he "was God" in the beginning (1:1). The challenge that Jesus's teaching presented in this regard did not go unnoticed among his Jewish opponents. Whenever Jesus made his audacious claims, the radical Unitarians of his day tried to kill Jesus. After each of the following instances, attempts were made to bring his life to an end: In John 5:18, Jesus was "calling God his own Father, making himself equal with God." In 7:29, Jesus said, "I am from him, and he sent me." In 8:58, Jesus asserted, "I assure you. Before Abraham was, I am." In 10:30, perhaps the most cited unity text, Jesus stated, "The Father and I are one." And in 10:38, Jesus cast their unity in the shape of mutual indwelling: "The Father is in me and I in the Father."

The Jews were not secretive with Jesus about their objections after these profoundly disturbing statements from him. They told Jesus the reason he should be stoned for blasphemy is, "You being a man make yourself God" (10:33). Finally, when they dragged Jesus before Pilate in order to demand his death, they laid out their theological rationale clearly: "He must die, because he made himself the Son of God" (19:7).

When the Son prayed to the Father, he referred to his preexistent unity with the Father. As noted above, he referred to his own unity with the Father not as a metaphor but as a reality toward which humanity must arrive: "May they be one even as we are one" (17:11). There is one unity between the Father and the Son, a mutual indwelling (17:21), which is subsequently offered as a unity by grace to the redeemed (17:21–23). The unity between the Son and the Holy Spirit is indicated by the fact that it is Jesus's very breath that is the Holy Spirit (20:22). This act of re-creating humanity through redemption, of course, parallels the original creation of humanity, when God breathed his own Spirit into the human body, giving it life (Gen 2:7). To complete the circle of unity between the three, we point again to the origin of the Holy Spirit as "proceeding from the Father" (15:26).

The earliest disciples also came to recognize the unity between the Father and the Son. Their confessions and interactions with Jesus are especially notable in the narrative of John's Gospel: The formerly blind disciple fell before his healer and cried out, "I believe, Lord!" The one with new sight also engaged in an act reserved only for God: "He worshipped him" (9:38). The grieving sister of Lazarus, Martha, was told she could have eternal life if she believed he was "the resurrection and the life." "Yes, Lord," she told Jesus, "I believe you are the Messiah, the Son of God who comes into the world" (11:27). And to affirm the truth of her faith, he wept with her and then called a man dead for four days to come back to life. To Philip, the disciple who wanted to see the Father and worship him, Jesus said, "Have I been among you all this time without you knowing me, Philip? The one who has seen me has seen the Father. . . . I am in the Father and the Father is in me" (14:9–11). And after his own resurrection, by the Father through the Spirit, Jesus showed himself with his wounds and called on a doubting disciple to believe. Thomas, with his hand in his master's death-dealing wounds, responded to Jesus, the crucified Lord of glory, the resurrected man, "My Lord and my God!" (20:28).

John includes each of these narratives, especially the explosive confession of Thomas near the end of his book, as an *inclusio* matched by the earlier ascription to Jesus of God (1:1, 18), in order to prompt reflection on Jesus's unity with God.

The Distinctions Between the Father, the Son, and the Holy Spirit Are Real

The distinctions between the three are real, and the unity of God does not change those distinctions. As noted above, the Word is God and "with" God (1:1). Moreover, while the Father and the Son are one, it is the corporate plural subject "we" and the distributive plural subjects "the Father and I" that comprise the unity. The plurality and unity are held simultaneously, without endangering either reality.

These real distinctions may be seen as contemporaneous within history and as eternal. Two historical events stand out in particular from the narrative of John's Gospel, one placed strategically near the beginning of the Gospel and the other at the end (as with the claims that Jesus is God, each serving as an *inclusio* investing the narrative with theological significance). First, at the baptism of Jesus, the Holy Spirit was seen by the Baptist to descend on the Son, and God the Father told him that Jesus is his Son. All three persons are active at the same moment in history (1:32–34). Second, at the commissioning of his disciples, which occurred after his resurrection and prior to his ascension, Jesus drew upon his Father's authority and granted authority to his disciples through breathing the Holy Spirit on them (20:21–23). Occurring as they do in singular moments, both events discount the modalist interpretation that God only appears to be three by manifesting himself differently at different times. Moreover, the language John the Baptist uses—"He is (ἐστιν) the Son of God"—is ontological language (1:34), not metaphorical.[17]

An event within the Gospel of John that signifies the historical reality of the distinctions but with eternal allusions concerns the particular relationship of the Son and the Holy Spirit. In his discourse on the community of God and the community of believers in John 14–16, Jesus teaches the Holy Spirit is related to himself in two ways. First, the Holy Spirit is intimately related to the Son as one person facing another. He is, like Jesus, a Paraclete (cf. 1 John 2:1), but he is "another Paraclete" (14:16).[18] The Spirit's ministry will be different

---

[17] This report is more poignant in the Synoptic traditions, for it is the Father himself who declares Jesus's sonship is not metaphorical but ontological: "You are (εἶ) my beloved Son." Appreciation is expressed to Craig Blaising for bringing this issue to my attention.

[18] Donald Carson warns against making too much of the use of ἄλλος, "another," here rather than ἕτερος. Many commentators translate ἄλλος as "another of the same type," in opposition to ἕτερος, "another of a different kind." For Carson, the term speaks not so much of the title of the counselor as the ministry of counsel. D. A. Carson, *The Gospel According to John*, Pillar New Testament Commentary (Grand Rapids, MI: Eerdmans, 1991), 499–500. I have argued for the traditional distinction. Yarnell, "The Person and Work of the Holy Spirit," in *A Theology for the Church*, rev. ed., ed. Daniel L. Akin (Nashville, TN: B&H, 2014), 494. Either way, Jesus's primary point is that his ministry will continue through the personal presence of the Holy Spirit.

in that whereas Jesus is a human being alongside other human beings, the Spirit will actually reside within believers (14:17). The distinction between the Spirit and the Son is strengthened by their divergent historical manifestations. The Spirit will not come to minister within believers until the Son has completed his earthly ministry. The Son presents the distinction between their divergent temporal ministries as a necessity; as the Son returns to dwell in glory, the Spirit comes to dwell in man (16:7). Second, the Holy Spirit is also closely identified with the Son. Referring to the impending ministry of the Holy Spirit, Jesus said, "I go away and I will come to you" (14:28a). With this statement, "Jesus' 'I' is virtually interchangeable with the person of the Holy Spirit, for it is the Paraclete who is to come at Jesus' departure."[19] The Son and the Holy Spirit are hereby both distinguished and identified, in a way similar to the relations of the Father and the Son mutually identified elsewhere in this Gospel.

The distinctions within God are not only historical; they are also definitely eternal. The time and place from which and to which Jesus goes is "heaven," a place and time that transcends matter and history even as it incorporates them. The Father is eternal, and the Son enters the world from there and returns there with his humanity.[20] The Holy Spirit, too, comes from the eternal Father, having been sent by the Father and the Son (14:26; 15:26). In summary, we note that the reality of the three is affirmed through their distinct manifestations within history and through their distinctions within eternity. We have not dedicated much space to the economic interrelations of the Trinity in this chapter, since we are primarily devoting our discussion to θεολογία, but the next chapter will raise them.

Our fourth pattern, concerning the reality of the distinctions between the Father, the Son, and the Holy Spirit, has shifted between discussions of eternity and history. The problem of transitioning between history and eternity raises two questions for theologians: First, how far shall we distinguish the eternal God from the economic God? Second, how far shall we correlate the eternal God with the

---

[19] Royce Gordon Gruenler, *The Trinity in the Gospel of John: A Thematic Commentary on the Fourth Gospel* (Grand Rapids, MI: Baker, 1986), 105.

[20] See "The Eternal God Who Comes and Goes" in chap. 5.

economic God? Some, for instance, among contemporary evangelicals, have emphasized the difference between the eternal Trinity and
the economic Trinity. Others, for instance, among followers of Karl
Rahner, have emphasized the equanimity of the eternal Trinity and
the economic Trinity. We must introduce that discussion here but will
reserve a fuller treatment for the economic Trinitarianism of Paul in
chapter 7.

Among evangelicals, some have decried the idea that there is a
subnumeration within the ontological Trinity. However, they have
also disagreed on how far the equality of the Father and the Son
extends into history. In a move that has drawn many evangelicals and
modern biblical commentators away from the Cappadocian doctrine
of the eternal processions of the Son and the Holy Spirit, Calvinist
theologians have deemed such language inappropriate. Where Basil
held simultaneously to Christ's self-existence and to his derivation
from the Father, B. B. Warfield argued, following John Calvin, that
subordination is restricted to the divine economy while the Son is
eternally αὐτόθεος, self-existent.[21] This comes, oddly, even after
Warfield has argued that the economic versus ontological distinction
is an extrabiblical way of thinking.[22] It also comes with a summary
denial of what later has become known as Rahner's axiom or rule.[23]
Calvin himself found the concept of eternal generation "difficult, if
not meaningless" and preferred to flatten the eternal relations.[24]

The subsequent radical equalization of the Trinity in evangelicalism has encouraged the development of a contrary hermeneutical rule
distinguishing between the ontological equality and the functional
subordination of the Son. Royce Gordon Gruenler is thereby led to
deny the eternal nature of redemption, dismiss the Cappadocians as
abstract, and build a case for an egalitarian view of gender relations.[25]
In recent years evangelical theologians have argued strenuously over

---

[21] Benjamin Breckenridge Warfield, *Biblical Doctrines* (Grand Rapids, MI: Baker,
1932), 163–71.

[22] Ibid., 161.

[23] Ibid., 166.

[24] Warfield, *Calvin and Calvinism* (Grand Rapids, MI: Baker, 1932), 247–79.

[25] Gruenler, *The Trinity in the Gospel of John*, xiv–xvii. Gruenler's theme is that
the Trinity is a family characterized by mutual disposability.

the theological and anthropological implications of the Calvinist rule that there is an ontological equality and functional subordination within the Trinity.[26] This author is convinced neither that the Calvinist rule is biblical, nor that it is helpful in theological construction, nor therefore that it will settle the raging gender debate. Perhaps the most important question contemporary Calvinist Trinitarian theologians should ask is: Is the radical disjunction between the economic and the ontological advantageous?

If John Calvin offered modern theologians a rule of disjunction between the ontological and economic Trinities, Karl Rahner offered modern theologians a rule of equivalence between the ontological and economic Trinities. As mentioned previously, Rahner stated that the economic Trinity is the ontological Trinity and vice versa. Rahner was attempting to redress the unitarian tendencies set loose in modernity through the retention of the medieval scholastic method of treating the divine unity prior to treating the divine Trinity. Rahner's axiom was seen as helpful but not without qualifications. Catherine LaCugna noted that there necessarily remains only a conceptual distinction between the economic and ontological.[27] Walter Kasper also pointed out that the equalitarian axiom may endanger God's freedom by making him necessarily act in a certain way, or it may merge the ontological Trinity into the economic Trinity.[28] In spite of these criticisms, most contemporary theologians recognize that Rahner's axiom is helpful in reframing God's salvation of humanity in explicitly Trinitarian terms.[29] Human salvation is impossible apart from the

---

[26] *The New Evangelical Subordinationism? Perspectives on the Equality of God the Father and God the Son*, ed. Dennis W. Jowers and H. Wayne House (Eugene, OR: Wipf & Stock, 2012).

[27] Catherine Mowry LaCugna, *God for Us: The Trinity and Christian Life* (San Francisco, CA: HarperCollins, 1973), 230–31.

[28] Walter Kasper, *The God of Jesus Christ* (London: SCM, 1983), 275–76.

[29] Rahner helpfully encouraged theologians such as Catherine LaCugna to reevaluate other aspects of traditional Trinitarianism. LaCugna used the opportunity to develop the idea that there arose historically a strong disjunction between the divine οἰκονομία and θεολογία, and this is why modern Christians could think of salvation without ever considering the Trinity. LaCugna's work contains many great insights, especially considering her leading role in the contemporary Trinitarian renaissance, but her work was also attacked for its generalizations. She was also lauded for trying to bring οἰκονομία and θεολογία back together but at the expense

Trinitarian pattern repeatedly made evident in the biblical text, as will become evident in the next chapter. For Rahner's contribution in this regard, we remain grateful, even if we may not hold with him to an exact correspondence between οἰκονομία and θεολογία.

The Distinctions between the Father, the Son, and the Holy Spirit Are Relational

We noted in chapter 1 that the Bible often uses "name" to speak of identity. The early church fathers dwelt on the importance of the divine names. Origen reminds us that the various names of the Son indicate the same being rather than diverse beings, as the Gnostics often argued.[30] After the Word becomes flesh in John 1:14, he is referred to with other titles, including often some derivative of "Son." Many of the first theologians distinguished between titles that are descriptive of some aspect of God and his proper names. Athanasius argued against his opponents that a name means something substantial, and they may not be easily dismissed. With regard to the proper names of "Father" and "Son," he says, "The name speaks of the relationship" and simultaneously "denotes the common bond."[31] Basil agreed:

---

of divine ontology. Declan Marmion, "Trinity and Salvation: A Dialogue with Catherine LaCugna's *God for Us: The Trinity and Christian Life*," in *Trinity and Salvation: Theological, Spiritual and Aesthetic Perspectives*, ed. Declan Marmion and Gesa Thiessen (New York: Peter Lang, 2009), 81–100. In denying access to the immanent Trinity, LaCugna also seems to argue directly against the Johannine prologue. Gerald O'Collins, "The Holy Trinity: The State of the Questions," in *The Trinity: An Interdisciplinary Symposium on the Trinity*, ed. Stephen T. Davis, Daniel Kendall, and Gerald O'Collins (New York: Oxford University Press, 1999), 19–21. The last three chapters have directly contradicted LaCugna's thesis that there is no immanent Trinity revealed in the Bible. LaCugna, *God for Us*, 22. I would add that LaCugna too easily restricts the pro-Nicene understanding of οἰκονομία to the incarnation. As we shall see in chapter 7, they would have placed all divine action, not just the incarnation of the Son, within the economy. LaCugna, *God for Us*, 39–41.

[30] Origen, *De Principiis, in Ante-Nicene Fathers*, vol. 4, ed. Alexander Roberts and James Donaldson, trans. Frederick Crombie (repr., Peabody, MA: Hendrickson, 1994), 1.2.4.

[31] Athanasius, *De Sententia Dionysii*, 17; cited in Thomas G. Weinandy, *Athanasius: A Theological Introduction*, Great Theologians (Burlington, VT: Ashgate, 2007), 67.

Each name explaining to us clearly the characteristic quality
[ἰδιότητα] of the One named, and in the case of each of
those names certain special characteristics [ἰδιωμάτων] being
with all reverence observed, the Father in the characteristics
of Fatherhood, the Son in the characteristics of Sonship, and
the Holy Spirit in his own characteristics.[32]

Gregory of Nazianzus provides a classification of biblical names
that may be helpful. The essence of God cannot be named, but his
existence is named through such terms as the Hebrew covenant name,
and the Greek θεός and κύριος. There are divine names of authority and governance, too, such as king, righteousness, and vengeance.
The previous nominal classifications may be used of any of the three.
However, the three are distinguished by their "proper" names: "the
Proper Name of the Unoriginate is Father, and that of the unorigi-
nately Begotten is Son, and that of the unbegottenly Proceeding or
going forth is the Holy Ghost." He goes on to describe the names of
the Son according to their divine and human indications.[33] Among
modern New Testament theologians, Udo Schnelle would agree
that the name of "Son," for instance, "is particularly appropriate
for expressing the unique relationship between God and Jesus of
Nazareth, and on the basis of the unity of Father and Son in their
essential being, is to be understood relationally and functionally."[34]
In the Gospel of John, Jesus is named "Son," "Son of Man," "Son of
God," and "one and only" or "only begotten Son."[35]

We have referred to the language of essence, but within the New
Testament scholars' guild, some wish to drive a wedge between the

---

[32] Basil, *On Faith*, 4; cited in Stephen M. Hildebrand, *Basil of Caesarea*,
Foundations of Theological Exegesis and Christian Spirituality (Grand Rapids, MI:
Baker, 2014), 62.

[33] Gregory of Nazianzus, *Fourth Theological Oration*, in *Nicene and Post-Nicene
Fathers*, Second Series, vol. 7, ed. Philip Schaff and Henry Wace, trans. Charles
Gordon Browne and James Edward Swallow (repr., Peabody, MA: Hendrickson,
1994), 16–21.

[34] Udo Schnelle, *Theology of the New Testament*, trans. M. Eugene Boring (Grand
Rapids, MI: Baker Academic, 2007), 689.

[35] Andreas J. Köstenberger, *A Theology of John's Gospel and Letters: Biblical
Theology of the New Testament* (Grand Rapids, MI: Zondervan, 2009), 380–82.

"functional" and the "ontological" understandings of Jesus's relation to God the Father. M. De Jonge, representing many other scholars, replies, "It does not make sense to play acting and being, function and nature, off against each other."[36] The functions of the Son in relation to the Father certainly may tell us something about the eternal nature of their relations. Nonetheless, even if one wishes to focus only on the ontological language provided in the Bible, there is enough there to describe their relationship. We have noted the ascription of generation to the Son's relation to the Father in the last chapter. However, the nature of the Son's relation, as we have seen with the quote from Basil immediately above, does not necessarily require the language of generation. "Begotten" may merely function as shorthand for the real relation of the Son to his Father.

There is yet other language that indicates the eternal relation between Father and Son, as we noted in the last chapter with the prepositions exposited by Basil. That the Father "sends" the Son is economic language, but the many ways the Son is said to be "from" the Father and returns "to" the Father indicates something more substantial than functional. This should have become clear within our discussion of the dialectic of ascent and descent that explicitly underlies the narrative structure of the Gospel, a narrative that seeks to transcend the boundaries of history. Because the Son is said to receive his "life" among the "all things" that he possesses from the Father, we may speak of the Son deriving his eternal being from the Father. This relation between Father and Son is true whether or not the exact language of "generation" is deemed acceptable. To deny the eternality of the Son's relation to the Father would, as Athanasius and many in the Nicene camp argued, also diminish the eternality of the Father.

From the perspective of an eternal derivation, it should also be recognized that the Son may be said to be "subordinate" to the Father without endangering the Son's equal possession of the Father's self. Such orthodox modern scholars as E. Earle Ellis can refer to the Son as being in "perfect subordination and unity with God," because their presentation holds the unity of God in a paradoxical but sustained way

---

[36] Quoted in G[eorge] R. Beasley-Murray, *Gospel of Life: Theology in the Fourth Gospel* (Peabody, MA: Hendrickson, 1991), 32.

with the subordination of the Son from the Father.[37] In the same way, the early church fathers were alternatively able to assign John 14:28, "the Father is greater than I," either to οἰκονομία or to θεολογία. The Nicene fathers who opted for the second option were able to do so, not because they were beholden to Arian subordinationism (to the contrary, they fought against it vehemently!), but because they also asserted that the Son's relation to the Father is eternal and thus essential.[38]

C. K. Barrett, a modern scholar, works through the historical and theological interpretations of this difficult passage and concludes that the theological aspect of the subordination in John 14:28 may not be glibly set aside in favor of a radical egalitarian Trinity. In Barrett's studied opinion, to divide the human function from the divine essence would threaten the integrity of the person of Jesus Christ.[39] Theologically, he has a point, a point that is instructive to those who wish to affirm an ontological equality yet a functional subordination. To drive a wedge between the function of Jesus and the essence of God preserves the divine Trinity in an unnecessary fashion, even as it sunders the humanity and deity of Jesus Christ. Modern theologians who summarily reject eternal subordination in order to preserve an orthodox Trinitarian doctrine simultaneously place orthodox Christology in danger, at least according to a Chalcedonian perspective. This is not to say that eternal subordination must be necessarily affirmed. Nor is it to say that affirmations of subordination without modifiers referring to eternity are acceptable. It is to say that one should be careful in summarily dismissing all language of subordination as unfaithful to the Nicene tradition.

A final issue from the Gospel of John and the eternal relations concerns the relationship between the Holy Spirit and the other two members of the Trinity. We have already noted that the early theologians pointed to the name of "Holy Spirit" as a proper name. "Holy" and "Spirit" may be applied individually to both the Father and the Son

---

[37] E. Earle Ellis, *The World of St. John: The Gospel and the Epistles* (Grand Rapids, MI: Eerdmans, 1984), 65–66.

[38] Maurice F. Wiles, *The Spiritual Gospel: The Interpretation of the Fourth Gospel in the Early Church* (New York: Cambridge University Press, 2006), 122–23.

[39] C. K. Barrett, "'The Father Is Greater than I' (John 14:28): Subordinationist Christology in the New Testament," in *Neues Testament und Kirche: Für Rudolf Schackenburg*, ed. Joachim Gnilka (Freiburg, Germany: Herder, 1974), 144–59.

as descriptions of their divine attributes, but only "Holy Spirit" may be applied to the third person of the Trinity as a proper title. Gregory of Nazianzus summarizes the multitude of names that apply to the Holy Spirit, many of which are unique to Him, others that indicate his relation to God: "He is called the Spirit of God, the Spirit of Christ, the Mind of Christ, the Spirit of the Lord, and Himself the Lord, the Spirit of Adoption, of Truth, of Liberty; the Spirit of Wisdom, of Understanding, of Counsel, of Might, of Knowledge, of Godliness, the Fear of God."[40] Nazianzus also summarizes the role of the Holy Spirit in the life of the Son. "Christ is born; the Spirit is His forerunner. He is baptized; the Spirit bears witness. He is tempted; the Spirit leads Him up. He works miracles; the Spirit accompanies them. He ascends; the Spirit takes His place."[41] In these ways the substantive personhood and relationality of the Spirit vis-à-vis the Son are suggested.

As noted at the end of the last chapter, the language of procession is used in John 15:26 to distinguish the Father and the Holy Spirit. The Son tells us that the Holy Spirit is going to be "sent," typically taken as an economic term, and then refers to the eternal relation between the Father and the Spirit. The Holy Spirit "proceeds from the Father" is typically taken as a theological term. Proceeding from the Father eternally, the Holy Spirit is also sent into the world to lead the disciples into the truth. This is only one biblical text, but it is nevertheless a strong one. The Cappadocian fathers helped make it widely accepted, and the language of procession with regard to the eternal relation of the Father and the Holy Spirit has entered into the theological vocabulary of Christianity through the Niceno-Constantinopolitan Creed they influenced.

This is well and good. However, it has also helped lead to a continuing division between Eastern Orthodoxy and Western Christianity. As is well known, the primary theological controversy between East and West concerns the *filioque*, the Western addition to the creed that derived the Holy Spirit from both the Father "and the Son."[42] While the Johannine language of the economic "sending" of the Holy Spirit

---

[40] Gregory of Nazianzus, *Fifth Theological Oration*, 29.

[41] Ibid.

[42] I have detailed these developments elsewhere. Yarnell, "The Person and Work of the Holy Spirit," 502–10. Statements similar to those of Cyril of Alexandria, mentioned above, represent perhaps the best mediating position.

is credited to both the Father and the Son (John 14:26; 15:26), it is instructive that the Spirit is theologically derived only from the Father in the biblical text. Augustine's argument that the Holy Spirit is the love between the Father and the Son, and therefore proceeds from both, is theologically thick, but it is exegetically thinner.[43]

Whatever position one takes with regard to the historical ecumenical crisis, whether that position is Eastern or Western or mediating, the Holy Spirit may be properly described as the Proceeding God. The Holy Spirit's eternal relation to the Father is one of procession, while the Son's eternal relation to the Father is one of generation. These are two different relations, and they are sufficient for distinguishing the Father from the Son, the Father from the Holy Spirit, and the Son from the Holy Spirit. The distinctions between the three persons of the one God are real, and they are relational.

Toward the Language of "Substance" and "Person"

While we have periodically alluded to and affirmed the language of οὐσία, "substance" (cf. "essence," "ontology," "being"), and ὑπόστασις, "person" (cf. πρόσωπον), we have not advocated their necessary use. This is because, as indicated, they are primarily postbiblical terms and are not required *per se* as a matter of authoritative revelation, although they may be standard in theological discourse. In this book we have sought to exegete the biblical text rather than assert a postbiblical theological formula. As helpful as a historical formula that has been advanced by so many graceful and erudite theologians may be, it may become stale and unfruitful when divorced from biblical exegesis. Theological discourse serves the church best when it focuses first on biblical exegesis while remaining in dynamic conversation with contemporary Christians seeking to witness within their diverse contexts and while respectfully though discriminately hearing the communion of saints who sought to do the same in their time and place at other points in history. (This is why ministerial degrees typically structure their courses around the biblical disciplines but also include the various practical fields along with church history and systematic theology.)

---

[43] Ibid., 505–8.

The early church fathers discovered that the term ὁμοούσιος, anathematized at the council of Antioch in AD 268/269 because of its use by Paul of Samosata, may be used positively at the ` of Nicaea in a little more than half a century. Likewise, the term ὑπόστασις, anathematized at the Council of Nicaea in AD 325, was no longer a major concern at the Council of Constantinople in AD 381. Moreover, ὑπόστασις soon became the normative theological language to describe the subsistent relations of the Father, the Son, and the Holy Spirit. In both the cases of ὁμοούσιος and ὑπόστασις, fifty-six years saw a normative *volte-face* in orthodox usage. And in both cases the shift has been largely retained within conservative Christian communities. The terminology has been helpful in positively, simultaneously maintaining the unity of God and the relationality of God. Or, to state it negatively, the terminology has been helpful in preventing a drift toward some form of Sabellianism, through the use of ὑπόστασις, or toward some form of Arianism, through the use of ὁμοούσιος.

Periodically, orthodox scholars have objected to the overuse or misappropriation of the orthodox terms. For instance, the leading Protestant theologian of the twentieth century, Karl Barth, famously objected to the language of "person," due to its individualizing anthropological tendencies. But others have pointed to the potential misunderstanding offered with Barth's preferred alternative of "modes of being."[44] Again, among biblical theologians, the tendency

---

[44] George Hunsinger summarizes Barth's position well: "Neither the Latin term *persona* nor the Greek term *hypostasis* is without liabilities. The former can tend toward tritheism (if it suggests three centres of consciousness), and the latter toward modalism (if it cannot distinguish itself from *ousia*). For lack of a better option, Barth finally settled for 'mode of being' as a literal translation of the concept *tropos hyparxeos* or *modus entitativus*. Nothing could be more superficial than to accuse Barth of 'modalism' for this choice." George Hunsinger, "Karl Barth's Doctrine of the Trinity, and Some Protestant Doctrines after Barth," in *The Oxford Handbook of the Trinity*, ed. Gilles Emery and Matthew Levering (New York: Oxford University Press, 2011), 300–301. Cf. Alan Torrance, "The Trinity," in *The Cambridge Companion to Karl Barth*, ed. John Webster (New York: Cambridge University Press, 2000), 81–84. Karl Rahner also objected to the modern notion of "person" due to its creation of three centers of consciousness within God, thus promoting tritheism. Rahner used the language of "modes of existence" (*Existenzweisen*), which is similar to Barth's "modes of being" (*Seinsweisen*). David Coffey, "Trinity," in *The Cambridge Companion to Karl Rahner*, ed. Declan Marmion and Mary E. Hines (New York: Cambridge University Press, 2005), 103–4.

has been to avoid the language of ontology, due to its Hellenistic tones, and to adopt the language of function. More recently there has been a happy movement back toward ontology with the biblical theologians' use of the language of "identity." In chapter 3, I used the language of "identity," in part because it could be taken in an ontological direction. I am also happy to recognize Barth's "modes of being" because I understand he was not using it in a "modalist" manner. However, I have retained the term "person" but only because I have learned to strip the latter term of its modernist anthropology. The contributions of the theologian John Zizioulas and the philosopher Robert Spaemann toward reclaiming a relational basis for personhood are especially helpful in this regard.[45] The point is, again like Athanasius, that we affirm an orthodox biblical meaning, whatever the particular postbiblical terms we employ.

As for any direct biblical basis for person, John Calvin has made a preliminary argument for the use of ὑπόστασις. Calvin noted that the ὑπόστασις of the Father is expressed in the χαρακτήρ ("image") of his Son in Hebrews 1:3. The Father's "person" is thereby both imaged in the Son's person and differentiated from the Son's person, allowing the language of personhood as indicative of distinct properties between the Father and the Son some exegetical basis. This is an ingenious move, a move Calvin took in order to show the word was not "humanly devised," but it is an argument that is not as yet well established in the secondary literature.[46] I am not aware of any

---

[45] Zizioulas is an Eastern Orthodox theologian who has shaped many contemporary theologians through his emphasis on divine being as a divine communion of persons. John D. Zizioulas, *Being as Communion: Studies in Personhood and the Church* (Crestwood, NY: St. Vladimir's Seminary Press, 1997), 18–19. Spaemann is a German philosopher who recognizes the contribution of Christianity to the concept of "person," especially with regard to relationality and dignity. Robert Spaemann, *Persons: The Difference Between "Someone" and "Something,"* trans. Oliver O'Donovan (New York: Oxford University Press, 2006), 37–39, 67.

[46] John Calvin, *Institutes of the Christian Religion*, ed. John T. McNeill, trans. Ford Lewis Battles, The Library of Christian Classics (Philadelphia, PA: Westminster, 1960), 1.13.2. Warfield dismissed Calvin's efforts in this regard: "It is not likely that this piece of exegesis will commend itself to us. Nor indeed is it likely that we shall feel perfect satisfaction in the logical analysis, even as a piece of logical analysis." However, Warfield then repeats Calvin's argument without a convincing explanation as to why it should be dismissed, except to say that Calvin is extending a

argument that οὐσία, as used in Nicene orthodoxy, has a linguistic biblical basis. There are near terms in the Bible, terms and ideas to which we have already pointed: "name," "mine," and "life," for instance. Unfortunately, for those with a philosophical cast of mind, none of the biblical terms approach the usefulness of οὐσία in abstract doctrinal discussions.[47] Then again, perhaps the Lord intended such propositional abstractions to receive little biblical sanction, because their absence[48] demands that his people return constantly in the spirit of prayer to the metaphors of the biblical text so that every theological thought might be taken captive, again and again, with joy to Christ. Christ interprets God through the Spirit who illumines the human reception of that interpretation.

Christological passage in a Trinitarian direction. Warfield, moreover, accuses Calvin of using "person" in an abstract manner rather than in a concrete manner. This author does not believe Calvin was using the term abstractly, for he makes clear that he is referring both to the Son's person and to the Father's person. Benjamin Breckenridge Warfield, *Calvin and Calvinism* (New York. Oxford University Press, 1932), 212–1b.

[47] For a defense of the usefulness of substance metaphysics in Trinitarian theology, see William P. Alston, "Substance and the Trinity," in *The Trinity: An Interdisciplinary Symposium on the Trinity*, ed. Stephen T. Davis, Daniel Kendall, and Gerald O'Collins (New York: Oxford University Press, 1999), 179–201.

[48] I use "absence" here in a positive sense as that which prompts humanity toward the divine presence, for God in his freedom may never be captured by the church or its clergy. Cf. Rowan Williams, *On Christian Theology* (Malden, MA: Blackwell, 2000), 183–96.

7

THE GOD WHO ACTS: O'IKONOMIA

He made known to us the mystery of his will, according to the good intention that he purposed in himself, in the economy [οἰκονομίαν] of the fullness of the times, to unite all things in Christ, things in the heavens and things on the earth.

Ephesians 1:9–10

We have periodically yet intentionally used the term *glimpse* in order to convey the biblical authors' presupposition that divine revelation provides both the certainty of human insight about God yet the incomprehensible nature of that insight. E. Earle Ellis says the Evangelists and Paul "represent the Old Testament as a hidden word of God, a divine mystery whose interpretation is itself a divine gift (χάρισμα) and act of revelation."[1] Gregory K. Beale and Benjamin L. Gladd contribute significantly to our understanding of the progressive nature and extent of divine revelation through their study of the Bible's use of the Aramaic רז (in the book of Daniel) and the Greek μυστήριον (in the Septuagint and the New Testament). Their

---

[1] E. Earle Ellis, *The Old Testament in Early Christianity: Canon and Interpretation in the Light of Modern Research* (Grand Rapids, MI: Baker, 1991), 117.

summary thesis is that "the revelation of mystery is not a totally new revelation but the full disclosure of something that was to a significant extent hidden."[2] According to Beale and Gladd, the mystery of Genesis 1:26 (human rule, lost in Genesis 3) was partially disclosed in Psalm 8:4 (rule of the Son of Man), prophesied in Daniel 7:13–14 (the rule of One like the Son of Man), and revealed in Ephesians 1:10, 20–22 (the rule of Christ Jesus).[3]

The mystery now revealed regards the οἰκονομία of God. Οἰκονομία, constructed from the words for "household" and "rule," may be translated as "economy," "administration," or "plan." It has also been rendered "dispensation," "stewardship," and "management."[4] This mystery was promised in concealed form to the people of Israel, but God has now revealed through his Spirit that the grace of God is for Jews and Gentiles in Jesus Christ (Eph 3:1–7). In Ephesians, the divine economy concerns the "unifying," "summing up," or "recapitulation" (ἀνακεφαλαιώσασθαι) of all things in Jesus Christ, the full and timely reconciliation of disorder in creation through submission to him as "head" (κεφαλή) over everything for the church (1:10, 22).[5]

Paul's economy of God provides a grand narrative that universally encompasses and personally suffuses heaven and earth, God and humanity (and angels), Jews and Gentiles, communities and individuals, husbands and wives, parents and children, masters and slaves, the world and the church. The Triune economy centers in Jesus Christ even as it comes from and returns to God the Father and is applied by the Holy Spirit. The Trinitarian economy concerns the work of God as

[2] G. K. Beale and Benjamin L. Gladd, *Hidden but Now Revealed: A Biblical Theology of Mystery* (Downers Grove, IL: IVP Academic, 2014), 30. רז (*raz*) occurs nine times in Daniel, primarily in chap. 2 but also in chap. 4. Cf. "Μυστήριον," in *New International Dictionary of New Testament Theology and Exegesis*, 2nd ed., ed. Moisés Silva, vol. 3 (Grand Rapids, MI: Zondervan, 2014), 350–57.

[3] Beale and Gladd, *Hidden but Now Revealed*, 148–59.

[4] "Οἰκονομία [etc.]," in *New International Dictionary of New Testament Exegesis and Theology*, ed. Silva, 3:465–68; Otto Michel, "Οἰκονομία [etc.]," in *Theological Dictionary of the New Testament*, vol. 5, ed. Gerhard Friedrich, trans. Geoffrey W. Bromiley (Grand Rapids, MI: Eerdmans, 1967), 149–53. Cf. C. C. Ryrie, "Dispensation, Dispensationalism," in *Evangelical Dictionary of Theology*, ed. Walter A. Elwell (Grand Rapids, MI: Baker, 1984), 321–23.

[5] Harold W. Hoehner, *Ephesians: An Exegetical Commentary* (Grand Rapids, MI: Baker, 2002), 218–22.

three and one, and it suggests immanent aspects of how God is three and one. In this chapter we shall focus on the apostle Paul's presentation of the divine economy and what it tells us about God. However, we must first consider profound challenges to such knowledge.

Theology Through Economy

In the last three chapters, which reviewed some of the Trinitarian portraits painted by John in his Gospel, we focused on the immanent Trinity. This was necessary because John often spoke of the divine Trinity from an *ad intra* perspective, God within Godself. However, other authors in Scripture primarily describe the Trinity from an *ad extra* perspective, demonstrating how God relates to his creation as the Father, the Son, and the Holy Spirit. While John was aware of and used the distinct yet common works of the Trinity, Paul relied even more on the works of God. A methodological problem that confronts us prior to an exegesis of Paul's economic Trinity has been raised at various times throughout this book. It remains one of the most critical issues in contemporary Trinitarian exegesis: Exactly what and how much does the economic Trinity reveal to humanity about the immanent Trinity? To answer this question prompts us to extend our conversation regarding the modern philosophical presuppositions that handicap evangelical hermeneutics. This will then allow the consideration of various responses to Rahner's axiom.

The Enlightenment's Hermeneutical Handicap

We noted previously that the biblical theology movement often introduced fractures into its exegesis. Ellis referred to these as "dialectical antitheses" that are rooted in the law/gospel dichotomy of traditional Lutheranism and expressed in the Hegelian forms that dominate many New Testament studies.[6] David Tracy takes a broader approach,

---

[6] Ellis, *The Old Testament in Early Christianity*, 152–53. Ellis, a Calvinistic Baptist affiliated with the author's own Southwestern Baptist Theological Seminary, might have also mentioned that these dichotomies were evident within Reformed biblical scholarship.

stating there are "three great separations" in modern Western culture
that inhibit our intellectual ability to appreciate the achievements of
premodern civilization, especially of Trinitarian thought. These three
are "the separation of feeling and thought; the separation of theory
and practice; the separation of truth and content."[7] Tracy believes the
first two great separations are being addressed, but the third requires
further solution. The modern era's separation of truth from content
undermines the premodern assumption that "form" held together
reality and our knowledge of it. The sundering of truth from content,
which the concept of form originally bridged, has been so success-
ful that it is difficult for modernity's "heirs of the fragmentation" to
comprehend even how this worked.[8] Murray Rae speaks similarly of
a widespread "disengagement" between history and eternity among
biblical interpreters.[9] The Enlightenment has handicapped Protestant
biblical hermeneutics through removing eternity from history, rendering real knowledge of either impossible.[10]

Tracy argues that all premodern philosophers, whether pagans
like Plato and Aristotle or monotheists like Jews and Christians, held
to some idea of form. According to Hegel, the thorough depen-
dence on form made Greek paganism a "religion of beauty" (but
then again from culture to religion to politics, everything for the
Greeks was filtered through beauty).[11] According to Tracy and Rae,
Christianity contradicts the separation of truth and history through

---

[7] David Tracy, "Trinitarian Speculation and the Forms of Divine Disclosure,"
in *The Trinity: An Interdisciplinary Symposium on the Trinity*, ed. Stephen T.
Davis, Daniel Kendall, and Gerald O'Collins (New York: Oxford University Press,
1999), 273.

[8] Ibid., 275.

[9] Murray A. Rae, "Creation and Promise: Towards a Theology of History,"
in *"Behind" the Text: History and Biblical Interpretation*, ed. Craig Bartholomew,
C. Stephen Evans, Mary Healy, Murray Rae, Scripture and Hermeneutic Series
(Grand Rapids, MI: Zondervan, 2003), 267–96.

[10] For a premodern narrative that eloquently weaves together knowledge of eternity and time in a realist fashion, see Augustine, *The City of God*, trans. Marcus Dods
(New York: Random House, 1993). For a premodern realist narrative that includes
personal knowledge of eternity, see Augustine, *Confessions*, trans. R. S. Pine-Coffin
(New York: Penguin, 1961).

[11] Hegel also recognized that the Greek emphasis on form did not allow them to
access the eternal realm of the Spirit. This was accomplished through the incarnation.

the incarnation in history of the eternal Word of God.[12] Hans Urs von Balthasar, who constructed a holistic theological aesthetics, would agree that the epistemological chasm is "the main problem": "How can the Absolute make itself present, definitively, in an ephemeral finite life form? From the world's perspective, this seems impossible." But, Balthasar continues, God the Trinity has overcome the impossible chasm through the incarnation of the Word, revealing his eternal self to humanity.[13]

We previously discussed the epistemological problem that Immanuel Kant helped create through his influential rejection of metaphysical knowledge.[14] Paul Tillich agrees that Kant's categorical method made it impossible for man to perceive God. And "almost everyone in the nineteenth and twentieth centuries accepted this criticism as a presupposition."[15] Tillich's point coincides with Tracy's claim that modernity has made God unknowable through the separation between the real and the perceptible, between ontology and epistemology. Rae develops this even further, registering how modern philosophers and biblical exegetes have brought this separation into dominance. Baruch Spinoza, for instance, denied the Bible's historical narrative is necessary for human knowledge of God. Rather than history, abstract propositions sufficiently convey truth.[16] Gotthard Lessing spoke famously of "a broad ugly ditch" that keeps contemporaries from accessing the history of the Bible, much less the eternal God to whom it claims access. The development of the historical

---

Georg Wilhelm Friedrich Hegel, *The Philosophy of History*, trans. J. Sibree, Great Books of the Western World (Chicago, IL: Encylopaedia Britannica, 1952), 2.2.1–3.

[12] Tracy, "Trinitarian Speculation and the Forms of Divine Disclosure," 276; Rae, "Creation and Promise," 291–93.

[13] Hans Urs von Balthasar, *Epilogue*, trans. Edward T. Oakes (San Francisco, CA: Ignatius, 2004), 94.

[14] See chapter 4 above.

[15] Tillich summarized Kant's thesis: "The finite mind is not able to reach the infinite." Paul Tillich, *Perspectives on 19th and 20th Century Protestant Theology*, ed. Carl E. Braaten (New York: Harper & Row, 1967), 64.

[16] "Nor can the belief in historical narratives, however certain, give us knowledge of God, nor, consequently, of the love of God." Moreover, "the divinity of Scripture must be established solely from the fact that it teaches true virtue." Baruch Spinoza, *Tractatus Theologico-Politicus*, trans. S. Shirley (Leiden: E. J. Brill, 1991), 4.104–5, 7.142; cited in Rae, "Creation and Promise," 271.

critical method has undermined the ability of both liberal and conservative evangelicals to interpret Scripture, due to their focus on evaluating the historicity of the Bible, much less human access to eternity through it.[17]

Both Tracy and Rae observe that these hermeneutical biases have hindered our ability to perceive God the Trinity in particular.[18] Tracy discusses how contemporary theology has adopted shifting meanings of "monotheism," eventually opting for a non-Trinitarian view. The solution to the problem of the modern bias toward an abstract monotheism, according to Tracy, is a recovery of the divine economy. "The fact that the Christian understanding of the one God is grounded not in a general philosophical theory of monotheism but in this concrete passion-narrative history of God's self-disclosure as agent in the cross and resurrection of Jesus of Nazareth provides the primary theological foundation for all properly Christian trinitarian understandings of God."[19] Where modern theologians have been largely working from an abstract view of an unapproachable God, some have begun to move toward a recovery of the view that God can make himself known to humanity and has done so concretely in Jesus Christ. Tracy points especially to the Trinitarian recovery fostered in the works of Karl Barth, Karl Rahner, and various Orthodox theologians.[20] Tracy then offers Rahner's famous axiom, which requires our elaboration.

Rahner's Axiom

Karl Rahner has been "universally hailed as the most influential contributor to the renaissance of trinitarian theology in the twentieth century." It has been claimed furthermore that his axiom is "the

---

[17] Rae, "Creation and Promise," 272–78. Hans Frei develops at length the narrative of the eclipse of historical realism in biblical hermeneutics. See his summative introduction. Frei, *The Eclipse of Biblical Narrative: A Study in Eighteenth and Nineteenth Century Hermeneutics* (New Haven, CT: Yale University Press, 1974), 1–16.

[18] Cf. Rae, "Creation and Promise," 286–87.

[19] Tracy, "Trinitarian Speculation and the Forms of Divine Disclosure," 284.

[20] Ibid., 287.

most fundamental issue," indeed "the crux of trinitarian theology."[21] While this is doubtless true within Roman Catholic circles, Rahner's contribution is an explicitly central concern for evangelicals, too. It will be remembered that Rahner brought the immanent Trinity and the economic Trinity into an equivalent relationship. By doing so, drawing upon Tracy's identification of modernity's great separation between content and form, we may conclude that Rahner overcame the separation with a vengeance. For Rahner there remains no distinction whatsoever between divine content and divine form: "*The 'economic' Trinity is the 'immanent' Trinity and the 'immanent' Trinity is the 'economic' Trinity.*"[22] If the modern theologians drove a wedge between the reality of God and human knowledge of God, Rahner did away not only with the modern wedge but also with any trace it ever should have existed. Rahner's God the Trinity is equivalent in act and being. The historical work of God is the eternal being of God.

Rahner did not pin the blame for the creation of the wedge on the modern theologians but on the medieval scholastic method, standardized in the authoritative works of Thomas Aquinas, of treating the divine unity separate from and prior to the divine threeness.[23] Surveying the contemporary landscape and recognizing that most Christian teachers and therefore most Christians were in practice "almost mere 'monotheists,'" Rahner was driven by the desire to reintegrate Christian piety with Trinitarian salvation.[24] Peter Phan notes that Rahner did not intend to posit two different trinities with his axiom, nor did he see the immanent Trinity as hidden behind the economic Trinity.[25]

Rahner believed that, although his axiom drove against the standing scholastic norm, it was conducive to the magisterium and concurrent with biblical revelation. In a move that could appeal to

[21] Peter C. Phan, "Mystery of Grace and Salvation: Karl Rahner's Theology of the Trinity," in *The Cambridge Companion to the Trinity*, ed. by idem (New York: Cambridge University Press, 2011), 192, 196.

[22] Karl Rahner, *The Trinity*, trans. Joseph Donceel (repr., New York: Crossroad Herder, 2004), 22. His italics.

[23] Ibid., 15–21.

[24] Ibid., 10.

[25] Phan, "Mystery of Grace and Salvation," 198.

conservative evangelicals, Rahner said that to contradict his thesis would be a denial that biblical revelation actually tells us who God truly is. That the immanent Trinity is identified with the economic Trinity "will be denied only by him who does not put his theology under the norm of Scripture, but allows the latter to tell him only that which he knows already from his textbook theology, cleverly and ruthlessly distinguishing all the rest away."[26] Those who argue the Trinity is different from how the Trinity reveals himself in Scripture place systematic theology before biblical theology.

Rahner next meets different objections to his argument. Opposing the scholastic tradition that any member of the Trinity could have become incarnate, Rahner says the acceptance of this Thomist thesis would make the personhood of the Son indistinct from the other persons. If any of the three could become the incarnate Son, what makes the Son different from the other two persons? Moreover, only the "Word" of God, who is the second person of the Trinity, may make available the divine words of God in flesh. Finally, Rahner argues, the human nature of the Son should not be viewed as an abstract addition to his person but as a necessary symbol of his fundamental reality.[27]

Rahner then puts forward his positive thesis regarding the Trinity. Theologians must begin not with a speculative analogy about divine being but with the concrete history of God's salvation of humanity. From this vantage he necessarily privileges the doctrines of divine transcendence, grace, and revelation. God communicates himself in love to humanity as Father, as Son, and as Holy Spirit.[28] This self-communication should not be seen as merely verbal but as a real gift of God himself.[29] The divine missions—the Father's sending of the

---

[26] Rahner, *The Trinity*, 22, 30. Phan characterizes this argument as *reductio ad absurdum*, but it is difficult to see how Rahner's exegetical logic is inconsistent. Phan, "Mystery of Grace and Salvation," 198.

[27] Rahner, *The Trinity*, 24–33.

[28] "The Father gives himself to us too as *Father,* that is precisely because and insofar as he himself, being essentially with *himself,* utters himself and *in this way* communicates the Son as his own, person self-manifestation; and because and insofar as the Father and the Son (receiving from the Father), welcoming each other in love, drawn and returning to each other, communicate themselves *in this way*, as received in mutual love, that is, as Holy Spirit." Ibid., 35.

[29] Ibid., 37–38.

Son, and the Father's and the Son's sending of the Holy Spirit—structure the self-communication of God in both the Old and New Testaments.[30]

When he turns to a systematic presentation of the immanent Trinity, Rahner chooses to follow the more scriptural, creedal, and Eastern Orthodox method of beginning with the Father rather than the divine essence.[31] Rahner's move in this regard is significant, for it places him firmly against any Western tendency to privilege the divine essence over the divine persons. The Father is hereby seen as the source of divine revelation and therefore of divine reality; the missions of the Son and the Spirit necessarily structure the internal processions of the Trinity. The Son is consubstantial with the Father, but he also derives from the Father's essence, being "begotten," which Rahner also calls "procession" (following the Western Augustinian tradition).[32] The Spirit also "possesses the one and same essence as the Father," but he "proceeds from the Father through the Son" (following some in the Eastern tradition).[33]

Rahner maintains his axiom to his logical conclusion. However, he apparently did not foresee some of the different directions his axiom might be taken. Rahner focused on the first part of his thesis, that the Bible's revelation of the economic Trinity, as verified in the tradition, truly reveals the immanent Trinity. He did not address whether the economic Trinity might also structure the immanent Trinity. Others would take up the implications of the second part of his axiom, the "vice versa."

Responding to Rahner

Both Catholic and evangelical theologians have crafted theological responses around Rahner's axiom.[34] Among evangelicals, Fred Sanders

---

[30] For instance, God manifested himself in the Old Testament, "mediated mostly by the 'Word' . . . and by the 'Spirit.'" Ibid., 41.

[31] Ibid., 58–61.

[32] Ibid., 61–66.

[33] Ibid., 66–68.

[34] A useful summary critique of Rahner's contribution to the discussion of the Trinity may be found in David Coffey, "Trinity," in *The Cambridge Companion*

and Scott Harrower have offered paradigms for classifying these various responses. Sanders pointed out the importance of Rahner's axiom because how a theologian responds to it "gives a particular stamp to a whole range of systematic concerns, which means that Rahner's Rule functions as a watershed between two types of trinitarian theology."[35] Sanders offered a twofold paradigm for classifying a range of ecumenical theologians in their responses, focusing some attention on the "vice versa" aspect of the axiom.[36]

Sanders's Paradigm. According to Sanders, the "tight interpreters" of Rahner's axiom are those theologians who bring God into close relation with the world. Piet Schoonenberg, for instance, so identified the immanent Trinity with the economic Trinity that God's triune nature became dependent on his relations with the world. "God would still be God if the salvation-economic events had not occurred, but would not in that case be triune."[37] Jürgen Moltmann similarly argued that "the economic Trinity not only reveals the immanent Trinity; it also has a retroactive effect on it."[38] Hans Küng, Wolfhart Pannenberg, and Catherine Mowry LaCugna are also classified as "tight interpreters" of Rahner's axiom. Against the strict interpretation, which may impinge upon divine transcendence and immutability, Sanders warns, "It is becoming apparent that there is a need for some slack in the line, lest God and world come to be constrictively entangled."[39]

The second group, the "loose interpreters," are those who agree in some sense with Sanders's warning. These include such notable

---

to Karl Rahner, ed. Declan Marmion and Mary E. Hines (New York: Cambridge University Press, 2005), 108–10.

[35] Fred Sanders, "Entangled in the Trinity: Economic and Immanent Trinity in Recent Theology," *Dialog: A Journal of Theology* 40, no. 3 (2001): 177.

[36] Sanders uses at least two sets of terms to describe these two tendencies: "tight" and "loose," or "radicalizers" and "restricters." Cf. Fred Sanders, *The Image of the Immanent Trinity: Rahner's Rule and the Theological Interpretation of Scripture* (New York: Peter Lang, 2005), 83–84.

[37] Sanders, "Entangled in the Trinity," 178.

[38] Jürgen Moltmann, *The Trinity and the Kingdom* (Minneapolis, MN: Fortress, 1981), 160; cited in Sanders, "Entangled in the Trinity," 179.

[39] Ibid., 181.

theologians as Yves Congar, Walter Kasper, and Thomas Torrance.[40] A further consideration of Congar's typically prudent response may be helpful here. Congar agrees that the axiom, especially the first part, is justified. First, we could not know the Trinity were it not for God's revelation of himself. Second, the incarnation is not simply appropriated to the Son as the result of a divine counsel but is proper to his person. Third, the history of salvation is not merely a revelation about God but a communication of God himself.[41] The loose interpretation willingly receives the first part of Rahner's axiom. Congar believes God's revelation of himself as Trinity really presents who he is as Trinity.

However, Congar is compelled to qualify the second half of the axiom for two reasons. First, is it really "true to say that God commits the whole of his mystery to and reveals it in his communication of himself?"[42] Congar reviews Schoonenberg's use of the vice versa of Rahner's axiom and affirms that we simply cannot submit the divine being to history in this manner. Second, the revelation of God the Trinity awaits his full self-communication for the beatific vision. Moreover, the way Scripture speaks of such things as κένωσις, the condescension of God to manifest himself, implies some "distance" between God in himself and his revelation.[43]

Congar concludes that the economic Trinity truly reveals the eternal Trinity but not entirely. We should remain cautious about the "vice versa" (i.e., that the immanent Trinity is the economic Trinity).[44] Tracy would agree with the reception of Rahner's axiom as advocated by these loose interpreters: "The immanent Trinity can be partly, analogously but really understood in and through the economic Trinity."[45] This author concurs with a judicious reception of Rahner's rule, as advocated by Congar and Tracy among others.

---

[40] Ibid., 180–81.

[41] Yves Congar, *I Believe in the Holy Spirit*, trans. David Smith (1979–80, 1983; repr., New York: Crossroad Herder, 1997), 3.11–12.

[42] Ibid., 13.

[43] Ibid., 15.

[44] Ibid., 16.

[45] Tracy, "Trinitarian Speculation and the Forms of Divine Disclosure," 286.

Harrower's Paradigm. Scott Harrower also constructs a twofold paradigm, but in order to describe primarily evangelical responses to Rahner's axiom. Harrower says the "strict realist reading" of Rahner's rule "affirms a strong epistemological connection between the economic and immanent Trinity." Evangelicals who affirm a strict realist reading would include Bruce Ware and Robert Letham. Harrower classifies Kevin Giles and Millard Erickson among evangelicals who hold to a "loose realist reading" of Rahner's axiom.[46] Erickson, for instance, argues against identifying "too closely the economic (the Trinity as manifested to us in history) with the immanent Trinity (God as he really is in himself)."[47] It must be stressed that Harrower's paradigm of "strong" and "loose" should not be conflated with Sanders's paradigm of "tight" and "loose." Harrower's context is an evangelical debate shaped by the relationship between genders as applied to Trinitarian relations, while Sanders's context concerns the ecumenical approach to the Trinity.

Moreover, Erickson, who is a "loose" interpreter according to Harrower, cannot be identified with a theologian like Congar, who is a "loose" interpreter according to Sanders. The differences between the two are paradigmatically prohibitive. Congar would argue that the Bible's description of the Son tells us something real about the Triune being, whereas Erickson argues the Bible's language of "Father" and "Son" is not absolutely normative. Congar would argue that the Bible's language of generation and procession are properly ascribed to the Son and the Spirit, whereas Erickson argues this language leads to eternal subordination and thus raises the specter of Arianism. As an alternative to the traditional τάξις, Erickson affirms a "mutual production," an equal procession of the three persons from one another.

---

[46] Scott D. Harrower, *Trinitarian Self and Salvation: An Evangelical Engagement with Rahner's Rule* (Eugene, OR: Pickwick, 2012), 3–13. Harrower's thesis does not argue so much for a loose realist reading as against a strong realist reading. He assumes Erickson's theological method in order to meet his goal. Ibid., 19–20.

[47] Millard J. Erickson, *Making Sense of the Trinity: Three Crucial Questions* (Grand Rapids, MI: Baker, 2000), 90. Erickson has three monographs dedicated to the Trinity, each of which extends the previous: *God in Three Persons: A Contemporary Interpretation of the Trinity* (Grand Rapids, MI: Baker, 1995); *Making Sense of the Trinity;* and *Who's Tampering with the Trinity? An Assessment of the Subordination Debate* (Grand Rapids, MI: Kregel, 2009).

In his first two monographs dedicated to the Trinity, Erickson makes forays into biblical exegesis but also draws heavily upon contemporary philosophical and social concerns to make his case.[48] Erickson stresses the equality of the three persons, remarking upon the various phenomenological orderings of the Trinitarian persons. His logic is that if the Spirit is merely manifested first, then there is not a proper τάξις ("order") within the Trinity. In his third and final monograph on the Trinity, he engages in more thorough exegesis, providing helpful examples of the indivisible works of the three persons. However, any underlying pattern of relations between the persons is not given serious treatment in any of Erickson's three monographs, except to stress that there is a fundamental equality.[49]

Similarly, on the key issue of whether the incarnation is proper to the Son's person, Erickson argues for a mutual covenant within the Trinity to decide which of the three divine persons would become human.[50] Again, in opposition to Rahner's axiom, Erickson is clear that the economic Trinity must not be brought too close to the immanent Trinity. The presupposition of an ontological equality may not be challenged with appeal to economic revelation.[51] Erickson believes any ontological appeal to economic differentiation puts one on a slope to the heresy of Arianism.

Evaluating the Evangelical Alternatives

Harrower's evaluation of the evangelical responses to Rahner's axiom may be helpful. His basic paradigm of a "strict realist reading" and "loose realist reading," however, requires supplementation. In particular, the loose realist reading of Rahner's axiom may actually slip

---

[48] Erickson, *Making Sense of the Trinity*, 62–63, 84–96.

[49] Erickson, *God in Three Persons*, 300; idem, *Making Sense of the Trinity*, 87–88; idem, *Who's Tampering with the Trinity?*, 109–38. It is notable that Erickson, like Gruenler before him, appeals to the contributions of Warfield as authoritative. Erickson, *God in Three Persons*, 299–303; idem, *Making Sense of the Trinity*, 88–89; idem, *Who's Tampering with the Trinity?*, 55–58, 117–22.

[50] Harrower, *Trinitarian Self and Salvation*, 10–12.

[51] Erickson, *God in Three Persons*, 291–95, 309; idem, *Making Sense of the Trinity*, 90.

into a statement of contradiction, as evidenced in the Warfield tradition's emphasis on distance between the economic and ontological Trinity. Drawing upon Warfield, and derivatively the Thomist legacy, Erickson argues for mutual derivation of the persons and a mutual covenant to send one of the persons to become incarnate. He then posits a distinction between the eternal equality of the three persons and the temporary subordination of one of the three.

Erickson and his evangelical opponents often refer to where their immediate concern resides, the gender debate between complementarians and egalitarians.[52] This tendency, which is common in evangelical circles, strikes me as potentially (even while trying not to do so) allowing a contemporary anthropological concern to drive classical Trinitarian theology. Whatever the particular position one takes in the debate over gender relations, perhaps a renewed commitment to move from careful biblical exegesis to theological formation and only thence to communal practice would be helpful. This is the method Erickson proposes in his deservedly popular *Christian Theology*.[53]

Moreover, does the "loose realist reading" Harrower describes in his introduction allow for a contradictory reading of the biblical text? Might it be accused of allowing for a special knowledge of how God is fundamentally different from the knowledge he has revealed? Or does it participate in the modern separation of the being of God from the revelation of God, as described by Tracy? At its worst, could it eventually participate in the Sabellian method, which concluded that the one God is not three eternal persons? For the Sabellian, God appears in these modes of being, but he really is not this way. Could advocates of Harrower's "loose realist reading" say that God appears to be moving as source, generation, and procession in certain passages, but he cannot be this way eternally? Could the concern not to allow eternal subordination, for fear of Arianism, drive some theologians to affirm the opposing error, Sabellianism? It is instructive that Randal

---

[52] Erickson concludes in his final monograph that the disagreements among evangelicals ultimately center on the issue of relative authority and admits the opposing sides frequently accuse each other of allowing the anthropological debate to shape their Trinitarian views. Erickson, *Who's Tampering with the Trinity?*, 17, 24.

[53] Millard J. Erickson, *Christian Theology*, 2nd ed. (Grand Rapids, MI: Baker, 2001), 70–84.

Rauser, from whom Harrower borrows his paradigm, concludes that Sabellianism is an ultimate possibility without Rahner's rule.[54]

Of course, I am also wary of a "strict realist reading" of Rahner's axiom, at least as presented by Harrower. Harrower argues that Rahner is not the most exegetically adept theologian and is readily dependent on tradition. However, Rahner's *Theological Investigations* do contain nuggets of exegetical insight that must be mined, and he was more than willing to depart from the tradition when his reading of Scripture required it. Moreover, Harrower's own thesis, that the strict realist reading is not a faithful reading of Luke and Acts, does not prove a loose realist reading is, by default, necessarily true. My own contention is that we need to provide a third category that will identify some of the loose realist readings as having actually moved in a contradictory direction.

Congar and Kasper and others have previously modified Rahner's axiom. If I might be allowed to offer my own statement for relating the economic Trinity with the immanent, it would be fairly brief: *The economic Trinity reveals the immanent Trinity truly but not exhaustively.* A comparison of this statement with the models proposed by Sanders and Harrower indicates a further need for adjustment in classification. I believe Sanders and Harrower would agree that I have adopted a "loose" interpretation according to Sanders's paradigm but a "strict" interpretation according to Harrower's paradigm. Along with many theologians, such as Sanders and Congar, I refuse to collapse the immanent Trinity into the economic Trinity because it endangers the transcendence of the divine being. On the other hand, I do believe that the immanent Trinity, including the relational differences, is realistically communicated through the economic Trinity. This is what requires the third category.

Both parts of the "truly but not exhaustively" portion of my own statement need to be taken seriously. While I believe, along with Rahner and Congar as well as Augustine and the Cappadocian

---

[54] Rauser argues that any interpretation of Rahner's Rule is alternatively trivial or possibly untrue. Randal Rauser, "Rahner's Rule: An Emperor Without Clothes?," *International Journal of Systematic Theology* 7, no. 1 (2005): 81–94.

Fathers,[55] that God's revelation of himself as Trinity—in a source, generation, and procession τάξις—indicates who he really is, I do not claim that this tells us everything about God. However, neither do I believe this allows for contradictory speculation, such as Rauser's conclusion that God may be a quaternity or a Sabellian monad.[56] The revelation of God as one who is defined by the distinct relations between Father, Son, and Holy Spirit reveals an unalterable divine reality. This calls for simultaneity in certainty and humility. We are certain that what God reveals about himself is eternally true. But we humbly admit that, as creatures, we will never fully comprehend the illimitable God, including in the eternal bliss where we expect to grow ever more appreciative of his boundless glory.

Correlating the various biblical passages that emphasize distinctions within the Godhead with those biblical passages that emphasize divine equality also requires simultaneity. That God reveals himself as a Trinity possessing an eternal order does not mean the divine τάξις overwhelms the περιχώρησις. To put it another way, the eternal order of the Trinity need not contradict the mutual equality of the Trinity, even if such esteemed theologians as Millard Erickson find this to be a "logical absurdity."[57] A properly stated eternal derivation need not oppose triune equality. The three subsistent relations may correlate with the common substance even without Erickson's mutual production. Kevin Giles, an egalitarian Trinitarian like Erickson, has performed an admirable service for evangelicals by demonstrating this at length.[58]

A Revised Paradigm. If I could modify the paradigms of Sanders and Harrower regarding theological responses to Rahner's axiom, I would offer the following threefold paradigm: First, a "strict"

---

[55] Note that Augustine's presentation of the processions depends on a different reading of the missions of the Son and the Spirit than that offered by the Cappadocians. I have discussed this more in detail in my previously referenced essay on the Holy Spirit. Cf. Jeremy D. Wilkins, "Why Two Divine Missions? Development in Augustine, Aquinas, and Lonergan," *Irish Theological Quarterly* 77 (2012): 41–48.

[56] Rauser, "Rahner's Rule," 94.

[57] Erickson, *Making Sense of the Trinity*, 87.

[58] Kevin Giles, *The Eternal Generation of the Son: Maintaining Orthodoxy in Trinitarian Theology* (Downers Grove, IL: InterVarsity, 2012).

reading of Rahner's rule would affirm both parts of the axiom but would face the problem of subjecting the eternality of God to history, as with Moltmann and Schoonenberg.[59] Second, a "modified" reading of Rahner's rule would primarily affirm the first part of the axiom, in a manner similar to the offerings of Congar, Tracy, and this author. (Sanders's group of "loose" theologians would likely coalesce with this position.) Third, we really should add a "contradictory" reading, which would include any theological position that denies the truthfulness of not just the second part but also the first part of Rahner's axiom. This may require the reallocation of at least some of the theologians in Harrower's "loose realist reading" category.

With regard to this third response to Rahner's axiom, Warfield's chronologically prior but continually influential antinomies, previously mentioned, are here brought into sharper relief. On the one hand, Warfield regarded the distinction between the economic Trinity and the ontological Trinity as extrabiblical.[60] On the other hand, Warfield soon after used that distinction even pushing it into a contradiction. With the contradiction he simultaneously affirmed the economic subordination of the Son and the Spirit but denied any biblical evidence for the eternal derivation of the Son and the Spirit. The followers of Warfield must decide three related questions: Does Warfield's admittedly extrabiblical separation between the economic and the immanent require an exegetical basis? Does his implicitly extrabiblical proposal, that there was an eternal covenant where the three persons agreed to work in different manners,[61] require the same? Is the

---

[59] It may be difficult to place Eberhard Jüngel in this category, but the possibility must be considered. Eberhard Jüngel, *God's Being Is in Becoming: The Trinitarian Being of God in the Theology of Karl Barth: A Paraphrase*, trans. John Webster (Edinburgh: T&T Clark, 2001). John Webster argues that the idea of a Triune "being-in-becoming is in no way to compromise his freedom or aseity; it is to attempt to describe the way in which that freedom and aseity are actual." J. B. Webster, *Eberhard Jüngel: An Introduction to His Theology* (New York: Cambridge University Press, 1986), 21.

[60] Benjamin Breckenridge Warfield, *Biblical Doctrines* (New York: Oxford University Press, 1932), 161.

[61] Ibid., 165–66.

evangelical correspondence theory of truth, which undergirds basic realism and biblical inerrancy,[62] endangered through Warfield's contradictory axiom? Millard Erickson's influential advocacy of the eternal covenant and his moral judgment of Rahner's axiom as "illicit"[63] demonstrate the relevance of all three questions. Warfield's heirs must ultimately choose whether Warfield's extrabiblical positions are worth retaining, require modification, or need jettisoning.

Evangelicals might also consider whether the Western emphasis on the essence of the Trinity, rooted in the medieval scholastic tradition and buttressed with modernity's abstract monotheism, might have helped prompt Warfield's influential contradictions. If so, then in a profound irony Warfield, the conservative evangelical, adopted the exact theological method that Rahner, the Roman Catholic, warned against. In response we remind evangelicals that the Reformation cry of *sola scriptura* demands that biblical theology, and by that we mean an immersive exegetical state, really must shape systematic theology and not vice versa. Our concern is that in their Western prioritizing of unity in essence, Warfield may have allowed some evangelicals to downplay the ontological import of the distinct relational passages within biblical revelation.

From a review of the relevant hermeneutical landscape, we now turn to a particular biblical example of how eternity and history relate in a Trinitarian manner. Perhaps an exegetical exercise focused on a Pauline masterpiece may suggest solutions for both evangelical and Catholic biblical scholars facing the problems that have come to light through Rahner's objection to the Thomist egalitarian Trinitarian tradition. How did Paul perceive the relationship between eternity and history? And what might his masterpiece tell us about how he

---

[62] Erickson places the correspondence theory within both the premodern and modern periods. He defines the theory thus: "Propositions are true if they correctly describe the realities they purport to describe, false if they do not." Erickson, *Christian Theology*, 161, 164.

[63] Although Erickson recognizes that even when the ordering is different, "it is clear that the Father has priority." However, to assume this reflects Paul's official teaching about the internal relations of God is "some illicit reference." Erickson, *God in Three Persons*, 191.

perceived the relationship of God in himself (the immanent Trinity) to God for us (the economic Trinity)?

Paul's Metaphysical Trinitarian Hymn

Udo Schnelle describes the apostle Paul as "the first Christian theologian" and says Paul's theology is centered on "the eschatological presence of salvation from God in Jesus Christ" and flows according to "an eschatological scenario."[64] F. F. Bruce opines that the epistle of Paul known as "Ephesians" is "the quintessence of Paulinism," while C. H. Dodd says Ephesians is "the crown of Paulinism."[65] Reflecting higher critical doubt about the book's authorship, G. B. Caird nevertheless agreed that Ephesians is "a masterly summary of Paul's theology."[66] From a literary perspective, Samuel Taylor Coleridge, famous poet and philosopher, described the epistle to the Ephesians as "the divinest composition of man."[67] Bruce says Coleridge was moved to make such a high valuation due to the epistle's "structural unity" as well as its "inner unity of conception and execution."[68]

---

[64] Udo Schnelle, *Theology of the New Testament*, trans. M. Eugene Boring (Grand Rapids, MI: Baker, 2007), 203, 205. Schnelle's summary of Paul's "eschatological scenario" is remarkably similar to my own understanding of the substance of Paul's great Trinitarian hymn in Ephesians 1: "Its foundation is God's saving will, its decisive act is the resurrection and parousia of Jesus Christ, its determining power is the Holy Spirit, its present goal is the participation of believers in the new being, and its final goal is transformation into spiritual existence with God." Ibid.

[65] F. F. Bruce, *Paul: Apostle of the Heart Set Free* (Grand Rapids, MI: Eerdmans, 1977), 424; C. H. Dodd, "Ephesians," in *The Abingdon Bible Commentary*, ed. Frederick Carl Eiselen, Edwin Lewis, and David George Downey (New York: Doubleday, 1929), 1224–25.

[66] G. B. Caird, *The Apostolic Age* (London: Duckworth, 1955), 133. Regarding the two different if related questions of Pauline authorship and the intended recipients of Ephesians, see the judicious and still largely influential work of W. J. Conybeare and J. S. Howson, *The Life and Epistles of St. Paul* (Grand Rapids, MI: Eerdmans, 1980), 702–5, 705n.

[67] On Coleridge and the fiduciary role of language in granting access to God, see Sandra M. Levy, *Imagination and the Journey of Faith* (Grand Rapids, MI: Eerdmans, 2008), 8–12.

[68] F. F. Bruce, The *Epistles to the Colossians, to Philemon, and to the Ephesians* (Grand Rapids, MI: Eerdmans, 1984), 230.

Ephesians and the Trinitarian Structure of Paul's Theology

While Paul's epistle to the Romans has received the lion's share of attention following the Reformation, primarily due to its doctrines of depravity, justification, election, and the role of Israel, contemporary systematic presentations of Paul's theology have mirrored the concerns of Ephesians.[69] When Ephesians is allowed to provide the framework for Pauline theology, it often reflects the Trinity. A survey of some recent substantial New Testament theologies, Pauline theologies, and commentaries on Ephesians demonstrates that, after the waning of Bultmann's influence, Paul's thought is frequently framed by God the Father, the Son, and the Holy Spirit, inevitably in that order. These commentators certainly recognize Paul did not structure his letters in a systematic format but addressed concerns raised within the context of the churches. However, as we saw in chapter 2 and shall see below, Paul's theology does present itself in an economic Trinitarian frame, and this encourages a Trinitarian ordering.[70]

Completing the modernist transformation of biblical theology into anthropology, Rudolf Bultmann viewed Paul as teaching kerygmatic anthropology. Bultmann treated Pauline theology under two primary rubrics: "man prior to the revelation of faith" and "man under faith."[71] Helping turn the tide against the dominant modernist

---

[69] Schnelle, a Lutheran biblical theologian, is adamant that the righteousness of God, so prominent in Romans, "is *not* the *key concept* of Pauline theology *as a whole*" (his italics). Justification is a major concept within the theology of Paul, but it was a response to the "nomology" that arose in the churches of Galatia, Philippi, and Rome. Schnelle, *Theology of the New Testament*, 262, 266.

[70] Because Ephesians is not engaged in polemics, perhaps this allowed Paul room to put his thought in a more systematic format than in most of his letters.

[71] Rudolf Bultmann, *Theology of the New Testament*, vol. 1, trans. Kendrick Grobel (New York: Scribner, 1951), 185–352. New Testament theologies offered by Southern Baptists often treat Paul within an integrated New Testament approach. Frank Stagg follows a combined systematic and anthropological ordering with little concern for the Trinity. Frank Stagg, *New Testament Theology* (Nashville, TN: Broadman, 1962). In his New Testament theology, Thomas Schreiner also integrates the biblical authors, centering their theology on Christ through eschatology. However, his largest section flows in a Trinitarian direction if not with an explicitly triadic structure. Thomas R. Schreiner, *New Testament Theology: Magnifying God in Christ* (Grand Rapids, MI: Baker, 2008), 119–67 (Father); 168–430 (Son); 431–506 (Holy Spirit). Schreiner's study of Paul follows similarly, though he centers Paul on

anthropological structuring of Paul, Leonhard Goppelt recovered Paul's theology through Christology. Goppelt certainly did not focus Paul's theology on the Trinity, for Jesus Christ was the center. Yet within this Christological presentation, Goppelt's first concern was Christ's relation with God. Goppelt then moved to Christ's human ministry. This was followed by "the continued ministry of Jesus" centered on the Holy Spirit. Goppelt's theology of Paul was not explicitly Trinitarian, but it was implicitly Trinitarian through a Christological lens.[72] George Eldon Ladd was heavily influenced by the historical critical tradition dominated by Bultmann. Although Ladd began structurally with "man outside of Christ," he first introduced Paul as "an uncompromising monotheist."[73] After setting the historical frame of human depravity, Ladd then discussed Christ's person and work, followed later by several chapters on soteriology.[74] Lagging Goppelt, Ladd nevertheless helped move commentary on Paul toward theology, as filtered through the locus of Christology.

After this important transition from anthropology to theology among biblical theologies of Paul, there appears a widespread adoption of a Trinitarian pattern. For instance, Leon Morris begins his *New Testament Theology* with Paul. Of four chapters the first centers on God; the next two concern Christ's person and work; and the fourth concerns life in the Spirit.[75] Harold W. Hoehner, in his massive exegetical commentary on Ephesians, agrees this letter is the "crown or quintessence of Paulinism." Hoehner provides a seven-part outline, with the first four entitled, "Trinity," "Fatherhood of God,"

God glorifying himself in Christ. Thomas R. Schreiner, *Paul, Apostle of God's Glory in Christ: A Pauline Theology* (Downers Grove, IL: IVP Academic, 2006), 37–72 (Father); 151–88 (Jesus Christ); 307–30 (Holy Spirit).

[72] Leonhard Goppelt, *Theology of the New Testament*, vol. 2: *The Variety and Unity of the Apostolic Witness of Christ*, trans. John E. Alsup, ed. Jurgen Roloff (Grand Rapids, MI: Eerdmans, 1982), 62–63 (on Paul's theological structure); 69–86 (Christ's relation to God); 87–106 (Christ's human ministry); 118–23 (Christ's continuing ministry in the Holy Spirit).

[73] George Eldon Ladd, *A Theology of the New Testament* (Grand Rapids, MI: Eerdmans, 1974), 396–407, 363.

[74] Ibid., 408–568.

[75] Leon Morris, *New Testament Theology* (Grand Rapids, MI: Zondervan, 1986), 19–90.

"Christology," and "Pneumatology."[76] In I. Howard Marshall's
presentation of "the theology of the Pauline letters," the first three
of fourteen subjects are "God—the Father," "God—the Son," and
"God—the Holy Spirit," while the remainder primarily concern salvation.[77] Marvin Pate analyzes word counts, which prompts him to
adopt a sevenfold structure for Paul's theology, giving pride of place
to "Theology Proper," "Christology," and "Pneumatology."[78]

To conclude this survey, we must consider three highly respected
contemporary interpreters of Pauline theology. Udo Schnelle, in his
magisterial *Theology of the New Testament*, believes pneumatology provides the integrative power that "enables Paul to impart a systematic
quality to his interpretation."[79] Schnelle perceives eight major subjects within Pauline theology, of which the first three are "Theology,"
"Christology," and "Pneumatology."[80] In his massive tome on Paul,
N. T. Wright strives to locate Paul within his intellectual context.
When he treats Paul's theology, he therefore structures it around the
"Jewish map" of monotheism, election, and eschatology. However,
he sees Paul "reworking" Jewish theology in a "Christological and
pneumatological" manner, which is then extended into contextual
theology. While not following a Trinitarian structure in presentation, Wright perceives within Paul a Trinitarian redefinition of Jewish
monotheism.[81]

James D. G. Dunn does not follow an explicitly Trinitarian structure. He begins with God, brings in humanity, and devotes most of
his book to Christology. In a consistent if troubling vein, Dunn allows
his peculiar "Spirit Christology" to subsume his discussion of the

---

[76] Hoehner, *Ephesians*, 106–14.

[77] I. Howard Marshall, *New Testament Theology: Many Witnesses, One Gospel*
(Downers Grove, IL: IVP Academic, 2004), 422–60.

[78] C. Marvin Pate, *Apostle of the Last Days: The Life, Letters, and Theology of Paul*
(Grand Rapids, MI: Kregel, 2013), 284–318.

[79] Schnelle, *Theology of the New Testament*, 269.

[80] Ibid., 203–359. In an earlier paradigm, Schnelle followed an eightfold struc-
ture but placed soteriology between Christology and pneumatology. Schnelle, *The
Apostle Paul: His Life and Theology*, trans. M. Eugene Boring (Grand Rapids, MI:
Baker, 2005), 387–597.

[81] Nicholas Thomas Wright, *Paul and the Faithfulness of God* (Minneapolis, MN:
Fortress, 2013), 609–18.

Holy Spirit under Paul's Christology and soteriology.[82] Dunn does not return considerations of Paul to anthropology, but he maintains theology in a binitarian rather than a Trinitarian frame. Dunn is definitely an outlier within this survey. Contemporary biblical theologians typically seem to detect within Paul's theology a Trinitarian structure, a structure especially evident within the epistle to the Ephesians.

The Trinity in Ephesians

Harold Hoehner says Ephesians is correctly known as "the Trinitarian letter."[83] Scholars have identified several Trinitarian texts within the epistle. Marvin Pate focused on one text as indicative of the Trinity.[84] Millard Erickson identified two Trinitarian texts;[85] Arthur Wainwright, four;[86] and James Leo Garrett Jr., five.[87] Hoehner found "the activity of the three persons of the Trinity" in eight passages;[88] Robert Letham identified nine "ternary patterns" in Ephesians;[89] and Clinton E. Arnold listed eleven with only cursory discussion.[90] Striving for a comprehensive picture of the Trinity in Ephesians, I have discerned the interrelated working of the three distinct divine persons in concert explicitly within twelve passages: 1:3–14, 17–20; 2:18, 20–22; 3:2–5, 14–17; 4:4–6, 23–24; 4:30–5:2, 18–20; 6:10–17, 18–24. If 1:3 was distinguished from 1:4–14, it could be listed as a thirteenth instance of the economic Trinity in Ephesians. These Trinitarian references

---

[82] James D. G. Dunn, *The Theology of Paul the Apostle* (New York: T&T Clark, 1998), 260–65, 413–41. For further discussion of Dunn's "Spirit Christology," see my "The Doctrine of the Holy Spirit," in *A Theology for the Church*, rev. ed., ed. Daniel L. Akin (Nashville, TN: B&H, 2014), 496–97.

[83] Hoehner, *Ephesians*, 106.

[84] Pate, *Apostle of the Last Days*, 244, 286.

[85] Erickson, *God in Three Persons*, 187.

[86] Arthur W. Wainwright, *The Trinity in the New Testament* (London: SPCK, 1962), 258–59.

[87] James Leo Garrett Jr., *Systematic Theology: Biblical, Historical, and Evangelical*, vol. 1 (Grand Rapids, MI: Eerdmans, 1990), 269–70.

[88] Hoehner, *Ephesians*, 106–7.

[89] Robert Letham, *The Holy Trinity: In Scripture, History, Theology, and Worship* (Phillipsburg, NJ: P&R, 2004), 73–85.

[90] Clinton E. Arnold, *Ephesians*, Zondervan Exegetical Commentary on the New Testament (Grand Rapids, MI: Zondervan, 2010), loc 13769–98.

come in the forms of hymn, prayer, soteriological description, and ecclesial description in the first half of the letter, which is doctrinal in focus (chaps. 1–3). They also come in the forms of exhortation, creed, anthropological description, ecclesial exhortation, missionary exhortation, worship, and prayer in the second half of the letter, which is ethical in focus (chaps. 4–6).

Among the Trinitarian passages in Paul's letter to the Ephesians, the *metaphysical hymn* in 1:3–14 serves as a theological introduction to the entire letter. Markus Barth called this passage, which is one long sentence composed of 202 words in the Greek, "a digest of the whole epistle."[91] I have classified the text as a "metaphysical" hymn because it provides a comprehensive vision of "ultimate reality,"[92] in which eternity is related to time, with God engaging the cosmos from creation to consummation, and because it assumes the epistemological availability to humanity through apostolic revelation of the simultaneously eternal and historical activity of God. It is metaphysical not only because it presents the progress of the cosmos but also because it presents a portrait of the God who both transcends the cosmos and becomes immanent to the cosmos. God the Father maintains the divine transcendence even as the Son and the Holy Spirit engage intimately with humanity: the Son becomes immanent through incarnation and death, the Spirit through the gift of personal presence.

I have classified the text as a metaphysical "hymn" due to its purpose and structure. The purpose of the text is declared in the threefold reference to "blessing" in verse 3. Similar to 2 Corinthians 13:14, which we exposited in chapter 2, it has therefore been identified as a benediction for use in Christian worship, or similarly as doxology or eulogy. The liturgical purpose of the hymn prompts only minor disagreement, but the structure of the text has exercised scholars.

---

[91] Markus Barth, *Ephesians: Introduction, Translation, and Commentary on Chapters 1–3*, The Anchor Bible (Garden City, NY: Doubleday, 1974), 97.

[92] We are using "metaphysical" in its earlier sense. D. W. Hamlyn, "Metaphysics, History of," in *The Oxford Companion to Philosophy*, ed. Ted Honderich (New York: Oxford University Press, 1995), 556. Peter van Inwagen and Meghan Sullivan, "Metaphysics," in *The Stanford Encyclopedia of Philosophy*, ed. Edward N. Zalta (accessed February 14, 2015, http://plato.stanford.edu/archives/win2014/entries/metaphysics).

If the formula that ends verses 6, 12, and 14—"to the praise of his glory"—is taken as a refrain; then it naturally divides into three major stanzas, each centering on the work of one of the members of the Christian Trinity. Martin Dibelius believed the recurrence of "in him" near the beginning of verses 4, 7, 11, [and 13] marked the beginning of stanzas.[93] If Dibelius's discovery were applied fully, that could yield a second Christological stanza, which would also account for the shift in verse 12 from the cosmic to the personal.

There are more complex schemes. However, Barth says "the majority of interpreters" still comment upon "the trinitarian structure which moves from the Father through the Son to the Spirit." If we accept the division according to the refrain, which is the most prominent literary feature, as Paul's way of emphasizing theology rather than anthropology, there unfolds a complementary triadic structure.[94]

> Blessed is the God and Father of our Lord Jesus Christ, who has blessed us with the Spirit's every blessing in the heavenly places in Christ. Just as he elected us in him before the foundation of the cosmos, so that we would be holy and blameless in his presence in love, he predestined us to adoption as sons to himself through Jesus Christ according to the good purpose of his will, to the praise of his glorious grace, which he freely granted us in the Beloved.
>
> In him we have redemption through his blood, the forgiveness of our sins, according to the wealth of his grace, which he lavished on us in all wisdom and understanding. He made known to us the mystery of his will, according to the good intention that he purposed in himself, in the

---

[93] Barth rehearses the hymn argument well but finds it "not convincing," preferring to emphasize unity around God's name. Barth, *Ephesians*, 99.

[94] We recognize verse 3 could serve either as an introductory stanza to the whole hymn or as the beginning of the first stanza. We also recognize the "in him" before verse 11 may start a second Christological stanza. However, even with these additional divisions, the Trinitarian structure of the metaphysical hymn would remain evident. For a helpful schematic showing how commentators since 1900 have divided the hymn, see Hoehner, *Ephesians*, 160–61. Those adopting a strictly Trinitarian structure include Innitzer, Coutts, Barkhuizen, and Hoehner. See also Pate, *Apostle of the Last Days*, 244.

economy of the fullness of the times, to unite all things
in Christ, things in the heavens and things on the earth.
In him we have also obtained an inheritance, having been
predestined according to the purpose of him who is working
all things after his will, so that we who have already hoped in
Christ might be to the praise of his glory.

In him you also, after hearing the word of truth, the
gospel of your salvation, in whom you also believed, you
were sealed with the Holy Spirit of promise, who is given as
the down payment of our inheritance, until the redemption
of God's possession, to the praise of his glory (Eph 1:3–14).

The Theology of Paul's Trinitarian Hymn

"Blessed is the God and Father of our Lord Jesus Christ, who has
blessed us with every spiritual blessing in the heavenly places in
Christ." Verse 3 serves as the introduction to the hymn, setting it
immediately in a Trinitarian frame with the Father as the origin of
divine movement. The Father's attribute of "blessedness" is emphasized here, although among contemporary theologians, according to
Fred Sanders, that attribute has been forgotten.[95] Hoehner argues
that the phrase, εὐλογητὸς ὁ θεὸς καὶ πατὴρ, "is not expressing a wish,
'blessed be God,' but rather a declaration, 'blessed is God.'"[96] In the
Genesis creation narrative, God is said to have blessed the earth thrice
(1:22, 28; 2:3). According to Thomas Aquinas, divine blessedness is
the attribute that embraces all other blessings. Blessing "belongs to
God in the highest degree," such that "God is the only beatitude,"
but he shares himself with his creatures, which allows us to speak
of humans being blessed.[97] This leading Roman Catholic theologian
allowed divine blessedness to function as the bridge attribute to his

---

[95] Sanders published four essays for *Reformation 21* in January 2015 on divine
blessedness (accessed January 29, 2015, http://72.47.212.95/fred-sanders).

[96] Hoehner, *Ephesians*, 162.

[97] St. Thomas Aquinas, *Summa Theologica*, trans. Fathers of the Dominican
Province (Westminster, MD: Christian Classics, 1911), Part 1, Question 26, Arts.
1, 3, 4.

discussion of the Trinity.[98] According to John Gill, the blessedness of God concerns "all the perfections of God put together." That leading Baptist theologian similarly allowed the attribute of blessedness to transition his discussion of the Trinity.[99]

The word *blessing* appears in three forms in verse 3, as a verbal adjective (εὐλογητὸς), as an aorist participle (εὐλογήσας), and as a noun (εὐλογία). The Father, the Son, and the Holy Spirit are respectively identified with distinct aspects of the one divine blessing. The Father, described with the verbal adjective, is closely affiliated with the divine being through an emphasis on the attribute of blessedness. The Son, as the indirect object ("in Christ") of the verb, is thereby identified as the active agent through whom the Father elected to bless humanity. The Holy Spirit is identified with the modification of the blessing placed "upon us" through the adjective, πνευματικός, attached to the noun.

Commenting on verse 3, Marshall opines, "The Spirit receives only passing mention at this point."[100] However, Barth, Fee, and Hoehner demonstrate that the Holy Spirit is typically included in Paul's use of πνευματικός, as seen for instance in 1 Corinthians 2:14–16; 3:1–4; and 15:44–46. According to Hoehner, spiritual benefits "have their source in the Spirit of God."[101] According to Barth, "Above all, those things or events are called 'spiritual' that are a result and evidence of the presence of the Spirit."[102] According to Gordon Fee, in his groundbreaking work on Paul's pneumatology, "spiritual blessing" is an inadequate interpretation, for it is often taken as a mere synonym of "heavenly." A more proper interpretation might be

---

[98] Cf. ibid., Questions 26 and 27.

[99] John Gill, *A Body of Doctrinal Divinity; or, a System of Evangelical Truths, Deduced from the Sacred Scriptures*, new ed. (London, 1839; repr., Paris, AR: Baptist Standard Bearer, [n.d.]), 122–40.

[100] Marshall, *New Testament Theology*, 380. He also states, "The structure is, however, not strictly trinitarian, with different aspects of salvation being assigned to different persons." Ibid. In response, we hope to demonstrate the Trinitarian nature of the hymn below.

[101] Hoehner, *Ephesians*, 167–68.

[102] Barth, *Ephesians*, 101.

"the spirit's blessings," "spiritual blessing," or "blessings that pertain to the Spirit."[103]

The movement of blessing in the benediction of Ephesians 1 is different from the Pauline benediction we considered in chapter 2 above. Following the pattern established in Numbers 6:24–26, a benediction where Yahweh is thrice called upon to bless the people of God, 2 Corinthians 13:14 also calls upon the Trinity to bless the people of God in a threefold way. Where Numbers 6 and 2 Corinthians 13 pray God to bless man, Ephesians 1 is an apostolic declaration that God is himself blessed. In Ephesians 1 man shares in divine blessing, derivatively from God through the Son in the Spirit; but Paul's emphasis is from beginning to end upon God as the blessed one. The first stanza (v. 3) and the repetitive nature of the refrain ("to the praise of his glory" in vv. 6, 12, 14) identify both the origin and the end of blessing as being in God himself. The second and third stanzas herald the Lord Jesus Christ and the Holy Spirit, respectively yet interrelated, as the locus, means, and end of the blessing God chooses to flow from himself into humanity.

The numerous prepositions Paul employs in Ephesians 1:3–14 perform "somersaults" that may confuse the unwary exegete into concluding this one long sentence is not a beautiful Hellenistic construction but a Pauline "monster."[104] However, according to Markus Barth, properly interpreted the prepositions reveal the internal literary structure of the hymn. An analysis of the hymn's prepositions simultaneously reveals the Triune economy. There is a definite movement in verses 4–14 that connects with verse 3's identification of the Father as the subject of blessing, the Lord Jesus as verbal agent of blessing, and the Holy Spirit as objective blessing. The purpose of God's activity of blessing is to incorporate humanity unto his glory.

First, grace comes from God the Father "according to" (κατά) his actions of election and predestination. Second, grace comes "through" (διά taken as a preposition of means) and "in" (ἐν taken as

---

[103] Gordon D. Fee, *God's Empowering Presence: The Holy Spirit in the Letters of Paul* (Peabody, MA: Hendrickson, 1994), 666–67.

[104] Barth's comments here should not be interpreted as affirming that Paul's Ephesian epistle is a literary monstrosity but as speaking tongue in cheek to the classicist. Barth, *Ephesians*, 77, 100.

a preposition of location) the Lord Jesus Christ by the sacrifice of his blood on the cross. Third, grace comes "with" or "in" (ἐν taken as a preposition of means or location) the Holy Spirit through his activity of sealing and insuring. This coordinated activity from the Father, through and in the Son, and with or in the Holy Spirit, then results in a reverse movement back toward God, once the divine grace has worked itself within the human object. Note that we have emphasized the use of the prepositions with reference to God the Son and God the Holy Spirit as locative as well as instrumental. Those preferring an anthropological focus, as manifested in the interpretation of divine election as individualistically particular,[105] tend to prefer the instrumental treatment of the Son and the Spirit.[106] Those preferring a theological focus, as manifested in the Christological and corporate

---

[105] For instance, an admired former Southwestern Seminary New Testament professor, Curtis Vaughan, treated Ephesians 1:3–14 as a benediction upon man rather than upon God. While Vaughan recognizes the triadic structure of the doxology, he never mentions the Trinity and prefers to organize his exposition anthropologically, according to the Christian life rubrics of "a description of the divine blessings" and "an enumeration of the divine blessings." He believes the "leading words and phrases" concern the predestination of human beings, taken in an individualistic direction. See "The Blessings of God's New People: A Prayer," in Curtis Vaughan, *Ephesians* (Cape Coral, FL: Founders, 2002), 17–30.

[106] For a pair of contrasting views on election in this hymn, consult first the Christological and incorporative approach of Markus Barth and then the point-by-point response of Harold Hoehner. Barth, *Ephesians*, 105–9; Hoehner, *Ephesians*, 185–93. Barth's treatment is convincing due to its Christological centeredness, which Paul himself makes a dominant literary theme through his use of "in Christ" and related terms some thirty-nine times in the relatively short book of Ephesians, as Hoehner himself details. Hoehner, *Ephesians*, 173–74. Hoehner's treatment of the subject is not ineloquent, but there remains an undefended presupposition in his distributive rather than corporate interpretation of the plural pronoun *hemas*, "us." We conclude that the Father's election treats Jesus Christ as the means and the end of election, as well as the locus of election. As God who has come *in flesh to shed his blood*, Jesus Christ is the *means* of our election; but *as God who has come* in flesh to shed his blood, Christ is the *origin* and *end* of our election. Among the "all things" about which Paul spoke in Ephesians 1:10, election may be said to be "summed up" in Christ. Jesus is the sum of election. Scripture does not appear to present eternal election as occurring beyond its locus, means, and end in the divine man Jesus Christ, neither through a predominant plan applied to particular individuals from eternity (*pace* Calvinism) nor through a foreknown result of how those individuals would respond (*pace* Arminianism). We leave the working out of this important soteriological issue for another venue.

interpretation of divine election, tend to prefer the locative treatment of the Son and the Spirit.

There is both an intermediate and ultimate purpose in the divine movement.[107] Intermediately, the unified yet distinct works of the Trinitarian persons are intended "for the purpose of" (εἰς taken as a preposition of purpose) the believers' adoption. The Father's incorporating election of believing humanity in Christ is intended to result in their holiness and blamelessness. The Father lavished his grace upon humanity through the blood of his Son, thereby redeeming, forgiving, and uniting believers in Christ. His grace becomes personally localized in the believer through the Holy Spirit's internalized presence. Yet humanity is not the final end of the divine movement. Ultimately, the election of the Father, the sacrifice of the Son, and the sealing of the Holy Spirit are intended "for" or "to" (εἰς) the praise of God's glory, which is offered by redeemed humanity "before" (κατενώπιον taken as a preposition of location) the Father.

Peter Toon recognizes the momentous nature of this divine movement through his treatment of Ephesians 1 as part of his discussion of the economic Trinity. In a chapter entitled "From the Father . . . to the Father," Toon builds a case for "the biblical theology of the economic Trinity." He believes the economic Trinity works according to a model of "descent" and "ascent," a patterned movement we also detected in the Gospel of John. First, grace flows to humanity "from the Father through the Son and in the Holy Spirit." Second, human worship and access to God flow "to the Father through the Son and in the Holy Spirit."[108] Through this movement the personal chasm between rebellious humanity and the holy God, as well as the epistemological chasm between history and eternity, is overcome by Triune grace. The prepositions within the book of Ephesians as well as within the Pauline corpus corroborate the orderly nature of this economic paradigm,[109] but because it is a movement from and to eternity, we must also see this as unveiling the eternal constitution of God.

---

[107] Vaughan, *Ephesians*, 22–23.

[108] Peter Toon, *Our Triune God: A Biblical Portrayal of the Trinity* (Wheaton, IL: Victor, 1996), 213–29.

[109] "The purpose of the compound prepositions in Eph 1 is clearly discernible. With the help of prepositions the origin and order of God's decision, the means and

In Ephesians 1:3–14, God the Father is the originating subject of the blessing; the Lord Jesus Christ is the active eternal agent that brings the blessing into history through the incarnation and the cross; and the Holy Spirit is the blessing made continually present to humanity. Where the metaphysical hymn of Ephesians 1 demonstrates the descent of divine grace, Ephesians 2:18 demonstrates the ascent of humanity to God. In the second chapter of Ephesians, the new humanity, composed of the formerly divided Jew and Gentile, is incorporated into Christ Jesus through the Holy Spirit. Incorporated with Christ and indwelt by the Holy Spirit, the new humanity is brought before the Father. "For through him [Jesus Christ; v. 13] we both have access in one Spirit to the Father" (Eph 2:18). Ephesians 1:3–14 evinces both the descent of blessing from God and the ascent in glory to God, but Ephesians 2 makes the ascent even clearer.[110]

The Economy of Paul's Trinitarian Hymn

Using the "blessing" of God as the encompassing divine attribute, Paul enabled us to glimpse the eternal being of God. He has also revealed that God the Father shares himself through blessing humanity in Christ with the Spirit (v. 3). Now we must consider in more detail how the Father communicates his blessing to humanity through the Son and in the Holy Spirit (vv. 4–14). Paul's metaphysical hymn encapsulates the universal history of the eternal God with his creation in a Trinitarian frame. As noted above, the hymn functions as an introduction to the book of Ephesians and as a summary of Paul's worldview. The hymn's economic thesis is that God has revealed the mystery of his working to restore order and unity to creation through the rule of Christ and the presence of his Spirit. The revelation begun in the hymn and more fully completed in the book of Ephesians

---

mode of carrying it out, and the goal and effect of its fulfillment are at one and the same time distinguished from one another and kept together." Barth, *Ephesians*, 100.

[110] Paul's portrait of the descent of grace to humanity from the Father through the Son in the Spirit, and the returning ascent of humanity to the Father through the Son in the Spirit, was abridged earlier in Galatians 4:6: "God has sent forth the Spirit of His Son into our hearts, crying, 'Abba! Father!'"

takes the form of a grand narrative that bridges heaven and earth, that shows the eternal God making himself really known through the incarnation, death, and resurrection of his Son, the Lord Jesus Christ. The divine incarnation grounds the historical revelation of the eternal economy, setting the stage for the central event of the cross and the resurrection. The life, death, and resurrection of the Lord Jesus Christ thus provide the perspectival center from which may be seen the beginning of the divine economy in election and creation and the end of the divine economy in the consummation and final judgment.

From an eternal perspective the economy of God includes a process of descent from eternity and ascent to eternity. Jesus Christ is the one who embodies and encompasses this divine movement: "He who descended is himself also the one who ascended far above all the heavens, so that he might fulfill all things" (Eph 4:10). This economy is centered in the Son but includes explicitly the entire Trinity. Paul draws attention to the distinct yet unitary working of God the Father, his Son, and the Holy Spirit. There is a Triune movement eternally in the Father's election from the kindness of his grace and unto the praise of his glory, in the Son's humble descent and triumphant ascent, and in the Spirit's omnipresent action in creation and redemption and omnipotent application of the resurrection. There is a perceptible historical movement in the universe from creation to cross to consummation, and there is a perceptible personal movement in human lives from election to redemption to resurrection.

Paul's metanarrative prompts us to speak of what Augustine termed the inseparable work of the Trinity on the one hand[111] and of what have come to be called the appropriated or proper works of the Trinity on the other hand.[112] First, every work of God is inseparably or indivisibly a work of all three persons. The Father, the Son, and the Holy Spirit are each involved in the major divine works of creation (cf. Gen 1:1–3; Ps 33:6; John 1:3; Rom 11:36), redemption (for instance, with the Father in sending, the Son on the cross,

---

[111] Augustine, *The Trinity*, trans. Edmund Hill (Brooklyn, NY: New City, 1991), 1.13.15, 1.13.18, 2.2.9.

[112] Ibid., 2.1–2. Note also that Augustine did not believe that either the missions, the sending of the Son and the Spirit from the Father, or the eternal processions endangered the equality of the Son and the Spirit with the Father.

and the Spirit through raising), and the consummation (the Father in planning, the Son in ruling, and the Spirit in calling). Yet, second, each divine person takes a lead in the unified activity of God through works appropriated or properly attached to that particular divine person. According to Ephesians, the Father leads in election (Eph 1:5–6) and creation (3:15), the Son in the cross (1:7) and the restoration of orderly rule (1:10, 20–22), and the Spirit in the application of personal regeneration (3:16–20; 5:18) and eschatological surety (1:13–14).

The Trinitarian economy of Ephesians 1:3–14 tells us much about God, but Paul relates the Trinity to humanity in many ways throughout the letter. As noted at the beginning of this chapter, there is a Triune movement with regard to dominion. The created gift of human rule (Gen 1:26)—which was subsequently compromised in the fall, prompting a consequent disorder in human hearts and of relations with God, one another, and creation (Gen 3:8–19)—is being restored by God through the rule of the man Jesus Christ (Eph 1:10, 20–22). There is also a Triune movement with regard to the nations, for the Spirit is incorporating humanity in Christ, who has reconciled Jew and Gentile, allowing both to approach God (Eph 2:18). There is a Triune movement within the church, which is God's dwelling built on Christ as the cornerstone through the Spirit's indwelling presence (2:20–22). There is a Triune movement in revelation: coming from the Father, the mystery of the Son is revealed through the indwelling of the Spirit (3:1–6). Paul concludes his doctrinal section by praying the Father will grant the Spirit to transform human hearts so that Christ may dwell therein by faith (3:14–17).

At the beginning of his moral exhortation, Paul includes a call to unity that has been interpreted as a nascent Trinitarian *credo* (4:4–6).[113] Paul presents the new humanity as an intimate Trinitarian reflection: "renewed in the spirit of your mind," "put on the new man," "created after God's likeness" (4:23–24). The church is to function with reference to the Trinity: grieving not the Spirit but following

---

[113] Bruce, *The Epistles to the Colossians, to Philemon, and to the Ephesians*, 335–38. *Credo* is the Latin term for "I believe." It is often used to describe the early creeds, especially the Old Roman and Apostles' Creeds.

God's example, loving as the Son loved (4:30–5:2). Christian worship requires a Trinitarian movement, too—filled with the Spirit, Christians are to sing to the Lord, giving thanks to God the Father (5:18–20). In the midst of the spiritual warfare between the ruler of this earth and the Lord of heaven, the church is to find its strength in the Lord, putting on "the armor of God," wielding "the sword of the Spirit" (6:10–11, 17). Finally, just as he began doxologically, Paul concludes the letter in Triune prayer, calling the people to pray "in the Spirit," asking for them to have peace "from God our Father and our Lord Jesus Christ" (6:18, 23). The Trinitarian economy of Ephesians extends from God into the world, bringing redeemed humanity back to himself.

Θεολογία through Οἰκονομία

In the last two sections as we tried to speak of θεολογία, the inner being of God as three in one, we inevitably transitioned to οἰκονομία, the external relations of God as three in one. As Warfield noted, the distinction between the eternal divine being and the historical divine working is a concept we bring to the biblical text. However, within Paul's metaphysical hymn, the transition from divine ontology to divine activity is pervasive. We noted this in the divine attribute and activity of blessing, which provides the overall structure of the eulogy. However, blessing is not the only concept that bridges eternity and history. The love of God and the holiness of God are likewise integral both in the divine being and in the Triune economy.

From the attribute of his love,[114] "the good intention [εὐδοκίαν] that he purposed in himself" (Eph 1:9; cf. 1:5), God the Father elected us "in love [ἀγάπη]" (1:4) and predestined us "in the Beloved [ἠγαπημένῳ]" (1:6). Here the Father is the sole actor in eternal election, while elsewhere the other persons become involved in electing.[115]

---

[114] John recognized that "God is love" (1 John 4:8, 16) and similarly exposited Trinitarian love as moving from God, toward humanity in Christ, and within redeemed humanity by his Spirit (1 John 4:7–21).

[115] Erickson demonstrates convincingly that all three persons participate in election in his *Who's Tampering with the Trinity?*, 124–25. What Erickson never shows

The Father elects not mechanically and grimly but benevolently out of the "person-to-person relationship of love" within the Trinity outwardly to humanity.[116] It is commonly accepted that "Beloved" is a reference to the Son of the Father (cf. Mark 1:11; 9:7), while Augustine identifies the love between the Father and the Son as the Holy Spirit. Because the Holy Spirit is the one who brings the Father's love close to us (Rom 5:5), we may conclude that God's identity as love pervades the Triune economy of love. God reveals himself as the one God who is love, through the love of his Spirit, in his beloved Son, because he is within himself dynamically moving in love.

Similarly, out of the character of his eternal being as holy, for his holiness is "before the foundation of the cosmos," God the Father elected us "so that we would be holy [ἁγίους] and blame-less [ἀμώμους]" (Eph 1:4). The concept of "blameless" belongs to the Old Testament economy of sacrifice, where the lamb that would redeem the people should be without blemish.[117] The Lord Jesus Christ is the holy one whose sacrifice provided "redemption through his blood, the forgiveness of our sins" (1:7). And it is the "Holy [ἁγίω] Spirit" who provides the down payment of our "redemption" unto holiness (1:13–14). As with divine blessing and divine love, so it is with divine holiness or blamelessness. In each case God the Father is the origin of the blessing, love, and holiness that characterize the eternal being of all three persons of the Trinity. In each case this divine attribute is then shared with humanity through the Lord Jesus Christ and in the Holy Spirit.

The Trinitarian economy is, according to Paul's metaphysical hymn, a reflection of the Trinitarian being. The immanent Trinity reveals the economic Trinity. God the Trinity—God as he really is—reveals himself in and through his Trinitarian acts. Or, to put it

---

from a biblical basis is his key contention that a Trinitarian council chooses the Trinitarian persons' roles on an egalitarian basis. Erickson believes this egalitarian election includes the choice of which person to incarnate. Alas, the eternal distinc-tions between the persons are thereby dissolved. Erickson's identification of prayer as directed to both the Father and the Son is helpful. Ibid., 131–32. For prayer directed toward the Holy Spirit, see Yarnell, "The Person and Work of the Holy Spirit," 540.

[116] Barth, *Ephesians*, 108.

[117] Exod 29:1, 38–42; Lev 22:19–25; Heb 9:11–10:18; Barth, *Ephesians*, 113.

another way: God reveals himself as God the Trinity because he really is God the Trinity. This reception of the hymn's pattern may suggest solutions to three of the major problems raised in this chapter. First, the reception of Paul's Trinitarian epistemology solves the dilemma posed by the Enlightenment's hiding of the metaphysical. Humanity is granted access to a real knowledge of God as the eternal Father reveals himself within history through his Son and in his Spirit. Second, the recognition that the immanent Trinity reveals the economic Trinity suggests the "strict" interpreters should be careful before adopting the "vice versa" of Rahner's axiom. While there is a return from history to eternity in the hymn, an "ascent," the ascent necessarily follows after the "descent." Economy is dependent on ontology and not vice versa. Third, the patterned correlation of Triune ontology with Triune economy through the communication of certain of the Triune attributes with humanity—in blessing, love, and holiness—suggests the "contradictory" interpreters should be careful before denying the movement from immanence to economy. Humanity has access to θεολογία, the being of God as Father, Son, and Holy Spirit, only through the grace of his οἰκονομία of revelation. Ephesians makes a sustained correlation between theology and economy. This does not subsume other scriptural paradigms, but the apostle Paul's grand theological portrait certainly presents the Triune being *through* the Triune economy and the Triune economy as moving *from* the Triune being.

8

THE GOD WHO IS COMING:
ʼΕΝ ΜΕΣΩ

> Then I saw One like a slaughtered lamb standing between
> [ἐν μέσῳ] the throne and the four living creatures and
> among the elders. He had seven horns and seven eyes,
> which are the seven spirits of God sent into all the earth.
>
> Revelation 5:6 (HCSB)

In *Painting the Word*, John Drury, former dean of Christ Church in
Oxford, demonstrates how orthodox Christian art operates from
a "two-world cosmology" composed of eternity and time.[1] Eternity,
where the Trinity dwells, is inaccessible to humanity except through
the "bridge" provided by the cross of Jesus Christ, who continues to
reveal God through the Holy Spirit. The cross is both historical and
eternal. It is historical in that it occurred once within time; it is eternal in that it has universal effect.[2] Tracking the progress of Christian
art into ever more incarnational forms, Drury shows how artists have
represented the twofold nature of reality in different ways. One of
the most effective has been captured visually in the long flight of
stairs at the Sainsbury Wing of London's National Gallery, which

---

[1] John Drury, *Painting the Word: Christian Pictures and Their Meanings* (New
Haven, CT: Yale University Press, 1999), 146.

[2] Ibid., 3–6.

ascends upward to Botticini's painting of this world being opened
further into a threefold heaven. The artistic idea of access into the
transcendent dwelling of God was prompted in part by "apocalyptic"
literature, wherein the concealed kingdom of heaven is unsealed for
believers to perceive.[3]

If Christian artists through the centuries have attempted to put
into visual expression the apocalyptic related in biblical literature, perhaps it is a response to the apostle John's Apocalypse originally being
a literary record of something he saw. When the apostle was "in the
Spirit" as he worshipped on the Lord's Day, he heard the voice of
"One like the Son of Man" command him, "Write on a scroll what
you see and send it to the seven churches" (Rev 1:10–13). Write what
you see—the book of Revelation is a literary record of John's visual
encounter with God. It depicts a lengthy vision of how eternity and
history are populated and of how the former guides the latter from its
beginning to its end. The beautiful style and content of John's resulting circular letter has prompted commentators to refer to it in highly
imaginative terms, from a philosophical perspective as "artistry" of
the transcendent,[4] from a historical perspective as a "tapestry"[5] or an
"unforgettable heavenly landscape,"[6] and from a literary perspective
as a product of "literary genius"[7] or "one of the great masterpieces of
early Christian literature."[8]

This book began with theological expositions of three passages
from both the Old and New Testaments, which were placed in the
context of worship. If the Christian life begins with the love of God
transforming human beings through the grace of Jesus Christ and the
fellowship of the Holy Spirit (chap. 2), it is publicly manifested in the
first act of Christian worship, baptism (chap. 1). This God, with whom

---

[4] Richard Bauckham, *The Theology of the Book of Revelation*, New Testament
Theology (New York: Cambridge University Press, 1993), 8.

[5] Ben Witherington III, *Revelation*, The New Cambridge Bible Commentary
(New York: Cambridge University Press, 2003), 15.

[6] Paige Patterson, *Revelation*, The New American Commentary (Nashville, TN:
B&H, 2012), 18.

[7] Robert H. Mounce, *The Book of Revelation*, rev. ed., New International
Commentary on the New Testament (Grand Rapids, MI: Eerdmans, 1977), 30.

[8] Witherington, *Revelation*, 48.

Christ Jesus is incorporated into Christian worship is, moreover, the one God of the Hebrew Bible (chap. 3). It is fitting, therefore, that this book end with a vision of the God who is the object of not only human worship but of worship by the cosmos (Revelation 4–5). In this final chapter we shall evaluate the Apocalypse's literary portrait of the God who creates, sustains, and comes to meet creation, a God who is Trinity. In the epilogue that follows, we shall offer some reflections on what we may garner from the various literary artists whom we have analyzed in this book, the prophets and apostles whose works are preserved in the Bible, works that vividly portray the God we are increasingly prepared to call "Trinity."

The Styles of Revelation

As we have seen already with a number of theologians from Christian history, although "theology" may be and often is inappropriately reduced to a series of abstractions, theology is truly inseparable from conversion and worship. A more appropriate "hermeneutic of piety" is expressed well in the writings of both Augustine and the Cappadocian Fathers, who saw the Christian's vision of the Trinity as beginning with glimpses of the divine light now, but finding completion only in the world to come.[9] Augustine famously traced our mental image of the Trinity through the gift of the *imago Dei*, its ruin in the fall, and its reconstruction by grace.[10] Gregory of Nyssa described Trinitarian salvation as human participation in the divine "circle of glory," of the Trinity's light radiating outward and reflecting back toward God, beginning with grace from God and ending properly in the return of worship to God.[11] From a systematic perspective John's

---

[9] Christopher A. Beeley, *Gregory of Nazianzus on the Trinity and the Knowledge of God: In Your Light We Shall See Light*, Oxford Studies in Historical Theology (New York: Oxford University Press, 2008), 231.

[10] Augustine, *The Trinity*, trans. Edmund Hill (New York: New City, 1991), books 9–15.

[11] "Thus divine life and grace stream down to us from the Father, through the Son, in the perfecting action of the Spirit, and either our praise or our blasphemies return again to the beneficent wellspring of deity, in the Spirit and through the Son." Gregory of Nyssa, *Adversus Macedonius*, 105–7; cited in David Bentley Hart, "The

vibrant portrait of worship before the divine throne has the double
advantage of presenting eternity as humanly accessible and of history as guided toward ultimate meaning. It uses particular styles in
genre and numeric symbolism to press these advantages toward triadic considerations.

A Threefold Genre

Such advantages are due to the threefold genre in which John's circular letter to the seven churches of the Roman province of Asia is
written. John begins his letter with the description of his work as an
ἀποκάλυψις, "revelation." While scholars debate the exact relations
between John's cross-genre combination of letter, apocalypse, and
prophecy, this work should doubtlessly be loosely classified alongside
the Jewish apocalyptic literature of the New Testament period.[12] The
widely cited definition of "apocalypse" from the Society of Biblical
Literature is that it is

> a genre of revelatory literature with a narrative framework,
> in which a revelation is mediated by an otherworldly being
> to a human recipient, disclosing a transcendent reality
> that is both temporal, insofar as it envisages eschatological
> salvation, and spatial insofar as it involves another,
> supernatural world.[13]

While we presume an incomparable perspective for eternity, we
note this definition's certainty regarding privileged access to transcendent reality, which has been mediated to human beings through the
gift of revelation.

According to literary genre Revelation is also an eschatological
prophecy, indicating that its recipients are allowed access not only to

---

Mirror of the Infinite: Gregory of Nyssa on the *Vestigia Trinitatis*," *Modern Theology*
18, no. 4 (2002): 555.

[12] Cf. Christopher Rowland, *The Open Heaven: A Study of Apocalyptic in Judaism
and Early Christianity* (New York: Crossroad, 1982).

[13] John J. Collins, "Introduction: Towards the Morphology of a Genre," in
Apocalypse: The Morphology of a Genre, ed. John J. Collins, Semeia 14 (Missoula, MT:
Scholars, 1979), 9.

eternity but also to the progress of history, including future history. The various methods through which to interpret the historical claims of the book of Revelation as an eschatological piece have been collated elsewhere.[14] Our goal is not to solve the eschatological debates surrounding especially the millennium of chapter 20, but it will be evident we hold to a futurist perspective, premillennialism in particular, and a holistic new creation that includes fulfilled promises to ethnic Israel,[15] even as we draw upon other perspectives taken by capable scholars. The eschatological nature of Revelation and the Trinity who grants revelation ensure that we pay attention to God, not only from the perspective of the ontological Trinity, and not only from the perspective of the economic Trinity but also from the perspective of what Brian Edgar has termed "the consummate Trinity."[16] We must not only show interest in who God is and how he works but also in where we will finally meet him in his fullness of glory.

The eschatological genre becomes important for theology proper when it is taken into account that the eternal God's relation to time is not only that of One who stands over the past in creation and the present in providence but of One "who is to come" (Rev 1:4). Jürgen Moltmann correctly draws theologians' attention to the fact that God is not presented abstractly as the One "who will be" (the future tense of εἶναι, "to be") but concretely as the One "who is to come" (the future tense of ἔρχεσθαι, "to come"). "God's future is not that he will be as he was and is, but that he is on the move and coming towards the world. . . . His eternity is not timeless simultaneity; it is

---

[14] Cf. Mounce, *The Book of Revelation*, 24–30; Leon Morris, *The Book of Revelation: An Introduction and Commentary*, rev. ed., Tyndale New Testament Commentaries (Grand Rapids, MI: Eerdmans, 1987), 17–20.

[15] Cf. Patterson, *Revelation*; George Eldon Ladd, *A Commentary on the Revelation of John* (Grand Rapids, MI: Eerdmans, 1972); John P. Newport, *The Lion and the Lamb: A Commentary on the Book of Revelation for Today* (Nashville, TN: Broadman, 1986); Craig A. Blaising and Darrell L. Bock, *Progressive Dispensationalism: An Up-to-Date Handbook of Contemporary Dispensational Thought* (Wheaton, IL: Victor, 1993).

[16] "A consideration of God 'at end of time'—the consummate Trinity—is a reflection on God who has embraced within God's own life the whole of creation, and is one that unites economic and immanent dimensions of Trinitarian thinking in the eschatological life of God." Brian Edgar, "The Consummate Trinity and Participation in the Life of God," *Evangelical Review of Theology* 38, no. 2 (2014): 120.

the power of his future over every historical time."[17] The eternally
transcendent God has been from before creation, continues to be
above creation, and will remain intimately involved in the progress
of creation and humanity. This means that divine transcendence may
never contradict divine immanence, even as transcendence grounds
immanence. Perhaps the Johannine (and Pauline) preference for a
Trinity originating in the Father buttresses the simultaneity of divine
transcendence in the Father and immanence in the Son and especially
in the Spirit.

If the genre of apocalyptic emphasizes the epistemological access
of humanity to eternity and the genre of eschatological prophecy
emphasizes the epistemological access of humanity to history from
beginning to end, the genre of the circular letter emphasizes both the
universality and the particularity of the message of John's Revelation.
Included within the book of Revelation are seven messages to seven
different churches, some of whom are prospering, others of whom
are slowly wasting, while yet others are under dire threat. The diversity of these seven churches in their various contexts, each of whom
receives the one revelation, demonstrates that there is a metanarrative, an eternal economy, that is relevant to every community's particular narrative. The genre of the circular letter, filled with different
messages for different contexts, yet presented as a universal story, is
in itself theologically profound. It demonstrates that one message can
be multivalent in its content and import for sundry human communities. From a Trinitarian perspective it also suggests that the God who
delivers such a multivalent message cannot himself be assumed to be
bound within a naïvely conceived monism. The God who constructs
a universal narrative for a diverse humanity, which is created in his
image and redeemed according to his perfect image through his perfecting Spirit, is not simply but complexly one.

---

[17] Jürgen Moltmann, *The Coming of God: Christian Eschatology*, trans. Margaret
Kohl (Minneapolis, MN: Fortress, 1996), 23–24. While we depart from Moltmann's
presentation of God as mutable, we affirm his emphasis on God as the sovereign
Lord who is coming to meet humanity in the ἔσχατον, molding history to receive his
glory. For a summation of Moltmann's eschatology, see Geiko Müller-Fahrenholtz,
The Kingdom and the Power: The Theology of Jürgen Moltmann (Minneapolis, MN:
Fortress, 2001), 200–218.

Triadic Patterns

Meaningful numeric patterns may be discovered throughout the book of Revelation. Paige Patterson summarizes the basic significance of this pervasive numeric symbolism: "one" refers to unity; "two," strength; "three," the divine; "four," the world; "five," humanity; "six," the sinister; "seven," completeness; and "twelve," organized religion.[18] Richard Bauckham goes further, showing how even the appearance of a term or action a certain number of times indicates a theological meaning for the author of the Apocalypse. For instance, the "seven spirits" are mentioned four times, which corresponds to the seven occurrences of the fourfold phrase that designates the peoples of the earth, both indicating the completeness of the Spirit's work in creation and the completion of humanity in creation. And when the world (four) and perfection (seven) are multiplied together, there are twenty-eight references to the Lamb, which indicates "the worldwide scope of the Lamb's complete victory."[19] While we would discourage constructing theology entirely from a symbolic numeric foundation, it may be instructive as a typological suggestion. In this suggestive sense the unity of "one" and the divinity of "three" may legitimately open the possibility of a theology of the Trinity in the Apocalypse.

Udo Schnelle cites a series of "triadic formulae" in the book of Revelation. Of his nine citations most have to do with a threefold ascription of past, present, and future existence and action to God (1:4, 8, 17–18; 4:8; 16:5; 21:6; 22:13), which may derive from the meanings of Yahweh as "I was," "I am," or "I will be" (Exod 3:14). One triadic formula concerns the life, death, and resurrection of Jesus Christ (Rev 2:8). Another, ensconced in a hymn, repeats the threefold Hebrew ascription of superlative holiness to God (Rev 4:8; cf. Isa 6:4). These triadic formulae do not teach the doctrine of the Trinity, but they do suggest John's awareness of a three-in-one paradigm regarding divine attributes and divine actions in how they "overlap and permeate each other."[20]

---

[18] Patterson, *Revelation*, 35.

[19] Bauckham, *The Theology of the Book of Revelation*, 109.

[20] Udo Schnelle, *Theology of the New Testament*, transl. M. Eugene Boring (Grand Rapids, MI: Baker, 2007), 752–53.

Reflecting a more personal triad at work in the book, Schnelle provides a rationale for choosing to list the theology of Revelation in the first three instances as "Theology," "Christology," and "Pneumatology." The structure of Revelation is "theocentric," the book's Christology yields a "theocentric profile," and the Spirit provides "internal coherence" to John's prophecy of God.[21] I. Howard Marshall similarly follows a tripersonal pattern of "God and his power," "Jesus Christ, Messiah and witness," and the Holy Spirit to start his theology of John. However, Marshall also believes that there is a great deal more angelology than pneumatology in the book.[22] Richard Bauckham has written the most substantial work devoted to the theology of the book of Revelation, and he intentionally follows a Trinitarian pattern, splitting Christology into the person and work of Christ. Bauckham finds explicit support for this in that the opening salutation is "deliberately trinitarian," though John does not conceive the doctrine in the fourth-century sense of the term.[23]

There are several passages in the book of Revelation in which the Trinity appears to be working together, while other passages suggest that God, the Lamb, and the Spirit exist together. These passages provide a sustainable basis for a hypostatic doctrine of the Trinity in the Revelation of John. While reviewing representative Trinitarian passages, we shall consider the placement of the Father, the Son, and the Holy Spirit in relation to one another, using the prosopological exegesis mentioned in chapter 1. Two of the most significant passages will require a deeper treatment of the Apocalypse's pneumatology, especially the reference to τὰ ἑπτὰ πνεύματα τοῦ θεοῦ, "the seven spirits of God" (Rev 1:4; 3:1; 4:5; 5:6). Modern scholarship is divided

---

[21] Ibid., 752, 755, 759.

[22] I. Howard Marshall, *New Testament Theology: Many Witnesses, One Gospel* (Downers Grove, IL: InterVarsity, 2004), 561–63.

[23] Bauckham, *The Theology of the Book of Revelation*, 23–24. Paul Rainbow combines the theology of John's Gospel, letters, and the book of Revelation into one theological whole. He also follows a Trinitarian pattern, but we have sublimated his contribution as we are seeking to allow Revelation's distinct genre to inform our analysis. Paul A. Rainbow, *Johannine Theology: The Gospel, the Epistles, and the Apocalypse* (Downers Grove, IL: InterVarsity, 2014).

on the identity of what H. B. Swete termed the *septiformus Spiritus*,[24] while there is general scholarly agreement on the distinctions between and relationship of God and the Lamb.

A Trinitarian Salutation?

While the apostolic epistles typically open with a salutation calling for grace and peace to come upon the recipients from God the Father and the Lord Jesus Christ,[25] the Revelation of John uniquely adopts a triadic salutation. The semicolon in the Holman Christian Standard Bible captures the threefold form of the Greek text well: "Grace and peace to you from the One who is, who was, and who is coming; from the seven spirits before His throne; and from Jesus Christ, the faithful witness, the firstborn from the dead and the ruler of the kings of the earth" (Rev 1:4b–5a HCSB). The first person who is regarded as the source of grace and peace is the eternal God, "the One who is, who was, and who is coming," who is also described as "Father" (1:6), is given a title of universal sovereignty, "Almighty" (1:8), and a set of titles to emphasize that he is the source and end of all things (1:8). The third person who is regarded as the source of grace and peace is Jesus Christ, who bears true testimony, who has risen from the dead, and who is sovereign ruler. It is with the second clause, which likewise is identified as the source of grace and peace, where difficulties arise.

The appearance of the *septimus Spiritus* between the Father and the Son provokes "surprise" because "it is strange to find them placed between the eternal God and Jesus Christ in this way."[26] Scholars have been divided over whether the seven spirits should be seen as a symbolic representation of the Holy Spirit, drawing particular attention to his work, or whether they refer to a class of angels.[27] Swete

---

[24] Henry Barclay Swete, *The Holy Spirit in the New Testament* (repr., Eugene, OR: Wipf & Stock, 1998), 275.

[25] Especially in the epistles of Paul and Peter but similarly in 2 John.

[26] F. F. Bruce, "The Spirit in the Apocalypse," in *Christ and the Spirit in the New Testament*, ed. Barnabas Lindars and Stephen S. Smalley (New York: Cambridge University Press, 1973), 333.

[27] "Are the seven spirits to be understood as equivalent to the Holy Spirit, the Apocalyptic writer having written *apo ton hepta pneumaton* for *apo hagiou pneumatos*

summarizes the attitude of many who argue for the identification of the seven spirits with the Holy Spirit from this passage. The positioning of the seven spirits between the Father and his Son would be "unsuitable even for the highest of created spirits in a salutation that is in fact a benediction."[28] Swete's argument against an angelic interpretation is persuasive. The Apocalypse draws a permanent divide between idolatrous worship and righteous worship. On the one hand, the worship of the beast results in eternal condemnation (13:8; cf. 14:9–12; 16:2; 19:19–20). On the other hand, the righteous may suffer in time for their worship and witness of the true God in Christ, but God will wipe away every tear and the Lamb will grant them eternal springs of living waters (7:9–17). `

Moreover, while John may be overcome with the weight of the disturbing visions he is granted, he is repeatedly warned against putting created angels in the place of God (19:10; 22:8). The angel before whom John inappropriately bowed afterward immediately exhorted John, "Don't do that! I am a fellow slave with you, your brothers the prophets, and those who keep the words of this book. Worship God." While the New Testament transformed Jewish monotheism to include the Son and the Holy Spirit with God the Father, it never compromised monotheism. Worship is reserved for God alone. Placing created angels between the Father and the Son, by including them within the source of grace and peace through a liturgical[29] benediction, would be tantamount to contradicting Christian monotheism. The better solution is to see the *septimus Spiritus* as a reference to the Holy Spirit, who is included by John within Christian worship, as he was similarly included in the liturgy of baptism by Matthew (Matt 28:19) and the liturgy of blessing by Paul (2 Cor 13:14).

---

for some reason connected with the peculiar purpose and style of his book? Or are the seven spirits to be understood as referring to created or imaginary spirits and not to the Spirit of God?" Swete, *The Holy Spirit in the New Testament*, 272–73.

[28] Ibid., 273.

[29] We are using "liturgical" and "liturgy" here in the New Testament Greek sense of public religious service. Cf. "Λειτουργέω," "Λειτουργικός," and "Λειτουργία," in *A Greek-English Lexicon of the New Testament and Other Early Christian Literature*, 2nd ed., ed. Walter Bauer, William F. Arndt, and F. Wilbur Gingrich (Chicago, IL: University of Chicago Press, 1979), 470–71.

A Vision of the Eternal Throne

Concluding an insightful response to Christopher Rowland's assertions about apocalyptic visions of God, Larry Hurtado said that Revelation chapters 4 and 5 should be construed as a unified and central vision for the book. The importance of the open door to heaven relayed in these chapters lies in its foundation for the remainder of the Apocalypse.[30] "Briefly put, Rev 4–5 gives the readers the heavenly realities, the sovereignty of God, the pure worship of his majesty, the relationship of the elect to God's throne, the triumph of the Lamb, that govern the rest of the scenes of the book."[31] Christopher Rowland agrees that chapter 4, which begins with John glimpsing an "open door" into eternity through which he was then ushered "in the Spirit," is the beginning of "the apocalypse proper" due to "the new dimension of John's experience."[32]

Patterson affirms chapters 4 and 5 should be considered together as "a transitional unit" that connects the churches of chapters 1–3 with their future in chapters 6–22 through the vision of "a magnificent heavenly throne room." Patterson, who emphasizes John's Old Testament proficiency, sets the scene well and touches upon its mysterious literary properties:

> The characters who participate in the massive throne room
> vision include the Lord himself, the Holy Spirit, four living
> beings, 24 elders, and innumerable hosts of angels. The
> adoration and worship of God is presented as exhibiting
> the most stirring emotional and volatile atmosphere
> imaginable. The reader can literally sense the excitement and

---

[30] Cf. G. K. Beale, *The Book of Revelation: A Commentary on the Greek Text*, The New International Greek Testament Commentary (Grand Rapids, MI: Eerdmans, 1999), 172–73.

[31] L. W. Hurtado, "Revelation 4–5 in the Light of Jewish Apocalyptic Analogies," *Journal for the Study of the New Testament* 25 (1985), 118.

[32] The apocalypse proper is distinguished from the prologue, salutation, and messages to the seven churches in Revelation 1–3 and the conclusion in 22:8–21. However, the seven messages are nonetheless integral to the structure and meaning of the book. Rowland, *The Open Heaven*, 414–15. While Rowland locates chapters 4 and 5 in the past, we prefer to see them as referring to eternal events that simultaneously transcend and incorporate temporal movement. Ibid., 420–21.

the grandeur of the scene unfolded by John, even though apparently John himself is groping for language adequate to describe what is presented to him by way of heavenly vision.[33]

In order to appreciate more fully the trinitarian significance of the throne room vision, we must consider those figures in chapters 4 and 5 who are most intimately related to the throne and the One who sits upon it.

The One Who Sits on the Throne

Occupying the center of the stage (the stage being universal reality) in this pivotal scene of the book of Revelation is a θρόνος, the throne of God. The ancient Near Eastern presentation of a throne is of a large piece of furniture upon which sits the king and/or deity. Only the rightful ruler may sit upon the throne, while his servants must bow in supplication or may stand in honor before him.[34] The occupant of the heavenly throne is here represented elusively and chastely, with never a precise description offered but only descriptions of the amazing effects he allows around himself. He is "the One who sits on the throne," a precise if limited designation used seven times in the Apocalypse (4:9; 5:1, 7, 13; 6:16; 7:15; 21:5).[35] The occupant of the divine throne is also described according to his attributes through the hymns of worship sung toward him by heavenly creatures. He is holy, eternal, and powerful in his character (4:8; 11). He is the Elector, Creator, and Sustainer of all things (4:11). He is worthy of glory, honor, and blessing (4:11; 5:13).

Some of the most important texts in the Old Testament, from the high Christological perspective of the New Testament, became so due to their portrayal of the Messiah in relation to God and his throne. In 2 Samuel 7:13, Nathan promised David his descendent would inherit

---

[33] Patterson, *Revelation*, 147.

[34] "Θρόνος," in *New International Dictionary of New Testament Theology and Exegesis*, ed. Moisés Silva, vol. 2 (Grand Rapids, MI: Zondervan, 2014), 468–69.

[35] Variations of the term are also used. Bauckham, *The Theology of the Book of Revelation*, 31.

an eternal throne. This promise "formed the primary link with the later hope of the everlasting throne of the Messiah."[36] Psalm 2:4–7 similarly presents Israel's king as being adopted by the enthroned Yahweh (cf. Rev 2:27; 11:15; 12:5, 10; 14:1; 16:16; 19:15). Psalm 110 portrays the Lord inviting a human priest and king, whom Yahweh names "my Lord," to join him in his eternal rule.[37] The most cited Old Testament text in the New Testament, Psalm 110, was used by Jesus Christ to suggest the solution to his own enigmatic participation in both humanity and deity (Mark 12:35–37). Jesus, moreover, said David was inspired to utter this prophecy while "in the Holy Spirit" (Mark 12:36).[38]

Isaiah 6:1–13 and 66:1–2 as well as Ezekiel 1:4–28 and 43:1–12 present heaven as Yahweh's throne and the temple as the access point for potential human interaction. The throne of the "Ancient of Days" in Daniel 7:9–10 was prophesied to be approached by "One like a Son of Man" in Daniel 7:13–14 (cf. Ezek 1:26–28; Dan 10:5–6), who would share in God's eternal sovereignty. Daniel's prophetic title, "Son of Man," was used by all of the Gospel writers to indicate Jesus's participation in divine rule,[39] and the title was likewise applied to Christ in Revelation 1:13 and 14:14. Other messianic titles in Revelation suggesting a share in divine rule include "the One who has the key of David" (3:7), "Lion of Judah" (5:5), "Root of David" (5:5; 22:16), and "Morning Star" (22:16; cf. Num 24:17). The explicit messianic title, "Christ," is used seven times, and "Lord" is ascribed to Jesus twenty-three times.[40] The throne of God would become the throne of the Messiah.

---

[36] Silva, "Θρόνος," 469.

[37] Derek Kidner, *Psalms 73–150: A Commentary on Books 3–5 of the Psalms,* Tyndale Old Testament Commentaries (Downers Grove, IL: InterVarsity, 1975), 391–96.

[38] Psalm 110 does not use the Hebrew term for "throne," but the royal context, invitation to ascend, accoutrements of a scepter and footstool, and acts of submission indicate its presence.

[39] Leon Morris, *New Testament Theology* (Grand Rapids, MI: Zondervan, 1986), 101–3, 124–25, 159–60, 234–25.

[40] Witherington, *Revelation*, 28; Bauckham, *The Theology of the Book of Revelation*, 66.

The Lamb

As important as messianic titles indicating rule are in Revelation, the
most important title for the Lord Jesus in the book is "the Lamb."
The context of cultic sacrifice for a lamb indicates its primary linguistic meaning of atonement (Exod 12:13; Isa 53:7), but the exact
positioning of the Lamb with regard to the divine throne and the
occupants of heaven stretches the meaning of the term far beyond
its original context. In order to convey the grandness of the vision,
"John has transformed this image to speak not only of a lamb slain
but of something else no early Jew who was not a Christian spoke
of—a lamb once slain but now glorified and powerful."[41] Next to
the throne's divine occupant, the Lamb is the central figure of this
pivotal vision.

Through careful comparison with the angelologies of noncanoni-
cal Jewish apocalyptic texts, Hurtado demonstrated that the angelic
hosts, though numerous, receive relatively minor attention. There
was no attempt by John to provide gradations among them. The four
living creatures, derived from Ezekiel 1, simply represent orders of
life. The twenty-four elders, who are unique in apocalyptic literature,
represent elect humanity. Hurtado appeals to elders being allowed
visions of God in the Old Testament (Exod 24:10; Isa 24:23) and the
widespread use of the term *elder* in the synagogues and churches. He
also notes that the elect of the seven churches were promised thrones
(3:21), white robes (3:5), and crowns (3:11), all of which graced the
elders in glory (4:4).[42]

Yet, while John was fascinated with the eternal throne and its
attendants, he was painfully reminiscent of the tangible vagaries of
Christian history. God held in his hand a scroll, but nobody was
found who was worthy to unseal it. The scroll represented the progress of universal history and the end of the churches. When John realized no attendant was worthy of approaching the divine throne to
reveal the eschatological progress of all things, he was overcome with
staggering sorrow (5:4). John was intensely aware of the historical

---

[41] Ibid., 30.
[42] Hurtado, "Revelation 4–5," 111–14.

nature of Christianity; in his Gospel and letters, he adamantly maintained the necessity of connecting heaven and earth through the
flesh of the Son of God. One of the elders, the representative of the
elect elders, admonished him to stop crying, for there is one who
has conquered who will open the scroll, "the Lion from the tribe of
Judah" (5:5). Turning and expecting a ruling king, the Messiah who
would ascend the eternal throne promised to David, John encountered instead a Lamb.

And the Lamb was "slaughtered" yet "standing." No wonder John was emotional. The multivalent delicacy of this moment,
which vividly captures the eternal-historical structure of Johannine
Christology, ought not go unnoticed. If the John of the Apocalypse
is also the John who leaned intimately on Jesus's breast (John 13:25;
21:20), and if he was the John who could never get over the fact that
he had touched with his hands and seen with his eyes the one who
derived his eternal being from the Father yet took on our human
flesh (1 John 1:1–2), then perhaps we may begin to understand the
spiritual and physical depth of this event. John knew human suffering, and John knew spiritual subtlety; and in the slaughtered Lamb
who yet stood in the place of eternal honor between the throne and
creation and in the place of suffering flesh between the elders, all of
reality reached its finale. The Lamb "slaughtered" is the Word (John
1:1; 1 John 1:1; Rev 19:13), who became flesh (John 1:14; 1 John
4:2; Rev 1:5) and died to propitiate the eternal Father through his
human blood (John 19:34; 1 John 2:2; 4:10; Rev 5:9). And this same
person, "like a slaughtered Lamb," was now "standing" as the resurrected One before him in eternity (John 20–21; 1 John 5:11; Rev
1:18), right there, between the throne and the living creatures and
between the elders.

With the gift of the Apocalypse, John was able to advance epistemologically further than he had ever seen before. The one who had
handled the incarnate God in the flesh had now entered in the Spirit
through an open door into eternity. While he knew beforehand that
the historical sacrifice of Christ had eternal consequences, here he
could see with his own eyes those eternal consequences. The Lamb
stands ἐν μέσῳ, "between," in two ways. The preposition of location, ἐν, joined with the adjective, μέσος, indicates one thing that

is situated with reference to at least two others. The theologically rich term μεσίτης, "mediator," derives from the adjective μέσος, "middle."[43] Again, in the heavenly throne room the Lamb is located in two ways. First, he personally stands between the divine throne and the living creatures, bridging the divide between eternality and deity on the one side and temporality and creatureliness on the other.

Second, he stands also ἐν μέσῳ, "between" or "in the midst" of the twenty-four elders. The verb "standing" is a perfect participle, indicating that he began this action and continues in it. The Lamb stands—incarnated from eternity into history, slain in history with eternal effect, and risen with history into eternity—in the midst of redeemed humanity. He stands in honor before the throne as Messianic human. He stands among humanity as the Lamb slaughtered and victorious, having conquered sin, Satan, and death through his death. While the Lamb stands in honor, having redeemed humanity, before the throne in chapter 5, he is said to stand "at the center" (ἀνὰ μέσον) of the throne in Revelation 7:17. From there he in turn shepherds the sheep—the risen Lamb is the divine Shepherd. Still later he shares the throne with the Father (22:1–3). The idea of standing "between" creation and God indicates that he has a proper place on the throne, such that he may grant to the saints a right to be seated on their own thrones under his dominion in Revelation 20:1–4.

As previously seen in the heavenly throne room, the twenty-four elders leave the grace of such rule behind through falling before the one great throne and casting their glorious crowns back toward the One who sits on it (4:10). It is also worth noting that the hymns of worship, worship being reserved exclusively for God, are directed to the Lamb in chapter 5. In ever increasing circles of praise, the Lamb alongside the Father is declared "worthy" to possess "power and riches and wisdom and strength," as well as "honor and glory and blessing" (5:9, 12). The divine attributes are ascribed in heaven equally "to the One seated on the throne, and to the Lamb, forever and ever" (5:13). The four living creatures respond for all of creation,

---

[43] "Μεσίτης," in *New International Dictionary of New Testament Theology and Exegesis*, 3:284.

"Amen," while the twenty-four elders respond for redeemed human-ity through falling down and worshipping (5:13).

Using his own "theological idiom," which avoids popular Greek and Hebrew abstractions, and working "as a literary artist rather than a philosopher,"[44] John has splendidly portrayed Christological mono-theism in its eternal and historical dimensions through the literary reconstruction of this moment. He has brought together the titles, the functioning, and the worship that indicate Jesus's equality with, yet subordination to, the Father in the one place where we can view them simultaneously, the eternal throne of God.[45]

The Seven Spirits

We must return to an issue raised above, the identification of the "seven spirits." Of the four appearances of the seven spirits, one is in the salutation (1:4), another occurs in the fifth message to the seven churches (3:1), and two are within the throne vision (4:5; 5:6). The seven spirits are not merely present but intimately related to the occupants of the divine throne. First, when the throne is revealed, the seven spirits are presented as occupying the personal space immedi-ately before the occupant of the throne. Second, the seven spirits gar-ner as much attention as the Lamb in the pivotal scene of Revelation 5:6, likewise being intimately related to the Lamb, yet more so.

The language of "seven spirits" has prompted some commen-tators to wonder whether John may be incorporating Hebrew angelology, which places seven angels before God's throne in a style reminiscent of Persian court practice.[46] They find two primary

---

[44] Bauckham, *The Theology of the Book of Revelation*, 62.

[45] "On the one hand, in Revelation Christ or the Lamb is clearly subordinate to God. . . . On the other hand, this clear primacy of theology in Revelation has its counterpart in the comprehensive participation of Jesus in the work of God, yielding a Christology with a theocentric profile." Schnelle, *Theology of the New Testament*, 755. "John stresses that Christ shares the names, the throne, the work, and the wor-ship of God." Witherington, *Revelation*, 30.

[46] Bruce, "The Spirit in the Apocalypse," 335. On angelology in Hebrew apoca-lyptic literature, including exalted angels, see Rowland, *The Open Heaven*, 88–113. On angelology in Persian apocalyptic literature, see John J. Collins, "Persian Apocalypses," in *Apocalypse*, 207–14.

arguments in favor of this interpretation. First, they cite such texts as
the apocryphal Tobit 12:15, where Raphael identifies himself as one
of the seven chief angels (cf. 1 Enoch 20:1–8). They conclude that
the seven spirits represent the closeness of creation with God through
the angels.[47] Second, there are references to groups of seven angels
within the book of Revelation. One group of seven angels stands
in the presence of God to blow the trumpets of judgment (8:2, 6).
Another group pours out the plagues in order to complete God's
wrath (15:1). Taking all the various evidence into account, Eduard
Schweizer arrives at a contradictory set of conclusions. The seven
spirits are, from a history of religions perspective, "simply the seven
archangels"; but from a theological perspective, they "represent the
Spirit of God in His fullness and completeness," "correspond to the
seven churches," "are simply the one Spirit of God," and "are simply
God's own action."[48]

In response, other commentators have raised three arguments
against equating John's seven spirits with the seven chief angels, and
we wish to add a fourth and a fifth argument.[49] First, while "spirit"
could be used of angels, as is often seen in the Dead Sea Scrolls,
John himself never makes that equation.[50] Second, while John may
be aware of apocalyptic literature within the biblical canon and
beyond, he feels free to use apocalyptic imagery in his own way. As
even Mounce recognizes, it would be a "strange intrusion" for John

---

[47] Among those deciding in favor of the identification of the seven spirits with seven chief angels are Witherington, *Revelation*, 75; Mounce, *The Book of Revelation*, 47–48.

[48] Eduard Schweizer et al., "Πνεῦμα, [etc.]," in *Theological Dictionary of the New Testament*, vol. 6, ed. Gerhard Friedrich, trans. Geoffrey W. Bromiley (Grand Rapids, MI: Eerdmans, 1968), 450–51.

[49] Among those deciding in favor of the identification of the seven spirits with the Holy Spirit are Bauckham, *The Theology of the Book of Revelation*, 110–15; Beale, *The Book of Revelation*, 189–90, 326–27, 355–56; Ladd, *A Commentary on the Revelation of John*, 24–25, 76, 88; Newport, *The Lion and the Lamb*, 129, 177; Patterson, *Revelation*, 58–60, 121, 153, 167; Stephen S. Smalley, *The Revelation of John: A Commentary on the Greek Text of the Apocalypse* (Downers Grove, IL: InterVarsity, 2005), 33–34. Anthony Thiselton also seems to conclude the seven spirits are "sovereign and omnipresent Spirit." Anthony C. Thiselton, *The Holy Spirit—in Biblical Teaching, Through the Centuries, and Today* (Grand Rapids, MI: Eerdmans, 2013), 156–60.

[50] Bauckham, *The Theology of the Book of Revelation*, 110.

to adopt Hebrew angelology.[51] Third, the book of Revelation presents the seven angels as fulfilling a role entirely different from that of the seven spirits.[52] Fourth, as Hurtado has underscored, John is not interested in pursuing any description of angelic hierarchies, in comparison with other apocalyptic literature.[53] Expanding upon Hurtado's discovery, we believe it would strike against John's focus on the divine throne to use the seven spirits as a description of chief angels in a hierarchy.

Finally, we offer a new argument, as far as we are aware, against interpreting the seven spirits as seven chief angels. Each of the distinct groups identified as having a place around the throne in chapters 4 and 5, including the four living creatures, the twenty-four elders, and the angelic hosts, are presented as worshipping God and the Lamb. However, in a blatant oversight, the seven spirits, if they were chief angels and therefore created beings, are never presented as joining in this universal worship. It would be an uncharacteristic imprecision on John's part to place the seven spirits at the throne twice but then exclude them from the other angelic groups worshipping God if the seven spirits were indeed angels. More likely John has not forgotten the seven spirits in his recounting of heavenly worship but subtly included them with God and the Lamb in the objective center of the worship directed toward the throne.

If the seven spirits are not created beings, chief angels in particular, then the most likely conclusion is that John is hereby referring to the Holy Spirit.[54] John does name "the Spirit" fourteen times in the Apocalypse. Of these fourteen instances, one regards the "Spirit of prophecy," which is related to the "testimony about Jesus" (19:10). According to the angel who refused John's worship, the blood of his prophetic brothers was shed because they refused to compromise their message on the lordship of the Lamb (19:10). Moreover, God is entitled, by the angel who refused worship, the "God of the spirits

---

[51] Mounce, *The Book of Revelation*, 47. Cf., Bauckham, *The Theology of the Book of Revelaton*, 9–12; Witherington, *Revelation*, 13–14.

[52] Bauckham, *The Book of Revelation*, 110.

[53] Hurtado, "Revelation 4–5," 107–8, 110–11.

[54] Patterson identifies five options for interpreting "seven spirits," three of which are easily dismissed and the two most important treated here. Patterson, *Revelation*, 58–59.

of the prophets." Similarly, the prophets are those who testify about Jesus (22:6). John's establishment of a parallel between the "Spirit of prophecy" and the "spirits of the prophets," through the angel who refused worship and through the testimony about Jesus, indicates a correlation between the person of the one Spirit and his active manifold witness through the prophets. The correlation is strengthened when the bride, the church, speaks after and in response to the speech of the Holy Spirit (22:17).

The primary work seems to be the promulgation of testimony regarding the Lamb. In two more of the fourteen references to "the Spirit," he works to emphasize the testimony about Jesus. Interestingly, in doing so he speaks on his own account. These two personal speech-acts clearly demonstrate that the Spirit possesses a hypostatic reality (14:13; 22:17). It is also indicative of his relation to the Lamb that he directs an exhortation toward the Lamb. Like the Father "who is to come" (1:4), the Lamb says he is "coming" (22:12), and the Spirit responds that he should "come" (22:17). This invitation is then turned in a triadic form toward the church and, intermediately, the world. In four more of the fourteen references to the Spirit, John refers to the agency of the Spirit in bringing the vision of God. John's person being moved "in the Spirit" concurrently forms the literary structure of the book and demonstrates that God inspired his book (1:10; 4:2; 17:3; 21:10).[55]

The seven remaining references to "the Spirit" appear at the end of the messages to the seven churches. While the Lord Jesus begins each message, the Spirit ends each message (2:7; 2:11; 2:17; 2:29; 3:6; 3:13; 3:22). The Son and the Holy Spirit are placed together to frame and deliver the messages of God to the churches. In these seven messages, as in the seven other references to "the Spirit," the emphasis is on the revelatory ministry of the Holy Spirit. This survey of the appearance of "the Spirit" in Revelation seems to indicate that John is using numeric symbolism to refer to the universal action of the Holy Spirit. The "seven spirits" indicates the multiple inspirations

---

[55] John is reflecting the influence of Ezekiel in such references to being "in the Spirit." Cf. Ezek 3:12, 14. Bauckham, *The Theology of the Book of Revelation*, 115–16.

by "the Spirit" of the prophet John, the spirits of the prophets, and the messages for the churches, and ultimately the world.[56]

But why "seven" spirits to represent the Holy Spirit? An Old Testament precedent has been suggested in the early Christian tradition's reading of the Septuagint's version of Isaiah 11:2, where seven gifts of the Spirit were said to come upon the Messiah.[57] A more likely candidate is found in Zechariah's prophetic vision of the sevenfold lampstand. When Zechariah saw seven lamps connected to one golden lampstand, along with two olive trees, he asked what it meant (Zech 4:2–5). The Lord responded through his angel with this Word: "Not by strength or by might, but by my Spirit, says the Lord of Hosts" (4:6). In Zechariah's apocalyptic vision, the seven lamps were clearly connected to one lampstand with the one Spirit of God providing the power for them all. The sevenfold working of the one God was given further emphasis by a subsequent explanation, "These seven eyes of the Lord, which scan throughout the whole earth" (4:10). The movement of the one God in a sevenfold direction to encompass the entire earth occurs through his powerful Spirit. The pervasive impact of the one Spirit of God's sovereign work upon the earth was symbolized in Zechariah with "seven lamps" and "seven eyes." The "seven" represented a universal movement by the one God through his Spirit.

John seems to have picked up this symbolism in his presentation of the "seven spirits." Recognizing the personal intimacy of the Spirit with God in Zechariah, where God speaks of "my Spirit" (Zech 4:6), John feels free to speak of "the seven spirits before his throne" (Rev 1:4). Drawing upon the Lord's disclosure that the "seven stars" are the "seven lampstands," who are the seven messengers to the churches (Rev 1:19–20), John can also loosely correlate the working of the "seven spirits" with the "seven stars" (3:1). F. F. Bruce notes that the καί connecting the seven spirits with the seven stars is not "epexegetic," explaining what the spirits are, but "copulative," listing two separate groups together.[58] The difference between

---

[56] "While there is but one Holy Spirit, he does not invest himself incrementally in the churches but is always available simultaneously, in his fullness, to all seven congregations." Patterson, *Revelation*, 59.

[57] Bruce, "The Spirit in the Apocalypse," 334; Smalley, *The Revelation of John*, 33.

[58] Bruce, "The Spirit of the Apocalypse," 335.

seven stars and the seven spirits (3:1), like the difference between the "spirits of the prophets" and the "Spirit of prophecy" (19:10; 22:6), is thereby maintained, even as it is recognized that the Holy Spirit works through the church's prophetic witness (22:17).

With this background the theological placement of the seven spirits in the throne room vision becomes intelligible. We are using *theological* now in its proper sense. The location and movement of the seven spirits before and from the throne indicate the Holy Spirit's participation in divine privilege. We base this claim on three aspects of the divine throne vision. First, the "seven spirits" are identified with God through τοῦ θεοῦ, which modifies πνεύματα in both Revelation 4:5 and 5:6. Τοῦ θεοῦ should be taken as a genitive of relation or genitive of source—these are the spirits "of God." The choice of a genitive of source is strengthened by the placement of the seven torches directly before the throne in Revelation 4:5 and their subsequent movement outward from the throne in Revelation 5:6.

Second, the descriptions applied to the seven spirits indicate divine attributes. Like the seven lamps of Zechariah 4, the seven torches placed directly before the throne in Revelation 4:5 represent the unlimited power of God's Spirit. Like the seven eyes of Zechariah 4:12, the seven eyes of the Lamb in Revelation 5:6 represent the unlimited insight of God's Spirit. The seven spirits are, moreover, "sent into all the earth." Divine omnipotence, divine omniscience, and divine omnipresence are ascribed to the seven spirits who work to bring the revelation of God about Jesus to the entire world through the churches. The "seven torches" and "seven horns" represent his power; the "seven eyes" represent his knowledge; the movement from the throne into the whole earth represents his presence. In every way the seven spirits are an extension of the divine attributes.

The third aspect indicating the participation of the seven spirits in divine privilege concerns the placement of the spirits. Not only are the seven spirits *before* the throne, causing "flashes of lightning and rumblings of thunder" to come "*from* the throne" (Rev 4:5), but the seven spirits are placed *within* the Lamb who is *in the midst* of the throne. The seven spirits are identified with both "the seven horns and seven eyes" that the Lamb possesses as part of his body (5:6). The pictorial relationship between the Lamb and the Spirit is not one of ontological distance but of personal presence. The Lamb is so close to the Father that he shares the throne with the Father, receiving the worship of creation; and the Spirit is so close to the Lamb that he shares in the body of the Lamb upon the throne. Such local intimacy on the exclusive heavenly throne and such local intimacy in the body of the Lamb suggest a unique ontological set of eternal relations between the three.

Eternal Relations

John's throne-room vision, which is so central to the book of Revelation, is focused on the throne. The throne room brings together the central event of time, the cross, and the worship of eternity. The throne is centered on the eternal God, the Lamb, and the sevenfold Spirit. The throne-room vision provides a profound portrait of the internal relations between the three on the one eternal throne, and this vision reaches its pivotal occasion in Revelation 5:6. Regarding the relations of the three, there is simultaneity of τάξις, order, and περιχώρησις, mutuality, in John's magnificent portrait of this eternal moment.

Τάξις. There is eternal subordination in John's portrayal of the three. God receives upon his throne the victorious Lamb whom he sent to be a sacrifice. And the Spirit is sent from the throne into all of creation through the Lamb in order to reveal God and the Lamb. There is no hint here that the subordination of the Lamb and the Spirit is merely historical or merely functional. This is an eternal setting, which includes time in its purview but is not necessarily limited to one point in time. The present tenses of the verbs "possesses" (ἔχων) and "are" (εἶναι) focused on divine relations, and the perfect active tenses of the verbs "standing" (ἑστηκὸς) and "sending" (ἀπεσταλμένοι) focused on divine action in Revelation 5:6, alongside the repetitive worship offered throughout the vision toward the occupants of the throne, suggest a continual state of relations.

Περιχώρησις. There is eternal equality in John's portrayal of the three, too. Mutual indwelling indicates equality when located in the context of the eternal being of God. We have already seen that placement upon the throne, reception of worship, and the ascription of divine attributes speak to the deity of each person. Again, the One who sits on the throne is the origin of all power; the Lamb is worthy to receive all power; and the seven spirits exercise all power. Again, the Spirit is the Spirit "of God," and the Lamb "possesses" the Spirit of God as his own eyes and horns. And again, the Lamb receives the worship that is due only to the One who sits upon the throne; and because of his intimate location within the Lamb, we may conclude that the Spirit also receives that worship.

The Apocalyptic Economy of Conquest

After witnessing the dynamic state of reality in the foundational vision of the throne room, a state of reality that is centered upon the occupants of the divine throne, the prophet John is granted further insight into what God has done, is doing, and will do with his rebellious creation. God gives John in the Spirit, through the mediation of angels, an all-encompassing vision of time that includes the creation, the cross, and especially the consummation. The vision has an all-encompassing spatial dimension, too, for it explicitly includes heaven and earth and all the inhabitants of both spheres of created reality. Angels, humans, and other creatures—all have their direct and indirect roles. But standing above and engaging all of these created beings is God, the Lamb, and the Spirit.

The Apocalypse's economy shares a basic form with the Pauline and Johannine economies already delineated. As with the Gospel of John and the Pauline epistles of Ephesians and 2 Corinthians, the book of Revelation presents an eternal plan hidden from the denizens of earth yet revealed through grace. Likewise, the apocalyptic economy grants Jesus and the Spirit divine roles alongside the Father at the beginning, the center, and the end of time. What the Apocalypse emphasizes, more than Paul and the Gospel of John, is the consummation of the economy, a consummation concluded through conquest. Richard Bauckham refers to God's eschatological conquering (νῖκος) of rebellious creation as "Revelation's key concept."[59] According to

---

[59] Bauckham, *The Theology of the Book of Revelation*, 69, 124.

Robert Mounce, "The Apocalypse is a broad canvas upon which the Seer paints without restrictions the ultimate triumph of God over evil."[60]

Commentators seem to agree that divine conquest is the central purpose of the Apocalypse's economy. Where they register profound disagreement is over exactly how the book's progress toward that ultimate triumph at the end of all things is to be interpreted as unfolding. Presuming the divine conquest over evil, Paige Patterson focuses on the temporal unfolding through Revelation 1:19, which he refers to as "the key to the book."[61] Jesus instructs John a second time to write what he sees but now with a programmatic sense of historic advancement: "Write what you have seen, what is, and what will take place after this." Where the literary divisions between past, present, and future aspects occur within the apocalyptic economy, and whether the future aspects unfold in strict chronological order or with a manner of reverberation—these are the issues that divide theological exegetes. While our own understanding of the book's historical progress favors a premillennial ordering with some intensifying repetition beforehand, and a holistic new creation that includes the fulfilled promises to Israel and the inclusion of the nations, we leave those debates for another venue and focus on the Trinity's role in the progress of divine conquest.

The conquest is anchored in the eternal throne and extends from the beginning of time to its end. While God is transcendent above the history of creation, he is intimately involved with it at every point, freely allowing his creatures the exercise of their freedom while guiding them unfailingly to their justly defined ends. Temporal progress is anchored in eternity through God's roles as Creator and Consummator, as relayed in his self-descriptive titles of "Alpha and Omega" and "Beginning and End" (1:8; 21:6). These are sovereign and transcendent titles in which the Lord Jesus eventually joins the Father (22:13), while hints that he would do so are found in the earlier ascription of "First and Last" (cf. 1:8, 17; 21:6; 22:13) and in his self-description as "the Originator of God's

---

[60] Mounce, *The Book of Revelation*, 32.
[61] Patterson, *Revelation*, 32.

creation" (3:14).[62] Temporal history begins in the eternal will of
the Father, and it continues to be guided by the ever-transcendent
Father, who is eternal, almighty, and invisible. The indefinite vis-
ibility of God the Father in the throne-room scene aids the reader
in perceiving his otherness, majesty, and transcendence, a transcendence he never surrenders. Even in his final coming to dwell
with creation, the Father's otherness is never compromised, for his
presence allows only the holy (22:3–5, 9). While the Father demonstrates the Trinity's transcendence, the Lamb and the Spirit demonstrate the Trinity's immanence in history.

God the Trinity's Work of Redemption

If history begins with the Father (and the Son shares with him in
such), history is nevertheless centered in the work of the Lamb.
From the beginning of the book, the first work of Jesus Christ that
is stressed is his death and resurrection (1:5, 7; cf. 1:18; 2:8). Within
the primary vision, that of the eternal throne, it is repeatedly stressed
by the worshippers that his redemption of people through his slaugh-
ter and blood prompts their inclusion of him in the worship of God
(5:9, 12–13). Thenceforward, the common title of "the Lamb" and
mention of his atonement continually remind the reader that Christ's
cross is central to human redemption. The Son conquers first and
foremost through his blood,[63] and believers are allowed to share in
his conquest through his blood and the testimony regarding his cross
and resurrection (12:11). Because Christ has died and risen, they can

---

[62] For a discourse and outline of how these three all-encompassing titles are
increasingly ascribed to both the Father and his Son, see Witherington, *Revelation*,
28–29; Bauckham, *The Theology of the Book of Revelation*, 54–58. For a unique
and convincing thesis that these titles should transform eschatology from a things-
oriented doctrine into a God-oriented one, see Adrio König, *The Eclipse of Christ
in Eschatology: Toward a Christ-Centered Approach* (Grand Rapids, MI: Eerdmans,
1989).

[63] Oscar Cullmann describes the first coming of Christ as providing the pivotal
victory, "D-Day," while his second coming results in the final conquest, "V-Day."
Oscar Cullmann, *Christ and Time: The Primitive Christian Conception of Time and
History*, trans. Floyd V. Filson (Philadelphia, PA: Westminster, 1950), 87.

remain faithful to his truth and be assured of their own resurrection through participation in him (7:14–17; 19:6–8; 20:4–6).

However, while the atoning work of Christ is completed on the cross, and the conquest of evil is definitely assured (the dragon knows his time is short, 12:12), there is still conquest to be accomplished. The continuing conquest of Christ occurs heart by heart and nation by nation, from ethnic Israel to the ends of the world. Through the witness of the prophets, exemplified in the coming ministry of the two witnesses, humanity is presented with one of two options: faith or destruction. In the letters to the seven churches, the truth-telling ministry of Jesus Christ was stressed and his people were called to join him in the ministry of the Word without hint of compromise. The churches of Ephesus, Pergamum, and Philadelphia are especially connected to the truth-telling ministry of Christ as the Word of God (2:1, 12; 3:7; 19:13, 15), and they are comforted and exhorted to stay true to proclaiming the word even to the point of death (2:2–5, 13; 3:8). A pivotal text showing that Christian conquest occurs through faith in Christ, which is mediated through faithful witness to Christ, is Revelation 12:11: "They conquered him [the dragon] by the blood of the Lamb and by the word of their testimony, for they did not love their lives in the face of death." We have already noted that the Spirit of prophecy empowers the spirits of the prophets to bear witness, and the people of God join the Spirit in issuing an invitation to the world to come to the One who is coming.

These scattered references make clear that God's eschatological conquest of the world through Christian ministry is a Trinitarian activity. A focal text wherein the Spirit of God joins the Father and the Son in the divine conduction of Christian ministry through proclamation is located in Revelation 11. The Spirit's resurrection of the two witnesses in verse 11, through the grant of "the spirit of life" (a recapitulation of the Spirit's origin of life in Gen 2:7), is quickly succeeded with the blowing of the final trumpet. It is announced at that time, in a first public saying, that the Son overcomes the kingdom of the world with his eternal reign (11:15). In a second public saying, this time voiced by the twenty-four elders, God begins this reign in two ways: first, through rewarding the saints, the prophets, and believers in his name; and second, through destroying those who are destroying his earth (11:18). To confirm this Triune movement of conquest through witness and judgment, the Spirit manifests the divine glory, as earlier, through the trembling of creation (11:19; cf. 4:5).

God the Trinity's Work of Judgment

In chapters 12 and 13, Satan, the primary opponent of divine rule, tries to emulate the powerful work of God the Trinity with his own satanic trinity. In an allusion to the protoevangelium of Genesis 3:15 having been fulfilled in Christ, the dragon pursued the child of the woman (Rev 12:5–6). War broke out in heaven and "the ancient serpent, who is called the Devil and Satan" is cast down with his deception (12:9). Although the woman, the eschatological church, is persecuted, the church conquers through the blood of the Lamb and testimony to the Word (12:12). The furious dragon continues to wage war against those who obey God's commands and testify to Jesus (12:17). The dragon, like an evil father, will send a beast out of the sea to which he gives authority. The beast boasts of himself and blasphemes God and deceives the wicked into worshipping him (13:8). Emulating the ministry of the Spirit, a second beast, also identified with prophecy, comes from the earth sounding "like a dragon" (13:11). He will exercise the first beast's power, perform signs, and compel false worship (13:12–13). In a perverse revision of the cross and resurrection of Christ, the second beast will give a "spirit" to enable an image of the first beast, now wounded, to speak and prompt false worship (13:12, 15).

This battle between the true Trinity and the false trinity, waged over the world through the means of violence as exercised by the wicked and through the means of testimony as exercised by the righteous, reaches a climax in the twofold judgment of the Trinity in Revelation 14. In the proclamation of the three angels, men are called upon to fear God (14:7). On the one side, the Father will send the full anger of his wrath to be accomplished against the wicked who worship the beast and his image, and the Son will carry it out (14:9–10). On the other side, the saints through perseverance will keep the Father's commands and continue their faith in the Son (14:12), while the Spirit assures them they shall receive their rest (14:13). The twofold end is reached as "One like the Son of Man" reaps the harvest of the righteous, ostensibly through the witness of the church (14:14–16), and an angel gathers the grapes of the earth to press the wicked in God's wrath (14:18–19).[64]

God the Trinity's Work of Renewal

On three occasions in the final chapters of Revelation, the work of renewing creation is clearly identified with all three members of the divine triad. The personal dimensions of the eschatological Trinity become evident through both correlation and individuality. God, the Lamb, and the Spirit exercise a common ministry and occupy a common place in worship, even as each exercises personal prerogative.

In the first instance, under consideration is the truthfulness of the invitation extended to the people of God to join in the marriage feast of the Lamb. The final conquest of the wicked and the certain blessing of the saints are assured with a threefold witness. The angel proclaims, "The words of God are true" (19:9). Then, while reminding the apostle of the irrevocable separation that exists between God and creation, the angel remarks that "the testimony about Jesus" prompts true worship of God. The "testimony about Jesus," moreover, "is the Spirit of prophecy" (19:10; my capitalization of HCSB). Access to divine blessing is available through a proper placement of worship vis-à-vis God, Jesus, and the Spirit over against creation.

In the second instance, the coming of the three is indicated in the fulfillment of the promise that God would dwell with humanity in the renewed creation. Subsequent to the casting of Satan, death, Hades, and the wicked into the eternal lake of fire, the redeemed are ushered into intimate life with God, the Lamb, and the Spirit. "Look, God's dwelling is with humanity, and He will live with them and be their God." The Father's unique role in this eternal relationship of intimacy is not the expected destruction of the rebellious but

---

[64] Bauckham has identified this twofold nature of divine judgment through a careful reconstruction of John's use of Old Testament allusions. Bauckham, *The Theology of the Book of Revelation*, 94–104.

the personal wiping away of every tear. Death, grief, crying, and pain will cease (21:3–4); the fullness of the sevenfold blessing will at last take their place (1:3; 14:13; 16:15; 19:9; 20:6; 22:7; 22:14). The people of God will be declared the "bride" of the Lamb, indicating an intimacy that human marriage can only imitate. This intimacy was made possible through the incarnation, cross, and resurrection of Jesus Christ, and sealed in the work of the Holy Spirit through faith; but it will be realized fully in the new creation that begins with the marriage supper of the Lamb (19:6–8; 21:9; 22:17).

The Holy Spirit's role in the blessed life is allusively established through his presence in the continual bestowal of life. In 22:1–3, the throne of God and the Lamb are permanently sited in the new Jerusalem that has descended to the new earth. The throne is, however, not the highlight of this scene. Rather, "the river of living water" is the focus, for it is out of the river that flows into the city from the throne that blessed life comes to the redeemed. As the seven spirits flow from the throne into creation (4:5; 5:6), so the river flows from the throne into renewed creation.[65] In the Gospel of John, the "rivers of living water" that will "flow" within the believer are thrice explicitly identified with "the Spirit" (John 7:37–39; cf. 4:10–11, 14).[66] In Revelation 21:22–24, the Apocalypse may also be drawing upon the biblical tradition of correlating the Spirit with the illumination (Prov 20:27; Dan 5:11, 14; cf. Eph 5:9; Heb 6:4) and glory (Ezek 3:12; 43:5; Dan 5:20; cf. Acts 7:55; 2 Cor 3:18; 1 Pet 4:14) witnessed by the joyous inhabitants of heaven.

Through the intimate presence of God, the Lamb, and the Spirit, the eschatological work of God is one of immanent blessing toward redeemed humanity. The three engage in the one divine work of blessing but through performing distinct actions: God removes sorrow,

---

[65] In the final vision of Ezekiel, whom John alluded to repeatedly, there is a renewing river of life flowing from the temple (Ezek 47:1–12; cf. Joel 3:18; Zech 14:8). The Spirit is earlier identified in Ezekiel as the bearer of renewed life (Ezek 36:27; 37:1–14). The Old Testament promises to Israel are kept in the Apocalypse, and this includes the coming of God to the temple in the new Jerusalem and the presence of the life-giving Spirit.

[66] Beale identifies the river with the Holy Spirit but then dissolves the river's physical reality in the eschaton. G. K. Beale, *A New Testament Biblical Theology: The Unfolding of the Old Testament in the New* (Grand Rapids, MI: Baker, 2011), 135.

the Lamb joins the bride in marriage, and the Spirit provides life. The common yet distinct activities of the eternal God are also seen in the distinct speeches of the three persons in the renewed creation. According to Robert Spaemann, one of the most important indicators of personhood is found in the capacity for self-objectification and self-relativization demonstrated in speech.[67] The three different speeches of the eternal Father, the slain and resurrected Lamb, and the Spirit of prophecy therefore indicate the personhood of each.

In the new creation the One seated on the throne speaks to creation directly. He does not speak mediately through an angel, nor does he speak instrumentally if more intimately through his Word. God declares he is remaking creation and that he is the source and end of all. God also promises that he will adopt the victor as a son and grant the victor a river of life, while he reserves eternal judgment for the wicked (21:5–8).[68] The Lamb also speaks regarding the new creation. He warns the reader that he is coming quickly (22:7, 12) and claims that he too is the source and end of life, incorporating the terms used of the Father (22:13). He provides the final blessing to the reader, who should wash his robes (through faith in his blood; 7:14; 19:13), and issues his own warning about the exclusion of the wicked (22:14–15). Finally, as exposited above, the Spirit also speaks to Jesus and the church, issuing an invitation to both to come. God, Jesus, and the Spirit speak independently yet coordinately—blessing or condemnation await those who read God the Trinity's invitations.

Economic Relations

Just as the eternal throne room shed light on the internal relations of the Trinity, so the coming of God in Christ as the Ὠ(μεγα), Ἔσχατος, and Τέλος (cf. Rev 1:8, 17; 21:6; 22:13) of history may illuminate for us the economic relations of the Trinity. God the Trinity's apocalyptic ministry of redemption, judgment, and renewal indicates the

---

[67] Robert Spaemann, *Persons: The Difference Between 'Someone' and 'Something,'* trans. Oliver O'Donovan, Oxford Studies in Theological Ethics (New York: Oxford University Press, 2007), 15.

[68] The Father speaks on his own twice in the book, here and in the prologue (1:8).

indivisible operations of all three persons of the Trinity. Each of the divine persons is explicitly involved in each of these divine workings. Yet in an indication that the patristic doctrine of appropriation or *proper operations* also has a basis in the text, we have seen that each person leads in various activities. This is exemplified for instance in the renewing work of the Trinity: the Father may be properly described through his blessing of the righteous as Benefactor; the Lamb as the one who enables the cleansing of the saints may be properly described as Redeemer; and the Spirit through his call to the church and the world may be properly entitled the Inviter.

We prefer to use the language of "proper operations," rather than "appropriated operations." This is because there is no idea in the Apocalypse that the three members of the Trinity entered a covenant with one another to appropriate certain works to certain persons. The question of appropriations, as we saw in the last chapter, has been centered on the issue of whether any person could have been appropriated the work of incarnation, death, and resurrection, or whether that work is proper to the Son. The book of Revelation does not evidence any covenantal act of appropriation. Rather, the primary title for the second member of the eternal Trinity is consistent from the eternal throne room to the end when all has been reconciled with God. The eternal description of the Lord Jesus, who is otherwise given various messianic titles and various transcendent titles, is that of "the Lamb." When eternity joins with history in the new Jerusalem, the throne is identified with the sacrificial victim who has been raised. The so-called second person of the Trinity is not merely functionally but eternally "the Lamb." It is his eternal property to be the one who would become human, be crucified, arise from death, ascend to the Father, and return as conqueror. He reigns eternally because he is the one who triumphed through his cross—Jesus is eternally "the Lamb" (cf. Heb 9:26; 1 Pet 1:20; Rev 13:8). As with the Father and the Spirit, Christ's work reveals Christ's person.

EPILOGUE

To this point each biblical text has been allowed to craft our theological presentation as we have sought to allow the text to speak
according to its literary movement within the author's historical context and purpose, cognizant of the canon. In chapter 1, we discovered that Jesus in the Gospel of Matthew presented God through the
premiere act of Christian worship as possessing a threefold singular
name. In chapter 3, we heard from Moses,[1] who presented a portrait
of God the Lord as worthy of singular devotion. In chapters 2 and 7,
we reviewed two of the apostle Paul's epistolary portraits regarding
the unitive work of God as a threefold movement, the Corinthian
benediction serving as a miniature, and the Ephesian hymn as a metaphysical frieze. In chapters 4–6, through a sequence of illuminative
impressions, the Gospel of John presented the divine being of God
as a differentiated triadic unity. And in chapter 8, we explored the
book of Revelation, which wove the Trinity into a vibrant apocalyptic
and eschatological tapestry. Only after the arduous work of critical
exegesis may one attempt, with some degree of confidence, to draw
general theological conclusions. Upon these close textual studies,
chastened with the need to be brief, the reader is offered ten theses
as a group appraisal of the eight portraits. These ten theses include

---

[1] Or the editors of Moses, if one accepts Wellhausen's speculative thesis. Duane
L. Christensen summarizes the critical literature. Christensen, *Deuteronomy 1–11*,
Word Biblical Commentary (Dallas, TX: Word, 1991), xlix–li.

exegetical reflections on Trinitarian reality, Trinitarian hermeneutics, and Trinitarian economy.

Trinitarian Reality

1. Unique Devotion to God. The Shema as the fundamental confession of the Hebrew religion must also be recognized as fundamental for Christianity due to the Lord's reception and promotion of that important text. There is only one God; and he is radically differentiated from his creation, which includes everything but God. The Lord God requires human beings to be singularly and uniquely devoted to him in their internal and external worship. However, this Christian "monotheism" resists other forms of monotheism. Within the New Testament understanding, monotheism includes the Lord Jesus Christ along with God the Father as the object of Christian devotion, and it includes the Holy Spirit of God, too. Christian or Trinitarian monotheism affirms that the simplicity of God encloses the Son and the Holy Spirit with the Father.

2. The Threefold Relations of God. The biblical canon reveals that within the simple unity of God, who remains the unique object of human worship, there is a threefold set of relations. This set of relations is shaped in a threefold manner through both identity and distinctions. The identity of the Father with his Son, and of the Father and the Son with the Holy Spirit, is manifested in the dominical and apostolic language of the common possession *inter alia* of "name," "mine," "light," "Lord," "life," "self," and "God." The simple identity of the three is also manifested through the common operations of the three and through the inclusion of the three in universal worship.

The distinctions between the Father and the Son and between the Holy Spirit and the Father and the Son are revealed through the personal dimensions of their diverse speeches, actions, and relations, as expressed through the biblical writers' own syntax with various nouns, verbs, and prepositions. Prosopological exegesis demonstrates that the distinctions between the three find their proper expression in the names of "Father," "Son," and "Holy Spirit." These proper names find corollary expression in the eternal derivations of the Son from the Father in generation and of the Holy Spirit from the Father through the Son in procession. The language of "substance" and "persons" when properly conceived is useful in speaking of the identity and distinctions within God.

3. *Eternal Περιχώρησις and Indivisible Operations.* The biblical descriptions of the eternal, intimate, and loving relations between God the Father, his Son, and the Holy Spirit were explored with the aid of the biblical exegesis performed by the great pastors of the fourth and fifth centuries. Athanasius, the Cappadocians, and Cyril of Alexandria in the East, and Augustine in the West discerned the eternal equality and differentiation of the three persons. Their exegesis of such texts as Matthew's Great Commission, the Corinthian benediction, and the Johannine portraits of the divine relations highlighted the eternal unity and threeness of God. The patristic contributions were condensed in dogmatic references to the shared substance of the three persons and in the doctrinal concept of περιχώρησις,[2] also known as circumincession, indwelling, or mutuality.

Even as God is eternally three persons who are one in identity, so the economy of God as three persons above and within history is one. The Augustinian tradition coined the language of "indivisible operations" to express Scripture's involvement of each of the three in the unified working of God. The Father, the Son, and the Holy Spirit are respectively involved in the great divine works of creation, redemption, and consummation. In general the Father originates the divine act, the Son performs the central actions, and the Holy Spirit perfects the divine activity.

4. *Eternal Τάξις and Proper Operations.* As the early church fathers engaged in theological exegesis, especially of the Gospel of John, they came to the conclusion that there is a proper ordering within the eternal Trinity. This τάξις for the orthodox does not entail any loss

---

[2] According to John of Damascus, the three persons "are made one not so as to commingle, but so as to cleave to each other, and they have their being in each other (*perichoresin*) without any coalescence or commingling." John of Damascus, *Exposition of the Orthodox Faith*, trans. S. D. F. Salmond, in *Nicene and Post-Nicene Fathers*, 2nd Series, vol. 9, ed. Philip Schaff and Henry Wace (repr., Peabody, MA: Hendrickson, 1994), 11.

of equality, but it does aid in maintaining awareness of the relations. The ordering of the eternal Trinity may be perceived as having its origin in the Father, the monarch. The Son is eternally generated from the being of the Father. The Holy Spirit eternally proceeds from the Father, according to the Eastern Christian tradition, and from the Father and the Son, according to the Western tradition. Some theologians in both the East and the West, including this author, prefer to speak of the procession of the Holy Spirit as occurring from the Father through the Son.

The eternal ordering of the Trinity is manifested in the economic ordering of the Trinity. The Son comes from the Father and is sent by the Father; the Son also returns to the Father. The Holy Spirit proceeds from the Father and is sent by the Father and the Son. The works of the three persons are indivisible, but particular works are ascribed to the distinct persons as an extension of their proper relations. Among other works the Father is primarily affiliated with election, blessing, and creation; the Son is involved in all the divine works but exclusively became human, died, and arose from death; and the Holy Spirit applies the work of God in creation, redemption, and consummation. In these eight biblical texts, there is no clear evidence of an eternal covenant between the three persons to appropriate distinct works to particular persons.

Trinitarian Hermeneutics

5. *The Accessibility of Human Knowledge to Eternity.* We have noted in both chapters 4 and 7 that the Enlightenment bequeathed to evangelical theologians the attitude that there is a profound gap between metaphysical reality and human epistemology. Part of our call for the revision of Protestant hermeneutics is an explicit affirmation of the communicability of eternal truth. Against Immanuel Kant and the various dichotomies established with the historical critical method, we desire the reclamation of aspects of the realism assumed in the early, medieval, and Reformation periods of the church. The divorce of eternity and history wrought through the Enlightenment made it difficult for Christian theologians to perceive the divine economy.

We believe a contemporary realist conception of Christian revelation must include the following traits. First, God may make himself knowable to humanity through the epistemological accommodation of his being and act for human conceptual abilities. Second, this accommodation is critically available in creation but redemptively available only in biblical revelation. Third, this accommodation does not reveal everything about God the Trinity, for he remains transcendent and may never be entirely comprehended; but what God does reveal remains trustworthy. Finally, the recognition of divine accommodation to manifest eternity within history must account for the distortions introduced into human accessibility to eternal truth through the fall of humanity.

6. The Correspondence between Appearance and Reality. Reclaiming a realist conception of revelation entails coordinate claims about theology proper and divine revelation. There is a striking agreement on this correspondence from both neoorthodox and evangelical theologians. First, according to Colin Gunton, the trustworthiness of God is not merely a claim about Scripture; it is a claim about God. Trustworthiness, the idea that God speaks truthfully, is a divine attribute that hangs on the divine attribute of immutability, the idea that God is steadfast in his being. Gunton brings these two attributes to bear on the doctrine of the Trinity.[3] Second, in an important essay during the conservative resurgence of the Southern Baptist Convention, L. Russ Bush argued that without biblical inerrancy, God's trustworthiness is cast into doubt.[4] Later, when the problem of open theism arose within evangelicalism, Bush argued as a principle that both

---

[3] God in his being is manifested in a trustworthy fashion through God in his work. "The way in which the three persons mutually constitute each other's being is eternal and unchanging. The Father is unchangeably the Father of the Son through the Spirit, and so on." This is supremely so in his love. Moreover, "the eternal love of the Father for his son is not denied but made actual in the complex of events from birth to resurrection." Colin Gunton, "Trinity and Trustworthiness," in *The Trustworthiness of God: Perspectives on the Nature of Scripture,* ed. Paul Helm and Carl R. Trueman (Grand Rapids, MI: Eerdmans, 2002), 281–83.

[4] L. Russ Bush, "Understanding Biblical Inerrancy," *Southwestern Journal of Theology* 50, no. 1 (2007): 20–56. Originally published as a rare and prized monograph in 1988.

theology proper and biblical inerrancy were simultaneously at stake. If Gunton and Bush are correct, then divine trustworthiness demands correspondence between divine revelation and divine reality.

We agree that there is a real correspondence between who God is and how God reveals himself to be. The economic Trinity truly reveals the immanent Trinity. If this is not the case, then both the divine attributes of trustworthiness and immutability and the biblical attribute of inerrancy are endangered. With every incremental step away from the first part of Rahner's axiom, divine trustworthiness and the eternal shape of the Trinity are deconstructed. If God's self-revelation is a revelation of God's self, then for the evangelical theologian, divine trustworthiness, biblical dependability, and the first part of Rahner's axiom must stand or fall together.

7. Human Knowing between Reason and Imagination. The reshaping of evangelical hermeneutics as a result of perceiving the Trinitarian idiom also requires a broader conception of the means for expressing theological truth. This was a major argument in chapter 1 and was buttressed in chapters 4 and 8. The calls to join in the recovery of patristic hermeneutics, to temper the overarching privilege granted to propositions, and to reconsider the truthfulness of the visionary are coordinate aspects of this broadened view of what constitutes the revelation of Christian doctrine.

New Testament theologian Christopher Rowland implied the same in his work on William Blake. "Blake," he affirms, "was a brilliant biblical interpreter—eccentric, perhaps, but one of Britain's most insightful exegetes."[5] Part of Blake's program was to push back against the rationalism of the Enlightenment. We could add other artists, writers, and musicians, such as J. R. R. Tolkien, C. S. Lewis, and George Frideric Handel, to complement Rowland's appreciation for nonpropositional forms of exegesis.[6] However, while the imagination

---

[5] Christopher Rowland, *Blake and the Bible* (New Haven, CT: Yale University Press, 2010), 1.

[6] John Ronald Reuel Tolkien's mother rejected her parent's Baptist beliefs and embraced Roman Catholicism. Ostracized from the family, after her early death, Tolkien was raised under the guidance of the Birmingham Oratory established by John Henry Newman. Christianity informed his dualistic cosmic fiction. Tolkien also helped convince the atheist Clive Staples Lewis to convert to Christianity. The

must be reclaimed as an aspect of the *imago Dei* and thus of theological communication, it must be done with care.

The imagination is a neglected anthropological constituency in contemporary Christianity, in spite of its biblical and historical prominence. And the imagination must again be brought alongside reason. But the imagination is also fallen and the source of great idolatry.[7] Through imagery the Trinity was revealed to John in the Apocalypse, and through the imagination his words can open the mind's eye to see the same *visio Trinitatis*. There is a need both for ὁ λόγος τοῦ θεοῦ, the Word of God, to discipline the human mind and for τό πμνεῦμα τοῦ θεοῦ, the Spirit of God, to transform the human heart. Both the Word and the Spirit are necessary to receive Christian doctrine. And in this Trinitarian hermeneutical movement, neither the Word with his sovereign reasonableness or the Spirit with his sovereign freedom may be suppressed, nor may they be divided. The best way forward for evangelical hermeneutics is to be open to the fruits of biblical typology[8] while being careful to guard against the endemic misuse of metaphors to impose a favored theology upon the biblical text.[9]

Christian fiction of both Tolkien and Lewis has had a deep impact on the contemporary imagination. Cf. Mark Atherton, *There and Back Again: J. R. R. Tolkien and the Origins of the Hobbit* (New York: IB Tauris, 2012); Alister McGrath, *C. S. Lewis: A Life: Eccentric Genius, Reluctant Prophet* (Carol Stream, IL: Hodder and Stoughton, 2013). Stefan Zweig describes Handel's intense psychological encounter with God and how it prompted the eighteenth-century composer's inspirational response of praise. The oratorio *Messiah* is still performed worldwide. Zweig, "The Resurrection of George Frideric Handel," in *Shooting Stars*, trans. Anthea Bell (London: Pushkin, 2013), 73–100.

[7] Gene Edward Veith Jr. and Matthew P. Ristuccia, *Imagination Redeemed: Glorifying God with a Neglected Part of Your Mind* (Wheaton, IL: Crossway, 2015). From an evangelical perspective, Veith provides the biblical, historical, and theological rationale for recovering the imagination, and Ristuccia exposits Ezekiel's visions to demonstrate the sanctifying power of the inspired imagination. Worthy of consultation from a Romantic perspective is Sandra M. Levy, *Imagination and the Journey of Faith* (Grand Rapids, MI: Eerdmans, 2008).

[8] E.g., Paul M. Hoskins, *That Scripture Might Be Fulfilled: Typology and the Death of Christ* (Maitland, FL: Xulon, 2009).

[9] Craig Blaising's critique of the spiritualist aspects of Reformed and New Covenant biblical theologies may be helpful here. E.g., Craig A. Blaising, "The People, the Land and the Future of Israel and Hermeneutics," in *The People, the Land, and the Future of Israel: Israel and the Jewish People in the Plan of God*, ed. Darrell Bock and Mitch Glaser (Grand Rapids, MI: Kregel, 2014), chap. 9.

Trinitarian Economy

8. The Trinity Reshapes Systematic Theology. Because God the Trinity reveals himself as God the Trinity, then we should expect that God the Trinity is the primary idiom not only for divine self-revelation but also for Christian reflection upon that divine self-revelation. In other words, if God the Trinity is both the idiom and content of the revelation of Scripture, then the Trinity must reshape our normal ways of engaging in systematic theology. This will have an impact on both its structure and content. With the renaissance of Trinitarianism in the twentieth century, many theologians began to restructure their reflections. Karl Barth is perhaps the most famous example. His *Church Dogmatics* masterfully moves forward the Trinity from the appendix to which Friedrich Schleiermacher had relegated it.[10] Among conservative evangelicals, the Trinity has begun to affect the arrangement of systematic theology. For instance, Thomas C. Oden arrays his systematic according to "The Living God," "The Word of Life," and "Life in the Spirit."[11]

The reshaping of systematic theologies away from the traditional loci approach toward a triadic format focused on the three persons of the Trinity should be helpful. However, bringing forward the Trinity, especially in his economy, reshapes not just the overall structure but also the internal content of systematic theology.[12] A recent movement toward recovering a vision of the entire divine economy as revealed in Scripture has been occurring among biblical theologians. Thomas R. Schreiner perceives both a Trinitarian dimension

[10] Regarding the widely accepted view that Schleiermacher reduced the Trinity to a second-level doctrine alongside his influential advocacy of the historical critical method, see Claude Welch, *The Trinity in Contemporary Theology* (London: SCM, 1953), 1–9. For a positive presentation of Schleiermacher's influence, see the fascinating essay by Christine Helmer, "Between History and Speculation: Christian Trinitarian Thinking After the Reformation," in *The Cambridge Companion to the Trinity*, ed. Peter C. Phan (New York: Cambridge University Press, 2011), 149–69.

[11] Thomas C. Oden, *Systematic Theology*, 3 vols (Peabody, MA: Hendrickson, 2001).

[12] Cf. John Webster, "Principles of Systematic Theology," *International Journal of Systematic Theology* 11, no. 1 (2009), 56–71.

and a "salvation-historical" dimension in New Testament theology.[13] G. K. Beale brings the Old Testament into the New Testament in his attempt to provide "a New Testament biblical theology." Through this cross-testament canonical perspective, Beale constructs both an Old Testament "storyline"[14] and a New Testament "storyline"[15] that are Trinitarian. Including the Trinity in the Old Testament narrative, at least implicitly, is a significant and welcome challenge to the long-standing dichotomy between the testaments in the discipline of biblical theology. Beale also rightly incorporates both the creational and the eschatological dimensions in his scriptural story line as it centers on Christ.[16] If biblical theologians are rediscovering the Triune economy, then systematic theologians should consider the impact of that recovery in their discipline. Examples come to mind.

For instance, evangelicals have inherited the placement of justification front and center since the necessary trauma of the Reformation in the history of the church. While the content of justification in evangelicalism should be retained, a redoubled effort needs to be made to locate justification in the context of the entire divine economy. Salvation is not merely a forensic declaration of righteousness,

---

[13] "The thesis advanced in this book is that NT theology is God-focused, Christ-centered, and Spirit-saturated, but the work of the Father, Son, and Spirit must be understood along a salvation-historical timeline." Thomas R. Schreiner, *New Testament Theology: Magnifying God in Christ* (Grand Rapids, MI: Baker, 2008), 23.

[14] "The Old Testament is the story of God, who progressively reestablishes his new-creational kingdom out of chaos over a sinful people by his word and Spirit through promise, covenant, and redemption, resulting in worldwide commission to the faithful to advance this kingdom and judgment (defeat or exile) for the unfaithful, unto his glory." G. K. Beale, *A New Testament Biblical Theology: The Unfolding of the Old Testament in the New* (Grand Rapids, MI: Baker, 2011), 16.

[15] "Jesus's life, trials, death for sinners, and especially resurrection by the Spirit have launched the fulfillment of the eschatological already-not yet new-creational reign, bestowed by grace through faith and resulting in worldwide commission to the faithful to advance this new-creational reign and resulting in judgment for the unbelieving, unto the triune God's glory." Ibid.

[16] G. K. Beale, "The Eschatological Conception of New Testament Theology," in *"The Reader Must Understand": Eschatology in the Bible and Theology*, ed. Kent E. Brower and Mark W. Elliott (Leicester: Apollos, 1997), 11–52. Cf. *From Creation to New Creation: Biblical Theology and Exegesis: Essays in Honor of G. K. Beale*, ed. Daniel Gurtner and Benjamin L. Gladd (Peabody, MA: Hendrickson, 2013).

though it is definitely that. Salvation entails not merely the removal of a state of condemnation. Salvation is also a real participation in the holy blessedness of the Triune life. This becomes clearer when the Trinitarian economy, as exhibited in chapters 7 and 8, is allowed to provide the metanarrative of Christian soteriology rather than a historical protest, necessary as that was to make and is to remember. The orthodox Eastern and Western doctrines of salvation as θέωσις,[17] which have been repressed in contemporary evangelicalism, will probably also require rigorous reevaluation.

A second instance concerns the Protestant view of the atonement. In his famous protest against the "Latin" and "humanistic" doctrines of the atonement, Gustaf Aulén felt he had rediscovered the "classic" idea of the atonement. He opposed the satisfaction view, which became the penal substitutionary theory favored among conservatives; but he also opposed the subjective theory favored among liberals. Aulén's rediscovered classic theory, however, requires resituating. Setting aside the question of redemption payment, we would argue that what Aulén really discovered was not merely the atonement but the lineaments of the Triune economy. While he correctly brings forward the divine "drama" and demonstrates its biblical roots, Aulén unfortunately dismisses both the central theory of the atonement, substitution, and minimizes the subjective effects of the atonement.[18] If the three "types" of the atonement are suitably placed, they need not be opposed. The classic idea of the divine drama of victory properly emphasizes the creative, redemptive, and consummative events of the divine economy; the objective vicarious substitution of Christ's sacrifice is the atonement itself; and the subjective appropriation of the cross is the Christian's response to that gift. The recovery of the Trinitarian economy may have other repercussions for systematic theology.

9. The Trinity Reshapes Human Relations. In systematic theology and the diverse fields of practical theology, a renewed emphasis on the economic Trinity is currently reshaping our conception of human

---

[17] Cf. Daniel A. Keating, *Deification and Grace* (Naples, FL: Sapientia, 2007).

[18] Gustaf Aulén, *Christus Victor: An Historical Study of the Three Main Types of the Idea of Atonement*, trans. A. G. Hebert (London: SPCK, 1931).

relations. If the first three chapters of Genesis are interpreted as a Trinitarian movement, and we believe that from a New Testament Christian perspective they are retrospectively foundational,[19] then the divine image as a Trinitarian image should inform our understanding of human personhood. The theological exegesis establishing this claim must await a third systematic volume, which should consider biblical anthropology. Strident debates have roiled both ecumenical and evangelical discussions as they consider the anthropological dimensions of the Trinity. We have only touched upon the evangelical debate on gender relations, and we have yet to introduce the ecumenical debate on the social Trinity.[20] The first debate focuses on relations within human families, and the second generally concerns relations within broader society, especially in its political dimensions. While we must delay consideration of these important discussions, we affirm here the importance of ascertaining the Trinity as the basis of Christian anthropology, especially regarding what it means to be a person, along with the effects on ethics, politics, and the family.

   10. The Trinity Shapes Worship. The first three chapters and the last three chapters of this book concerned texts that taught Trinitarian monotheism through acts and visions of worship. Early church fathers like Athanasius, Basil, and Augustine were driven to Trinitarian orthodoxy through concern for worship and salvation. Soteriological concerns similarly drove theologians like Karl Rahner, Karl Barth, and John Zizioulas to spark a Trinitarian renaissance in the twentieth century. More pointedly, this study did not begin when the writing of this book began, nor did it begin with research in biblical theology, historical theology, and systematic theology. This study began when I was a child and God grasped me powerfully with his Spirit as I read his Word. The brilliance of that experience has never departed. He has shaped my personal and communal worship from the initial crisis of baptism to the vision of the cross continually refreshed in the

---

[19] Cf. Beale, *A New Testament Biblical Theology*, 29–87.

[20] Jason Sexton distinguishes the "social Trinity" from the "relational" model of the Trinity, which is advocated by Paul S. Fiddes. Jason S. Sexton, "Introduction," in *Two Views of the Doctrine of the Trinity*, ed. idem (Grand Rapids, MI: Zondervan, 2014), 20. Cf. Paul S. Fiddes, *Participating in God: A Pastoral Doctrine of the Trinity* (Louisville, KY: Westminster John Knox, 2000).

Lord's Supper. And in the quiet of this study, surrounded as I am by Bibles and books about the Bible and its history of reception, he comes pouring back in an overpowering way. God reveals himself to be Trinity because he is Trinity.

The Trinity is the idiom of Scripture because he inspired his Word as such, and the Spirit illumines him as prominently and inextricably woven into the warp and woof of the text. Every time I open the Bible, I am struck that he would deign to reach down and renew this sinful mind and enlighten this dark soul. Because it is the Father reaching out through his Son in his Spirit to save a person for life with himself as Trinity, it is difficult to comprehend how a Christian could speak of being saved by God while denying him as Trinity. And because God holds the teacher to a greater standard, it seems impossible to believe a true minister of his Word could deny the Trinity. To return to our introductory questions, we asked whether God as Trinity is biblical and whether God as Trinity is necessary to be believed. The answers from this study to both questions are affirmative, attested exegetically and existentially. My prayer for you is that God the Trinity will transform you through his gracious revelation of himself as the one God who is the Father, the Son, and the Holy Spirit.

Appendix
Three Primary Trinitarian Creeds
(newly translated)

Symbolum Apostolicum
(The Apostles' Creed)[1]

I believe in God the Father, omnipotent, Creator of heaven and earth.

And in Jesus Christ, his unique Son, our Lord; who was conceived by the Holy Spirit, born of the virgin Mary; he suffered under Pontius Pilate, was crucified, died, and was buried; descended to hell; on the third day he rose again from the dead; he ascended to heaven [and] was seated at the right hand of God the Father omnipotent, from where he will come to judge the living and the dead.

I believe in the Holy Spirit, the holy church universal, the communion of saints, the forgiveness of sins, the resurrection of the body, and life eternal. Amen.

---

[1] Scholars dismiss the legend that each apostle contributed a phrase, but generally agree the creed reflects apostolic teaching. Some oppose the late addition of *descendit ad inferna*, but proponents of the doctrine may be found within each of the major Christian traditions. Latin text provided in J. N. D. Kelly, *Early Christian Creeds*, 3rd ed. (New York: Longman, 1972), 369.

Symbolum Nicaeno-Constantinopolinatum
(The Nicene Creed)[2]

We believe in one God, the Father; Ruler of all, Maker of heaven and earth, of all that is seen and unseen.

And in one Lord Jesus Christ, the only Son of God; who was begotten from the Father before all the ages, light from light, true God from true God, begotten not made, one essence with the Father; through whom all things came into existence. Who, for us human beings and for our salvation, descended from heaven and took flesh by the Holy Spirit and the virgin Mary and became human. Who was crucified on our behalf under Pontius Pilate and suffered death and was buried; and he rose again on the third day according to the Scriptures; and he ascended into heaven and is sitting at the right hand of the Father; and again he will come with glory to judge the living and the dead; his kingdom will have no end.

And in the Holy Spirit, the Lord and Life-giver; who is proceeding from the Father;[3] who with the Father and the Son is together worshiped and together glorified; who spoke through the prophets. [We believe] in one, holy, universal, and apostolic church. We confess one baptism unto the forgiveness of sins. We anticipate the resurrection from the dead and life in the coming age. Amen.

---

[2] This creed was ostensibly adopted at the Council of Nicaea in 325 but was revised at the Council of Constantinople in 381; it is more properly referred to as the Niceno-Constantinopolitan Creed. Greek text provided in Kelly, *Early Christian Creeds*, 297–98.

[3] The West later inserted *filioque*, "and the Son," here.

Symbolum Quicunque
(The Athanasian Creed)[4]

Whoever wants to be saved should above all hold this as a tenet of the universal faith. Whoever does not guard it whole and inviolable will doubtless perish eternally. This is the universal faith: We worship one God in Trinity and Trinity in Unity, neither confusing the persons nor separating the substance. For the Father is one person, the Son is another, and the Spirit is another. But the deity of the Father and Son and Holy Spirit is one, equal in glory, coeternal in majesty. What the Father is, so is the Son, and so is the Holy Spirit; uncreated Father, uncreated Son, uncreated Spirit; infinite Father, infinite Son, infinite Holy Spirit; eternal Father, eternal Son, eternal Holy Spirit—and nevertheless not three eternals, but one eternal; thus also not three uncreated nor three infinites, but one uncreated and one infinite. Likewise, omnipotent Father, omnipotent Son, omnipotent Holy Spirit—and nevertheless not three omnipotents, but one omnipotent. Therefore God the Father, God the Son, God the Holy Spirit—and nevertheless not three gods, but one is God. Therefore Lord Father, Lord Son, Lord Holy Spirit—and nevertheless not three lords, but one Lord.

Because Christian truth compels us to confess each distinct person as God and Lord, therefore universal religion prohibits us from saying there are three gods or lords. The Father is neither made nor created nor begotten. The Son is from the Father alone, neither made nor created but begotten. The Holy Spirit is from the Father and the Son, neither made nor created nor begotten but proceeding. Thus one Father, not three fathers; one Son, not three sons; one Holy Spirit, not three holy spirits. And in this Trinity, none is before or after, none is greater or less, but the entire three persons are coeternal and coequal. Thus it is completely as has been said above: We must

---

[4] While using the name of the fourth-century bishop of Alexandria, this creed first appears clearly in the West in the early sixth century. Latin text provided in *Enchiridion Symbolorum: Definitionum et Declarationum de Rebus Fidei et Morum*, 31st ed., ed. Henrici Denzinger (Rome: Herder, 1957), 17–18.

worship Unity in Trinity and Trinity in Unity. As a result, whoever would be saved should think thus about the Trinity.

But it is necessary to eternal salvation that the incarnation of our Lord Jesus Christ be faithfully believed. For this is the right faith that we believe and we confess: That our Lord Jesus Christ, God's Son, is God and man. He is God, begotten from the substance of the Father before the worlds, and he is man, born from the substance of his mother in the world; perfect God, perfect man, subsisting with a rational soul and a human body, equal to the Father according to divinity, less than the Father according to humanity. Although he is God and man, nevertheless he is not two but is one Christ; one moreover not because he has converted divinity into flesh but because he has assumed humanity into God; one entirely not by confusion of substances but by unity of person. For as the rational soul and body are one man, thus God and man is one in Christ. He suffered death for our salvation, descended into hell, on the third day rose again from the dead, ascended into heaven, sitting at the right hand of the Father omnipotent, from where he will come again to judge the living and the dead. At whose coming all human beings shall rise bodily to give account for what they have done. And those who have done well will enter eternal life; those who have done evil will enter eternal fire. This is the universal faith, which unless one believes it faithfully and firmly one may not be saved.

NAME INDEX

H

Hall, Christopher A. 88, 96
Hamlyn, D. W. 182
Harnack, Adolf 92, 127–28
Harrison, Nonna Verna 105
Harrower, Scott 10, 168, 170–71
Hart, David Bentley 197
Haykin, Michael A. G. 95
Hays, Richard B. 12, 97, 110, 119
Healy, Mary 162
Hebert, A. G. 236
Hegel, George Wilhelm Friedrich
    103, 163
Heine, Ronald E. 123–24
Heiser, Michael S. 70
Heller, Reinhold 29
Helmer, Christine 234
Helm, Paul 102, 231
Hemphill, Ken 17
Hewison, Robert 4
Hildebrand, Stephen M. 52, 130,
    150
Hill, Edmund 26, 40, 117, 190, 197
Hines, Mary E. 155, 168
Hodge, Charles 94
Hodgson, Leonard 14
Hoehner, Harold W. 160, 179–81,
    183–85, 187
Holmes, Stephen R. 84, 95
Honderich, Ted 102, 136, 182
Horton, Douglas ix, 26
Hoskins, Paul M. 233
House, H. Wayne 148
Howson, J. S. 177
Humphreys, Fisher 10–11, 14, 24
Hunsinger, George 155
Hurtado, Larry W. 72–74, 78, 82,
    205, 208, 213

I

Ice, Laura M. 11, 25
Innes, James 109
Innitzer 183
Issler, Klaus 10

J

Jackson, Blomfield 40, 127
Janzen, J. Gerald 63, 68–70
Jenson, Robert W. 25
John of Damascus 138, 229
Johnson, Aubrey R. 67, 70
Johnson, Keith E. 140
Jowers, Dennis W. x, 10 148
Jüngel, Eberhard 175

K

Kant, Immanuel 102, 103
Kapic, Kelly M. 10, 103
Kasper, Walter 148, 169
Keating, Daniel A. 52, 236
Kehler, Heinrich x, 10
Kelly, J. N. D. 240–41
Kendall, Daniel 24, 149, 157, 162
Kerr, Hugh Thomson, Jr. 89
Kidner, Derek 80, 207
Kittel, Gerhard 41, 58, 114
Kleinknecht, H. 114
König, Adrio 220
Köstenberger, Andreas J. x, 111,
    113, 121–23, 140, 150
Kramer, Fred 89

L

Labahn, M. 140
LaCugna, Catherine Mowry 148,
    149, 168
Ladd, George Eldon 79–80, 83, 179,
    199, 212
Letham, Robert 10, 51, 170, 181
Levering, Matthew 24, 46, 59, 115,
    155
Levy, Sandra M. 177, 233
Lewis, C. S. 232, 233
Lewis, Edwin 177
Lim, Paul C. H. 90–91
Lindars, Barnabas 203
Locke, John 93
Long, V. Philips x
Lossky, Vladimir 105
Louth, Andrew 117

SUBJECT INDEX

SCRIPTURE INDEX